YOU ARE ASKED TO WITNESS:

The Stó:lō in Canada's Pacific Coast History

Edited by Keith Thor Carlson

Stó:lō Heritage Trust

Chilliwack, British Columbia, Canada

YOU ARE ASKED TO WITNESS: *The Stó:lō in Canada's Pacific Coast History*

Edited by Keith Thor Carlson

PUBLISHED BY

Stó:lō Heritage Trust

Building 1 - 7201 Vedder Road, Chilliwack, British Columbia, Canada V2R 4G5

Canadian Cataloguing in Publication Data

Carlson, Keith, 1966-

You Are Asked To Witness:
the *Stó:lō* in Canada's Pacific Coast History

Includes bibliographical references and index.

ISBN 0-9681577-2-6 (bound).—ISBN 0-9681577-0-X (pbk.)

1. Stalo Indians—History. 2. Indians of North America—

British Columbia—Fraser River Region—History.

3. Fraser River Region (B.C.)—History.

I. Carlson, Keith Thor. II. Sto:lo Heritage Trust.

E99.S72Y68 1997   971.1'37004979   C96-910841-9

Funding for earlier versions of material presented in this volume provided by Stó:lō Nation, the B.C. Ministry of Education (Aboriginal Education Branch), School District #33 Chilliwack, School District #35 Langley and Parks Canada. In addition, the B.C. Heritage Trust has provided financial assistance to this project to support conservation of our heritage resources, gain further knowledge and increase public understanding of the complete history of British Columbia.

Cover Photos by Gary Fiegehen and the British Columbia Archives & Records Service.

Layout and design by Jan Perrier Design, Box 1097, Fort Langley, B.C. V1M 2S4 (604) 513-0227.

Printed and bound in Canada by Hignell Printing Limited, Winnipeg, Manitoba.

First printing December, 1996; second printing June, 1997; third printing February, 1999; special hard cover edition(500 books) February, 1999; fourth printing April, 2000.

FRONT COVER: **The transformer rocks shown are *Tewít* the hunter, with *Tahl* his spear beside him and farther downriver is *sqwémay* his dog. The elk he was hunting is not shown.**

INSET: **Contemporary *Stó:lō* speaker Herb Joe.**

BACK COVER: **"We take our name from the word that we give the river: *Stó:lō*."** *(Ernie Crey)*

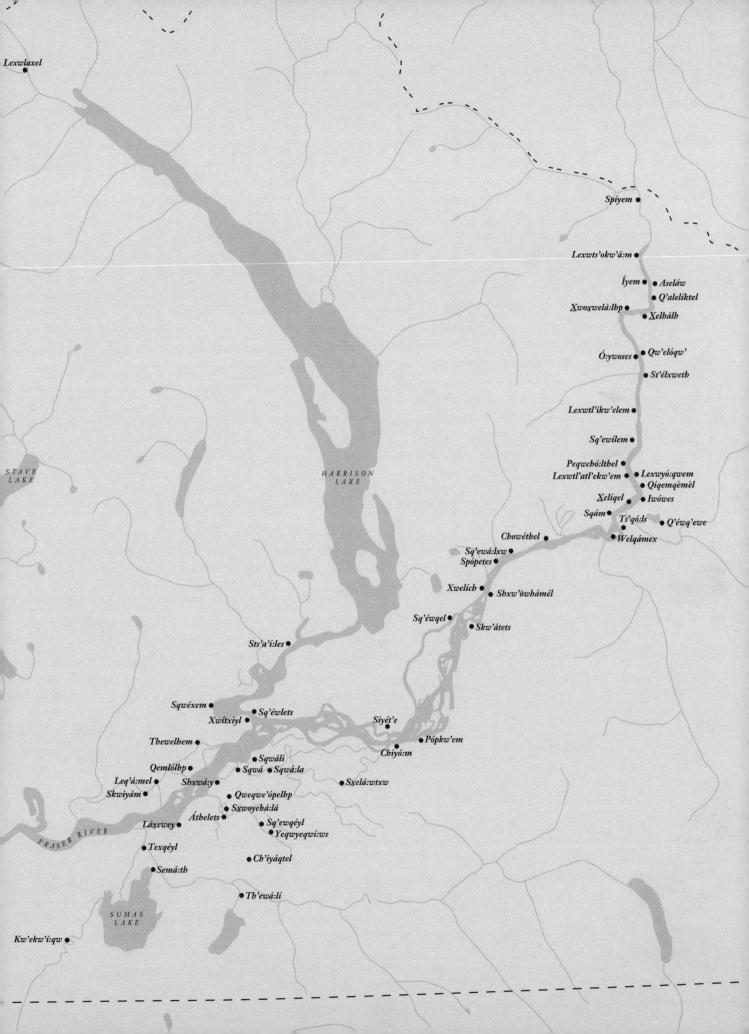

Lexwlaxel

Spíyem

Lexwts'okw'á:m

Íyem ● Aseláw
● Q'alelíktel
Xwoxwelá:lhp ● Xelhálh

Ó:ywoses ● Qw'elóqw'
● St'élxweth

Lexwtl'ikw'elem

Sq'ewílem

Peqwchó:lthel
Lexwtl'atl'ekw'em ● Lexwyó:qwem
● Qíqemqèmèl
Xelíqel ● Iwówes
Sqám ● Ts'qó:ls ● Q'éwq'ewe
● Welqámex

STAVE
LAKE

HARRISON
LAKE

Chowéthel
Sq'ewá:lxw ●
Spópetes ●

Xwelích ●
● Shxw'ōwhámél

Sq'éwqel ●
● Skw'átets

Sts'a'í:les ●

Sqwéxem ●
Xwítxiyl ● ● Sq'éwlets
Siyét'e ●
● Pópkw'em
Thewelhem ● Chiyó:m
Sqwáli
Qemlólhp ● Sqwá ● Sqwá:la
Leq'á:mel ● Shxwá:y ● Sxelá:wtxw
Skwiyám ● Qweqwe'ópelhp ●
● Sxwoyehá:lá
Láxewey ● Áthelets ● Sq'ewqéyl
FRASER RIVER ● Yeqwyeqwí:ws
Texqéyl ●
Ch'iyáqtel ●
Semá:th ●
Th'ewá:lí ●

SUMAS
LAKE

Kw'ekw'í:qw ●

For Edie, Antoine,

Katherine, John,

Charles, Robert,

Kenneth, and Peter McHalsie.

TABLE OF

C O N T E N T S

Preface

For many years it has been an objective of *Stó:lō* leaders to better inform *Xwelítem* society (mainstream Canadians) about the history and culture of the *Stó:lō* people, as well as the history of *Stó:lō-Xwelítem* relations. *Stó:lō* leaders recognize that by promoting cross-cultural awareness, prejudice and racism can be broken down and suspicion and resentment replaced with respect and understanding. This book, *You Are Asked To Witness*, is just one of many recent programs and projects initiated by the *Stó:lō* Nation to achieve this goal. Others include *Shxwt'a:selhawtxw* (The House of Long Ago and Today), a hands-on educational interpretive centre designed primarily to provide school students with culturally appropriate and historically balanced information about the *Stó:lō*. *Shxwt'a:selhawtxw* is located on *Stó:lō* Nation's Coqualeetza grounds in Chilliwack. Another dynamic avenue for accessing first hand information about the *Stó:lō* is the *Xá:ytem* Interpretive Centre in Mission. There visitors are exposed to aspects of *Stó:lō* spirituality and archaeology.

While plans for a book of this nature have been percolating in many *Stó:lō* people's minds for a long time, the project did not begin until the winter of 1992. At that time, a secondary school principal from Hope requested that a report dealing with "traditional *Stó:lō* leadership" be adapted for use in schools. The enthusiastic response of high school teachers to this hurriedly prepared curriculum supplement convinced *Stó:lō* Nation management and staff to look for ways to produce more comprehensive cross-cultural educational material. At a subsequent meeting of the Langley School District's Aboriginal Education Committee, (which includes *Stó:lō* Nation representatives), it was determined to begin a large scale *Stó:lō* curriculum development program, and to invite other school districts to participate. Shortly thereafter, the twenty-one *Stó:lō* communities represented by the *Stó:lō* Nation, and six Fraser Valley school districts formed the *Stó:lō* Curriculum Consortium, and work began in earnest.

In the spring of 1996, after a series of reviews by various *Stó:lō* Elders and cultural experts, a total of eighteen *Stó:lō* curriculum units ranging from science to social studies to physical education were ready to be introduced to the high school system in printed "binder" format. Following this, the *Stó:lō* Nation decided to take the project one step further and to publish as a book those units with the broadest appeal. To reach a more varied audience, and to contribute to the larger academic discourse, each of the selected units (now chapters) were exposed to the scrutiny of peer review prior to publication. Each chapter was subsequently sent to three anonymous academic reviewers and at least one additional *Stó:lō* reviewer. All reviewers are acknowledged experts in their field. *Stó:lō*

leaders recognized that it was not in their long term interests to produce a book whose content or interpretation could not be defended. Moreover, they did not want a book which in its attempt to address stereotypes inadvertently created new ones. Accordingly, within the pages of this book readers will find a complex cultural history describing both *Stó:lō* agency as well as Aboriginal reaction to *Xwelítem* actions.

You Are Asked To Witness is arranged in six roughly chronological thematic sections:

Section I: An Introduction to the *Stó:lō*
Section II: Early Encounters
Section III: Facing Government Coersion
Section IV: Venturing Into the *Xwelítem* World
Section V: Whose Land and Resources?
Section VI: Oral Narratives

While the entire book is designed to present a complete story, each section, and even every chapter within each section, can be read in isolation. This format is designed to engage a broader readership and attract people with focused interests who might not otherwise have consulted a larger monograph.

A brief introduction to each chapter outlines the major themes and content found within. At the end of each chapter readers will find detailed citations. To attract readers to what might otherwise be the least consulted sections of the book a beautiful motif designed by George Pennier has been shadowed behind all the endnotes. The compelling original art work found on the introductory page of each chapter has been contributed by renowned *Stó:lō* artist Stan Greene. Before commencing his work Stan sat down with draft copies of each chapter and acquainted himself with their content and "feel." He then spent many months carefully seeking inspiration so that his art would intimately complement the writings.

Readers will find that *Halq'eméylem* words within the text are presented in italics. This has been done to expose people to the continuance of the *Stó:lō* language and to provide readers with new words through which to view a culturally loaded landscape. (A guide to the proper pronunciation of *Halq'eméylem* words is found immediately following this preface.) Likewise, readers will find three separate font styles used throughout the book. This has been done to heighten the distinction and perspective of *Stó:lō* oral sources, *Xwelítem* archival sources and the writings of the authors.

In the *Halq'eméylem* language the word for mainstream Canadians of European descent is *Xwelítem*. Its application throughout enables us to avoid describing people in the negative (non-Aboriginal); in stereotypical racial terms (white); or in temporally or geographically inaccurately ways (Euro-Canadian or European). Moreover, the literal translation of *Xwelítem* is "hungry people," an expression with deep historical as well as metaphorical meaning. This linguistic context and the fact that the word continues to be used by contemporary *Stó:lō* adds another layer of meaning to each of the texts.

Readers will find that the expression "Aboriginal" is used to the exclusion of "Native" or "First Nation." This decision was made upon the recommendation of a number of *Stó:lō* who felt this term was more appropriate. The word "Indian" is used within quotes or when referring to specific things people said within a specific historical context.

The main title, *You Are Asked To Witness*, comes from the expression *Stó:lō* "speakers" use when inviting respected guests to become witnesses at gatherings. In this context the expression refers to the speaker's request that guests witness and pay attention in a respectful manner. It is in this way that the *Stó:lō* share their culture and history. For a more detailed description readers are encouraged to consult the final chapter of this volume.

———■———

A special acknowledgement must be given to those *Stó:lō* Elders, cultural experts, Chiefs, and family leaders, past and present, who have consistently articulated the need for cross-cultural awareness programs and for research directed toward sharing *Stó:lō* history and knowledge.

A few people have been especially helpful in seeing this project through to fruition, some more visibly than others. Listed alphabetically, they are: Chief Michelle Douglas of Matsqui, who while holding the education portfolio on the *Stó:lō* Nation's Special Chief's Council made clear to staff the importance of cross-cultural awareness initiatives; Sarah Eustace, who came late to the project, but whose enthusiasm and critical reading skills contributed significantly to the final product; Gary Fiegehen, for capturing aspects of *Stó:lō* life on film; Rosaleen George, one of the most kind and generous people I have ever met. I would like to acknowledge her commitment to sharing her extensive knowledge including the *Halq'eméylem* language; Tracey Joe, who contributed not only her increasingly keen research skills, but also her insightful understanding of aspects of *Stó:lō* culture; Albert "Sonny" McHalsie, who as Cultural Advisor of the Aboriginal Rights and Title Department not only ensured that the chapters conveyed material of significance to *Stó:lō* community members, but also kept authors from presenting "too positive" a view of *Stó:lō* cultural history; Heather Myles, whose undaunting dedication to the refinement of earlier versions of the curriculum project helped make the final publication possible; Jan Perrier for sharing her skills in graphic design and layout; Clarence Pennier, Executive Director of the Aboriginal Rights and Title Department, who provided general direction and inspiration for the entire project as well as constructive critical comments on every chapter; Gwen Point, who as Education Manager at *Stó:lō* Nation steered the research into fruitful directions; the late Wesley Sam, a great *Stó:lō* historian who I was privileged to call a friend; and David Smith, who not only provided critical feedback and constructive comments on various chapters, but who in his capacity as *Stó:lō* Nation Archivist co-ordinated the process of anonymous peer review and compiled the book's index. My own chief intellectual debt is to Dr. Wesley T. Wooley.

The other authors and myself would also like to acknowledge certain other people who have played direct roles in the production of this book:

As Elders and/or Cultural Advisors: Edna Bobb, Joan Chapman, Bill Pat-Charlie, Jimmie Charlie, Rosaleen George, Stan Greene, Matilda "Tilly" Gutierrez, the late Sylvester Joe, James Louis, Mervyn "Skip" Malloway, Mary Malloway, Frank Malloway, Albert "Sonny" McHalsie, Clarence "Kat" Pennier, the late Bertha Peters, the late Nancy Phillips, Steven Point, the late Wesley Sam, Anabel Stewart, and Harold Wells.

For their assistance with the *Halq'eméylem* Language: Dr. Strang Burton, Diane Charlie, Rosaleen George, Matilda "Tilly" Gutierrez, Albert "Sonny" McHalsie, and Tess Ned.

For their assistance in research: Sarah Eustace, Tracey Joe, Gloria Morgan, Heather Myles, and David Smith.

For their artistic contributions: Stan Greene, and George Pennier.

For Graphics/maps/photos: E.W. Carlson, M. Teresa Carlson, Gary Fiegehen, Tracey Joe, Neil LaHaise, Albert "Sonny" McHalsie, Anne Mohs, Jan Perrier, Ryan Ross, Brian Thom, The British Columbia Archives and Records Service, The Chilliwack Museum and Archives, The Royal British Columbia Museum, The Vancouver Museum.

For their critical editorial review of certain chapters: Al Barry, Sarah Eustace, Helen Joe, Albert "Sonny" McHalsie, Heather Myles, Clarence "Kat" Pennier, Norm Poggemoeller, Steven Point, Gwen Point, David Smith, Brian Thom, Dr. Lionel Adey, Dr. Jean Barman, Dr. Brian W. Dippie, Hamar Foster, Dr. Brent Galloway, Dr. Cole Harris, Dr. Michael Kew, Dr. Ralph Maud, Dr. Robert A. J. McDonald, Dr. Bruce Miller, Dr. Alf Siemens, Dr. Paul Tennant, Dr. Elizabeth Vibert and Dr. Wendy Wickwire.

Archivists and curators from the British Columbia Archives and Records Service, the Chilliwack Museum and Archives, the Royal British Columbia Museum and the Stó:lō Nation Archives, in particular Brian Young, Ron Denman, Kelly Stewart, Dan Savard and David Smith.

For their patient clerical assistance: Rhonda George, Tracey Joe, Dilhia Hall, Lori Kelly, Tara Kelly, Kim Stevenson, and Gail Thomas.

All the teachers who were involved in developing instructional strategies or in piloting earlier versions of this material: Brian Alexander, Dianne Anderson, Lori August, Carmen Babin, Katherine Baker, Mat Born, Anne Bourque, Sharon Bradley Green, Gerald Charlie, Ji Ai Cho, Mary Ellen Campbell, Marilyn Connoly, Roberta Cooper, Ingred Cunningham, Donald Dale, Judy Dallin, Deborah LaFontane, Stacy DeVries, Will Dirks, Tammy Fox, Ernestine Franson, Brad Fuller, Donna Frost, Vic Gladish, Jan Gladish, Alison Guy, Dave Hague, Bev Holroyd, Dianne Hopton, Vic Janzen, Jon Jordan, Ulpu Kauppi, Dianna Kay, Alan Klein, Colleen Kennedy, Sarah Killby, Marlyn Lamarre, Marsha Lemon, Ron MacFarlane, Karen Mak, Anne McLaverty, Mark Milliron, Don Nelson, Ann Penner, Brenda Point, Tammy Quirring, Jackie Ross, Selina Shaffer, Karen Schultz, Dale Servatious, Sigrid Singlton, Don Sparks, Patrick Stedman, Ray Steiguilas, Gary Taylor, Dan Theissen, John Tymoshuk, Cynthia Weldon, Ruby Williams, and Jill Wight

Recognition is also due to Judy Dallin, Brian Domney, Mel Folkman, Heather Hansen, Jim Latham, Rhoda Peters, Norm Poggemoeller, Heike Sasaki, Laura Smith, and Robert Stan Watchorn. In any project of this size it is inevitable that some people who deserve special recognition will be inadvertently left out. If I have forgotten to include anyone's name, I apologize.

This volume is only a series of interpretations. It is not *the* interpretation. With the Stó:lō Nation leaders, I encourage others to publish additional interpretations which might, challenge, oppose or complement those presented here. Moreover while the Stó:lō Nation sponsored this project, interpretation and all errors of fact are the sole responsibility of the individual authors.

Notes on Contributors

Laura Cameron wrote her Master's Thesis, *Openings to a Lake*, in history at the University of British Columbia. In it she explores the ways different communities remembered and experienced the draining of Sumas lake. A published version of her thesis is forthcoming from the University of Toronto Press. She also has an article on the history of Sumas lake appearing in the upcoming issue of *Native Studies Review* (Summer 1997). She was born and raised in the Fraser Valley and is an earnest advocate of environmental protection. Currently she is completing her PhD at Cambridge University in England.

Keith Thor Carlson began his association as historian for the Stó:lō Nation in 1992, subsequent to finishing his Masters Degree in History at the University of Victoria. His MA thesis, *The Twisted Road To Freedom*, analyzes the decolonization process in the Philippines and was published by the University of the Philippines Press in 1995. He is the author of two recent articles on aspects of Stó:lō history: "The Lynching of Louie Sam" (*BC Studies*, Spring 1996), and "Stó:lō Exchange Dynamics" (*Native Studies Review*, Summer 1997). While still working for the Stó:lō Nation, he is also in the process of completing his PhD at the University of British Columbia.

M. Teresa Carlson designed the interactive exhibits at *Shxwt'a:selhawtxw* (The House of Long Ago and Today) and now works as the curator of this Stó:lō hands-on educational interpretive centre in Chilliwack. Many of the programs she co-ordinates at *Shxwt'a:selhawtxw* involve Stó:lō Elders sharing their traditional knowledge with the younger generation. She has a degree from the University of Victoria in English Literature and a particular interest in written or "captured" Aboriginal oral narratives. She is currently completing a post-graduate program in Cultural Resource Management at the University of Victoria and is exploring issues of race, culture and appropriation of voice.

Vincent Harper began his association as a biologist for the Stó:lō Fishing Authority and the Stó:lō Nation between 1991 and 1995. Aside from biology, he also has extensive experience and educational training as an archaeologist, working at the Hatzic Rock excavation among other projects. Currently he works as a freelance environmental assessment agent in the Fraser Valley.

John Lutz is an Assistant Professor of history at the University of Victoria. He was one of the first scholars to seriously study the involvement of Aboriginal people in the post-fur trade economy. Extracts of his Doctoral dissertation *After the Fur Trade: The Aboriginal Labouring Class in British Columbia, 1849-1890* have been published in article form in The *Journal of the Canadian Historical*

There are ten consonants written with an apostrophe: ch', k', kw', p', q', qw', t', th', ts', tl'. These are popped or glottalized consonants. Th occurs in English wi<u>dth</u> and brea<u>dth</u>.

'   glottal stop. It is found in a few words in English like, "mu<u>tt</u>on" or "bu<u>tt</u>on" or Cockney English "bo<u>tt</u>le" (spelled with "tt") or beginning each "uh" in "uh-uh" (the sound meaning "no") or the sound beginning "earns" in "Mary earns" when pronounced differently from "Mary yearns".

lh   made by putting your tongue in position to say an "l" but then blowing air (like an "h") around the sides of the tongue. This sound may be heard in English after "k" sound in a few words like "clean" (klhin) or "clear" or "climb".

There are four blown x sounds. These sounds are made by raising the tongue to narrow the passage of air till you hear the friction of the air

x   made with the middle of the tongue raised roughly in the same place is it is put to make a y as in "yawn". But instead of using your voice you just blow air and it produces a friction sound between the middle of the tongue and the front of the hard palate. English has this sound first in "Hugh" or "hew".

xw   made with the tongue raised a little further back, by the middle off the hard palate (roof of the mouth), but it also requires rounded lips. It sounds a lot like wh in some words in English but with more friction on the roof of the mouth.

$\underline{x}$ made still further back, in fact with the back of the tongue raised close to the soft palate (where the q is made). German has this sound in "ach" for example, and Scottish has it in "lock" meaning "lake".

$\underline{x}$w   made in the same back place as $\underline{x}$ but is also made with round lips. It is like a blown qw while $\underline{x}$ is like a blown q.

Footnotes

1   See Brent Galloway, *Tó:lméls ye Siyelyólexwa: Wisdom of the Elders. Coqualeetza* Education Training Center, Sardis, 1980. The exception for the use of the *Halq'eméylem* orthography is for words in other Aboriginal languages. *Halq'eméylem* words cited from a source where they appeared phonetically have been changed to the *Stó:lō* orthography, were possible.

2   See Galloway, p. 23-27 in *The Chilliwacks and Their Neighbors,* edited by R. Maud, B. Galloway and M. Weeden, Talonbooks, Vancouver 1987. This article also lists the Americanist International Phonetic Alphabet (IPA) equivalents to the *Stó:lō* writing system.

For Graphics/maps/photos: E.W. Carlson, M. Teresa Carlson, Gary Fiegehen, Tracey Joe, Neil LaHaise, Albert "Sonny" McHalsie, Anne Mohs, Jan Perrier, Ryan Ross, Brian Thom, The British Columbia Archives and Records Service, The Chilliwack Museum and Archives, The Royal British Columbia Museum, The Vancouver Museum.

For their critical editorial review of certain chapters: Al Barry, Sarah Eustace, Helen Joe, Albert "Sonny" McHalsie, Heather Myles, Clarence "Kat" Pennier, Norm Poggemoeller, Steven Point, Gwen Point, David Smith, Brian Thom, Dr. Lionel Adey, Dr. Jean Barman, Dr. Brian W. Dippie, Hamar Foster, Dr. Brent Galloway, Dr. Cole Harris, Dr. Michael Kew, Dr. Ralph Maud, Dr. Robert A. J. McDonald, Dr. Bruce Miller, Dr. Alf Siemens, Dr. Paul Tennant, Dr. Elizabeth Vibert and Dr. Wendy Wickwire.

Archivists and curators from the British Columbia Archives and Records Service, the Chilliwack Museum and Archives, the Royal British Columbia Museum and the Stó:lō Nation Archives, in particular Brian Young, Ron Denman, Kelly Stewart, Dan Savard and David Smith.

For their patient clerical assistance: Rhonda George, Tracey Joe, Dilhia Hall, Lori Kelly, Tara Kelly, Kim Stevenson, and Gail Thomas.

All the teachers who were involved in developing instructional strategies or in piloting earlier versions of this material: Brian Alexander, Dianne Anderson, Lori August, Carmen Babin, Katherine Baker, Mat Born, Anne Bourque, Sharon Bradley Green, Gerald Charlie, Ji Ai Cho, Mary Ellen Campbell, Marilyn Connoly, Roberta Cooper, Ingred Cunningham, Donald Dale, Judy Dallin, Deborah LaFontane, Stacy DeVries, Will Dirks, Tammy Fox, Ernestine Franson, Brad Fuller, Donna Frost, Vic Gladish, Jan Gladish, Alison Guy, Dave Hague, Bev Holroyd, Dianne Hopton, Vic Janzen, Jon Jordan, Ulpu Kauppi, Dianna Kay, Alan Klein, Colleen Kennedy, Sarah Killby, Marlyn Lamarre, Marsha Lemon, Ron MacFarlane, Karen Mak, Anne McLaverty, Mark Milliron, Don Nelson, Ann Penner, Brenda Point, Tammy Quirring, Jackie Ross, Selina Shaffer, Karen Schultz, Dale Servatious, Sigrid Singlton, Don Sparks, Patrick Stedman, Ray Steiguilas, Gary Taylor, Dan Theissen, John Tymoshuk, Cynthia Weldon, Ruby Williams, and Jill Wight

Recognition is also due to Judy Dallin, Brian Domney, Mel Folkman, Heather Hansen, Jim Latham, Rhoda Peters, Norm Poggemoeller, Heike Sasaki, Laura Smith, and Robert Stan Watchorn. In any project of this size it is inevitable that some people who deserve special recognition will be inadvertently left out. If I have forgotten to include anyone's name, I apologize.

This volume is only a series of interpretations. It is not *the* interpretation. With the Stó:lō Nation leaders, I encourage others to publish additional interpretations which might, challenge, oppose or complement those presented here. Moreover while the Stó:lō Nation sponsored this project, interpretation and all errors of fact are the sole responsibility of the individual authors.

Notes on Contributors

Laura Cameron wrote her Master's Thesis, *Openings to a Lake*, in history at the University of British Columbia. In it she explores the ways different communities remembered and experienced the draining of Sumas lake. A published version of her thesis is forthcoming from the University of Toronto Press. She also has an article on the history of Sumas lake appearing in the upcoming issue of *Native Studies Review* (Summer 1997). She was born and raised in the Fraser Valley and is an earnest advocate of environmental protection. Currently she is completing her PhD at Cambridge University in England.

Keith Thor Carlson began his association as historian for the *Stó:lō Nation* in 1992, subsequent to finishing his Masters Degree in History at the University of Victoria. His MA thesis, *The Twisted Road To Freedom*, analyzes the decolonization process in the Philippines and was published by the University of the Philippines Press in 1995. He is the author of two recent articles on aspects of *Stó:lō* history: "The Lynching of Louie Sam" (*BC Studies*, Spring 1996), and "*Stó:lō* Exchange Dynamics" (*Native Studies Review*, Summer 1997). While still working for the *Stó:lō* Nation, he is also in the process of completing his PhD at the University of British Columbia.

M. Teresa Carlson designed the interactive exhibits at *Shxwt'a:selhawtxw* (The House of Long Ago and Today) and now works as the curator of this *Stó:lō* hands-on educational interpretive centre in Chilliwack. Many of the programs she co-ordinates at *Shxwt'a:selhawtxw* involve *Stó:lō* Elders sharing their traditional knowledge with the younger generation. She has a degree from the University of Victoria in English Literature and a particular interest in written or "captured" Aboriginal oral narratives. She is currently completing a post-graduate program in Cultural Resource Management at the University of Victoria and is exploring issues of race, culture and appropriation of voice.

Vincent Harper began his association as a biologist for the *Stó:lō* Fishing Authority and the *Stó:lō* Nation between 1991 and 1995. Aside from biology, he also has extensive experience and educational training as an archaeologist, working at the Hatzic Rock excavation among other projects. Currently he works as a freelance environmental assessment agent in the Fraser Valley.

John Lutz is an Assistant Professor of history at the University of Victoria. He was one of the first scholars to seriously study the involvement of Aboriginal people in the post-fur trade economy. Extracts of his Doctoral dissertation *After the Fur Trade: The Aboriginal Labouring Class in British Columbia, 1849-1890* have been published in article form in The *Journal of the Canadian Historical*

Association. He completed his Masters degree at the University of Victoria and his Doctorate at Ottawa. Since finishing his studies he has secured a number of post-doctoral fellowships.

Albert "Sonny" McHalsie has been working as a researcher and more recently as the cultural advisor for the *Stó:lō* Nation since 1985. In this capacity he seeks to ensure that *Stó:lō* culture and history are interpreted accurately and respectfully. In the past three years he has begun presenting papers on aspects of traditional *Stó:lō* culture at various academic conferences. He has recently co-authored an article dealing with the exploitation of *Stó:lō* slaves at Fort Langley which is forthcoming in *BC Studies.* He continues to exercise his Aboriginal right to catch and sell salmon from his hereditary family owned fishing spot in the Fraser Canyon. He is the father of eight children and sits as the representative of his extended family on the *Shxw'ōhamel* Band council.

Siyémches **(Chief Frank Malloway)** is the hereditary leader of the Yakweakwioose Band in Chilliwack. His "Indian name" can be traced back to one of the original four brothers of the Chilliwack people. *Siyémches* is the leader of the *Yeqwyeqwi:ws* longhouse where he and many other *Stó:lō* people practise the traditional Coast Salish Winter Dance ceremonial. He has been an active advocate of *Stó:lō* rights and a vigorous promoter of the revival of *Stó:lō* traditional culture. With other Elders, he currently advises *Stó:lō* Nation Chiefs on matters of culture.

Brian Thom received his MA in Anthropology from the University of British Columbia in 1995. His primary interest is in Coast Salish ethnography and archaeology. He has been working for the *Stó:lō* Nation since 1994, co-ordinating their traditional use study, developing high-school cirriculum and conducting research on *Halq'emélem* place names. Before his current position, Brian worked with the U.B.C. Museum of Anthropology, Semiahmoo First Nation, Saanich Native Heritage Society, Upper Skagit Tribal Council and Cowichan Tribal Council.

You Are Asked to Witness

Key to the *Stó:lō* Writing System for *Halq'eméylem* used in this book...

Halq'eméylem was traditionally an oral language, having no written form. Work in the 1970s and 1980s by *Stó:lō* Elders at the *Coqualeetza* Cultural Center and Brent Galloway (a linguist who was then with University of California, Berkeley) has produced a standardized "orthography," or way of writing the language as it is heard. This orthography is used throughout this book.[1]

Brent Galloway published an excellent discussion of the orthography and the pronunciation of *Halq'eméylem* sounds in his short article "The significance of the *Halkomelem* Language Material". This is reproduced and slightly summarized here.[2]

The vowels in *Halq'eméylem* are:

a　　as in English fat, bat (when under ´ or ` or before w or y) or as in English "sell" or "bet" (elsewhere).

e　　as in English sill, bill (when between palatal sounds l, lh, x, y, s, ts, ts', k, k') or as in English "pull" or "bull" (when between labialized sounds m, w, kw, kw', qw, qw', xw, xw) or as in English "mutt", "what" (elsewhere).

i　　as in English "antique", "beet", "eel".

o　　as in English "pot", "mop", "father", "brother".

ō　　as in English "no", "go", "crow".

u　　as in English "Sue", "soon", "moon", "flu".

Most vowels can be followed by [y] or [w] in the same syllable:

aw　　as in English "cow".

ay　　rare in English, some have it in "sang".

ew　　as in Canadian English "about".

ey　　as in English "bait".

iw　　as in English "peewee" minus the last "ee".

iy　　as in English "beet".

ōw　　as in English "ah well" minus the last "ell".

oy　　as in English "bite".

ow　　as in English "bowl".

´ *or* `　　Almost all *Halq'eméylem* words have at least one stressed vowel (like á or à or í for example). Some words have several stressed vowels. The stress marks are needed to tell which part of the word is said louder and higher. Without this a speaker will have a foreign accent or say the wrong word. Stress (´ or ` does not change the pronunciation of a vowel (qwá:l "mosquito" and qwà:l "talk" both rhyme with English "pal"). Stress means the vowel is pronounced fairly loud and with a higher melody than if the vowel was unstressed. High stress (shown by ´ over a vowel) has the highest pitch, about four notes above a vowel without a stress mark. Mid stress (shown by ` over a vowel) has a medium pitch, about two notes above a vowel without stress.

:　　means that the sound before the colon is prolonged or dragged out twice as long as a sound without a following colon.

The only consonants which are pronounced like those in English are:

p　　as in English "pill" and "spin".

t　　as in English "tick" and "stand".

ch　　as in English "church".

ts　　as in English "rats".

k　　as in English "king" and "skill".

kw　　as in English "inkwell" and "queen".

th　　as in English "thin" (but not voiced as in "this" or "the").

sh　　as in English "shine".

s　　as in English "sill".

h　　as in English "hat".

m　　as in English "man" and "bottom".

l　　as in English "land" and "camels".

y　　as in English "yes" and "say".

w　　as in English "wood" and "how".

This leaves eighteen sounds, most of which do not even occur in English.

q　　made by raising the very back of the tongue to touch the soft palate

qw　　made just like the *q* but with rounded lips

There are ten consonants written with an apostrophe: ch', k', kw', p', q', qw', t', th', ts', tl'. These are popped or glottalized consonants. Th occurs in English wi<u>dth</u> and brea<u>dth</u>.

'   glottal stop. It is found in a few words in English like, "mu<u>tt</u>on" or "bu<u>tt</u>on" or Cockney English "bo<u>tt</u>le" (spelled with "tt") or beginning each "uh" in "uh-uh" (the sound meaning "no") or the sound beginning "earns" in "Mary earns" when pronounced differently from "Mary yearns".

lh   made by putting your tongue in position to say an "l" but then blowing air (like an "h") around the sides of the tongue. This sound may be heard in English after "k" sound in a few words like "clean" (klhin) or "clear" or "climb".

There are four blown x sounds. These sounds are made by raising the tongue to narrow the passage of air till you hear the friction of the air

x   made with the middle of the tongue raised roughly in the same place is it is put to make a y as in "yawn". But instead of using your voice you just blow air and it produces a friction sound between the middle of the tongue and the front of the hard palate. English has this sound first in "Hugh" or "hew".

xw   made with the tongue raised a little further back, by the middle off the hard palate (roof of the mouth), but it also requires rounded lips. It sounds a lot like wh in some words in English but with more friction on the roof of the mouth.

    x̲   made still further back, in fact with the back of the tongue raised close to the soft palate (where the q is made). German has this sound in "ach" for example, and Scottish has it in "lock" meaning "lake".

    x̲w   made in the same back place as *x̲* but is also made with round lips. It is like a blown qw while *x̲* is like a blown q.

Footnotes

1   See Brent Galloway, *Tó:lméls ye Siyelyólexwa: Wisdom of the Elders.* *Coqualeetza* Education Training Center, Sardis, 1980. The exception for the use of the *Halq'eméylem* orthography is for words in other Aboriginal languages. *Halq'eméylem* words cited from a source where they appeared phonetically have been changed to the *Stó:lō* orthography, were possible.

2   See Galloway, p. 23-27 in *The Chilliwacks and Their Neighbors,* edited by R. Maud, B. Galloway and M. Weeden, Talonbooks, Vancouver 1987. This article also lists the Americanist International Phonetic Alphabet (IPA) equivalents to the *Stó:lō* writing system.

CHAPTER 1

THROUGH THE EYES OF *Siyémches te Yeqwyeqwí:ws*

Siyémches (Frank Malloway)

INTRODUCTION

The following edited transcript of an interview with *Siyémches te Yeqwyeqwi:ws* (Chief Frank Malloway of Yakweakwioose) was conducted by Heather Myles and *Hychblo* (Tracey Joe) in June 1996 in *Siyémches' Yeqwyeqwi:ws* longhouse. The questions were prepared in advance and relate to issues discussed by academics in other chapters of this book. Heather was working as assistant curriculum coordinator with *Stó:lō* Nation at the time, and *Hychblo*, or Tracey as she is known in English, was the historical research assistant in the *Stó:lō* Aboriginal Rights and Title Department. This was the first time Tracey or Heather had ever formally interviewed an Elder on tape. Heather asked most of the questions, but because Tracey is related to *Siyémches* and a member of his *Yeqwyeqwi:ws* longhouse, her presence undoubtedly contributed to the ambiance and gave context for *Siyémches'* responses. Both Heather and Tracey chose *Siyémches*, "Frank," because of his extensive knowledge of *Stó:lō* culture.

Like his late father, the highly respected Chief Ritchie Malloway, Frank is heavily involved in *Stó:lō* spirituality as expressed in the Winter Dance/Spirit Dance ceremonial. Over the years Frank has played a key role in the preservation and promotion of traditional cultural knowledge. As he explains in his answers to Heather and Tracey's questions, he has made effective use of learning opportunities from both *Stó:lō* and mainstream Canadian society. In this interview Frank speaks on a variety of topics, some of which might be considered controversial. There may be others with different interpretations of the events, situations and people he discusses. Frank recognizes that he does not speak for all *Stó:lō*. When reviewing the typed transcript he was careful to point out that he does not know everything: "I can only tell you what I know. None of us know everything. We have to tell it the way it was told to us by the Elders. We can't change it." Clearly, *Siyémches'* knowledge is deep and varied.

Siyémches: Most of the time when you read of our *Stó:lō* history you read about fishing. Fishing has always been important. Like where you have two canoes going down the Fraser river with a bag net between them. I was never taught too much about that because we're from the *Ts'elxwéyeqw* (Chilliwack) tribe and most of our fishing is done at that Chilliwack River. Very seldom did we venture out into the Fraser. I remember my father going to the Fraser river to purchase, or barter, fish. My father *Th'eláchiyatel* (Grand Chief Richard Malloway) wasn't a fisherman, he was a dairy farmer. He never had time to go out to the river and so he usually purchased all his fish.

Fishing on the Chilliwack River

My grandfather went up the Fraser canyon for about six weeks to preserve his salmon for the winter but he did a lot of his fishing in the Chilliwack River. But I guess I was lucky that I went with him once. I must of only been about eight years old at the time. You see, I went into the hospital when I was eleven or twelve and my grandfather died six months after I went into the hospital. So I must have been quite young. But I remember this one trip where we asked my father if we could use his wagon – he had a horse and wagon. So I went with him and my grandmother and grandfather and we went right around to where Albert Cooper lives (you know where that first house is going up to Chilliwack Lake by the Vedder bridge), there was a big field there at that time. And we went through the field and down to the river. It must have been Coho season. It didn't take long and he had his fish. In those days, he used to hook them with the gaff hook. I couldn't see the fish when they were in the water, but he would reach out with his pole and then he would have one.

I imagine that before the gaff hooks came into existence they used spears. You used to see a lot of people who were re-creating the fishing methods of a long time ago – by using spears for example. Ed Leon used to talk about the spears, and he drew or even made one. I think they had one at Coqualeetza there, where the tips were made of bone or something like that. They were detachable you know, as soon as they went through the fish, you pulled it out, it would get stuck on the other side. My grandmother butchered them on the beach and we put them in the wagon and we came home. And they smoked them and salted them for the winter...

There was another method of fishing that they used to use in the Sweltzer Creek area. I'm not sure if they used it in the Chilliwack River, I never saw it set up there. It was a cone shaped basket like the ones you see in *National Geographic* used by the tribes in Africa. Well, the Chilliwack people used them too. They built a weir across the river. I've never seen one in operation, but Stan Mussell had a model of one in his living room. He used to make a lot of things, and I guess he used to use them to teach his children or something. He never ever used them himself. It was a big trap, you know, and when I went in there he showed it to me and said, "You get trout, you get everything, and they get trapped in there." I wish I could have seen it set up.

Heather: Did many people perform the First Salmon Ceremony?

First Salmon Ceremony

The First Salmon ceremony. I questioned Ed Leon about it, and he told me about the teachings behind it and the prayers. He used to tell a lot of stories that were passed on to him about when the world was created. You know that it went that far back. And he was talking about why we got salmon. He said, "Us Indian people in the Fraser Valley and the tributaries of the Fraser never ate meat very much. We only ate meat when we ran out of salmon." He said, "That when the creator first made mother earth, he had all kinds of meat around here, bear, deer, elk. When you eat meat you get that heavy feeling and you don't want to move too much because meat weighs you down. They used to pray to the creator to send them food that didn't bog them down." Yes, there is a difference between fish and meat – if you eat meat it slows you down. You don't want to get up and do things. He said that one of the *shxwlá:m* [Indian Doctors] had a dream that the creator was sending something up the river and told him to go down to the river and scoop their dip nets, and it was the salmon. They told them how to respect the salmon and thank the ones that sent the salmon. The salmon people from out in the ocean, you pray to them and thank them for what they sent. He used the word children.

I don't hear it often but, he used the word children. The salmon people sent their children up to you so you'd have something different to eat that gives you better energy. Those are the words that Ed Leon used. I don't see them written down like that anymore. Now they just talk about the salmon people sending the salmon up the river. But the words that Ed Leon used to describe it was as children. You have to just thank them; take the bones and send them back after you have eaten the first salmon. He said that if you didn't do that you weren't showing your respect for the salmon people and they would quit sending their children out to you. So you have to show respect for the things that people give to you in the *Stó:lō* way.

Families used to do the first salmon ceremony, but they never made a big thing about it. It was something sacred, something private. When Ed described it to me, he said it was done by the chief and the whole village was included in the ceremony. The ceremony happened when the first fisherman went out and got a fish. When you went out and caught your first Spring salmon of the season you never kept it for yourself. You always gave it away. If you didn't give it away then you'd be unlucky for the rest of the year. You really had to practice that.

The fishing area that I got up the valley its not what you'd call a good Spring hole. Well there are certain parts of the river that people say are good spring holes. But at my hole you'll catch anything but Spring salmon there. I guess it's the deep water, the fast water that the Springs go in. I did get one spring salmon once and we were so hungry for Spring salmon that I brought it home and we ate it, and I didn't give anything away. The rest of the season I only got two more. That's all that I got that season – three Springs. I told my wife Mary, "See I didn't give that first Spring away and I only got two more all season - bad luck." So I had to stick by those practices. My partner, Francis Phillips, he gives his first Spring away. Another one who does that is Darwin Douglas. He walked into my house last year and brought me a great big Spring salmon. He said, "We just went fishing and we are giving some of our first fish to our Elders." He has always been lucky, he and his cousin, and they practice the old culture. But other than that it's a change from the First Salmon ceremony to not keeping the first one for yourself. That's the change that has happened but some people still practice it the old way – like Sonny McHalsie. His whole extended family gets together to practice the traditional first salmon ceremony.

Usually when I get a big salmon I call all my children and we have a meal here. But I haven't done that yet this year cause I really haven't caught one for myself; I've given them all away. I guess that when I do catch one then we will go through that ceremony. One of the other things that I never did was bring the bones back to the river. I've just shared it with my family. I haven't sent any bones back. A lot of families practice it but they leave little things out I guess. Instead of bringing the village together I bring my family together.

Heather: What were the popular fishing techniques that were used out on the Fraser?

Out on the Fraser in the Canyon it was the dip net.

Heather: How did that work exactly?

There were two different methods of using a dip net. One you set it down there in a back eddie and wait for the fish to swim in it and the other you use in fast current when you scoop. I've never ever heard them talk about any other method of fishing other than the dip net. Sometimes I went with my grandfather and his brothers and they made a platform out over the deeper spot. When he stood out on the platform he held the net tight in. He didn't scoop it. He just held it, and as soon as the fish hit the net he'd release the bag and the top end of the bag would close. Then he'd pull it in. That time that I was with him, he caught two sockeye at a time. They had themselves tied up to the bank so they wouldn't get pulled in in case they caught a big Spring. But in the canyon you see them scooping too – that's the second type of use for the net. They get into a spot, it's mostly where there is no back eddie, and the river goes right through in a swift spot and then they just scoop their net right through it. They scoop down river with the current. They get a lot of fish that way.

Dip and Still Nets
on the Fraser

Heather: With the dip nets did people make them themselves or did they buy them?

I imagine if you go back two hundred years ago everybody had that skill to make them themselves, cause it was a required skill to survive. They used to use the stinging nettle fibres for the net – for the web part of it. I've always wanted to learn how to make the string from stinging nettles. I tried once, but I kept breaking the fibres and so I just quit. But I was over at the X̱á:ytem interpretive centre and this lady was showing me the twine that they made from the stinging nettle and it looked like the cotton twine that you buy in the store. It was real nice. I was talking to Darwin Douglas about it and he was saying that it takes a long time, it really takes a long time to make the nettle fibre; its real fine work. So if its that difficult to do I guess that I will never learn [laughs]. Right now we have a fellow who can weave dip net bags. His name is Kenny Wallace. He's good at it and he used to teach at Coqualeetza. Whenever we had a program we would bring him in he would make the bags. And he makes the hoops for the dip nets too.

Heather: After a fish was caught what were some of the popular methods of preserving?

I think that it depends on the time of the year. Because in the summer time it was wind dried. Somebody told me, I'm not sure about this, but somebody told me they bartered for salt. They knew how to salt salmon before the Hudson's Bay traders even came in They got the salt from a special place in what is now the United States. I'm not exactly sure where it came from. We always asked him to tell us, and he would just point to the States.

Wind Dried Salmon

Every way that you cook a salmon it tastes different. Salt salmon, people crave for salt

salmon. Certain parts of salmon. You know the belly of the Spring is very rich. When we went up to a gathering at Katz – Katz landing up at Chawathil – Chief Herman Peters said that there is salt salmon on the table, and we went rushing over there and everybody grabbed a piece of salt salmon. And Allan Williams from Scowlitz he says, "Oh I don't like salt salmon." I asked, "Why?" He said, "I eat too much potatoes." That's because he separates them. When my wife cooks them she mixes it together. She will cook the salt salmon and then she will boil the potatoes and then she will mix them together. But the way that we were brought up by our grandmothers, they'd put the salt salmon on the table and then the potatoes and you mixed them together yourself. And it's really good. And that's all that you do is eat it, just salt salmon and potatoes. You don't have anything else. It's a delicacy too. I guess a lot people don't like it. I guess you can't eat it every day, but it's a treat when you do get it. Smoked salmon. My wife says she can eat smoked salmon three times a day and still not get enough of it.

Heather: How do you smoke a salmon?

Smoked Salmon

You just filet the salmon, but it has to be done in the cooler part of the season. We don't smoke salmon till about October when the weather is cool out. We have October weather right now. Flies and the heat will spoil them you know. But now-a-days with our deep freezer we only smoke them for two or three days and then we take them down and put them in the freezer. But before you would smoke them for a week or two weeks and get them hard as a board. Then they didn't require any refrigeration. You just kept them out of the dampness. Some people used to soak them. Because they were dried out so much they would soak them for a day before. If you wanted them for an evening meal you would soak them in the morning and cook them in the evening.

But there's a difference between the way *Stó:lō* people and the way *Xwelítems* [Euroamericans] eat salted and smoked salmon. If you smoked a Spring salmon and put

You Are Asked To Witness

it on the table *Xwelítems* will eat it straight without steaming it or boiling it first. We don't do that. There's a danger of being poisoned if you don't steam or boil it. One guy I know didn't believe Francis when Francis told him "You've got to boil that first before you eat it." He just wouldn't believe him. You have to cook it. Then it finally dawned on me that I did the same thing when I smoked a Spring salmon. It was the only fish that I had in my little smoke house because I caught it too late in the year, and the skin was just black when I took it out of the water. Nobody wanted to buy it off of me. So I said, "I'll filet it and smoke it." I took it down and showed it to my mechanic. He was always asking me about smoked salmon. I brought it down and asked him, "Is this alright? Is this the way you want it?" And gee he got a knife out and they started slicing it and he started eating it just like that. I looked at him and I almost gagged. "Oh gee, are you eating it like that? We usually steam it or boil it first." But he just ate it: "Oh its good, its good." I guess it was good to them. I couldn't have eaten it. [laughter]

Difference between
Stó:lō and *Xwelítem*

Heather: How long will smoked salmon last?

Indefinitely. When they are smoked really good – when they're smoked as hard as a board – they last a long time. I've noticed that if you keep wind dried salmon too long it starts to fall apart. It just turns to powder. I went up to the canyon and it was late in the season and a lady that I knew I asked me if I had gotten my dried salmon yet. She used to be married to a man in Chehalis and she could never dry salmon there because there isn't a strong dry wind like there is in the Fraser Canyon. Then when she went home to Lytton where the weather was different and so she started to dry salmon again. She asked, "Frank, did you get your dried salmon?" I said, "No," and she said, "Oh I got some." Then she gave me two, but by the time that I got home they were just all in flakes. She had them so long that they just flaked out almost like powder. So she kept them too long.

Heather: Did you want to talk about family now?

Traditional Transportation

Oh, I'll talk about transportation. I've got that on my mind. We went through this at Coqualeetza when we were developing elementary school curriculum there as to methods of travel. It is done mostly by canoes and I guess before the Hudson's Bay traders

came, I guess before our country was all dykes and drainage ditches, there was a lot of tributaries or sloughs and it was really easy to travel up and down the Fraser Valley because these slough along the Fraser. Take the Hope Slough, for example. That was a big river before, a part of the Fraser river. But they blocked it at one end and now you can't get through. I guess at one time it used to go right up to Rosedale. Rather than stay on the swift Fraser you'd take a side tributary.

Shovel Nose Canoe

One of the popular canoes for travelling on the Chilliwack River and the sloughs was the 'shovel nose canoe.' Burns Mussell used to describe the shovel nose canoe and I think that I owe a lot to Burns Mussell. Like I said, my father never fished, and Burns Mussell was the one that used to take people up and teach them how to fish. He would help them for one or two years and after they learned how to fish Burns Mussell would leave them on their own. Then he would grab other ones and teach them how. He said, "I don't care as long as they learn how to fish and provide for their family." He used to use a dug out canoe in that Choate area in the Fraser River. And they were heavy. The bottom was not like the racing canoes that you see today. You know the racing canoes are only inch and a half thick on the bottom. But these fishing canoes are about three inches, four inches thick.

Heather: This is a shovel nose canoe with the thick bottom?

Any river canoe. You know they were really thick bottomed. It was mostly so that they wouldn't be so tippy. With a heavy bottom and thin sides and it would never tip. When you were pulling in nets, you could stand on the edge of it and not tip over. But if you do that with a racing canoe, there is no weight on the bottom and you'll just flip right over. Or even these fibre glass canoes; they may be wide but there's no weight on the bottom and they would flip over. If you had a sharp nose canoe like a racing canoe it would go where the current would move you but a shovel nose canoe would just ride on top of the waves. The river wouldn't control you, you'd control the canoe. It was just like a sled, you would ride over the waves. That's the way that Burns described it. When you were coming down the river the canoe would go where you wanted it to, instead of just getting thrown around by the current.

When you go up the river there was a method of poling. You know that was a skill in itself. A person would pole right up the Fraser along the edge of the river. I think that there was a real skill in it because I tried it and I couldn't keep the canoe straight. I would push on one side and the canoe would head out the other way. You had to have a skill to learn how to do that. They used to talk about the meaning of *Ts'elxwéyeqw* (Chilliwack): "What does *Ts'elxwéyeqw* mean?" But if you heard our Chief Louie, he would say "*Ts'elxwéyeqw* means as far as you can get up the river using a paddle. Then when you had to switch to a pole, and that's where *Ts'elxwéyeqw* was." So that made sense to me, and that was the name of our tribe – my people. Those are the only two types of canoes that ever heard Elders talk about.

The Meaning of Chilliwack

During the gold rush time. They used to pack supplies into the mines beyond Chilliwack Lake, only they couldn't get them because Chilliwack lake is quite rough and there were no good trails. So Chief Billy Sepass built a huge freight canoe out of a cedar log. And his picture is in that book *The Chilliwacks and their Neighbours*. A lot of canoes we see in the early pictures are not our shovel nose design. After doing some research we learned that our people traded with the Nootka people for those sea going canoes. They used to use them in Harrison Lake or for raiding parties. Even though today all the *Stó:lō* villages are closely knit, in earlier times there were disputes among different *Stó:lō* tribes. There was always some people trying to claim more territory. They used to use these big war going canoes for those raids.

Intervillage Disputes

Heather: Do you know how often these raids occurred?

No I don't know how often they happened, but in every community there was always one leader who would lead his people and try to get more territory or wealth. It stopped when he was killed or whatever. We never hear how often these things happen.

Heather: Who usually started these disputes? Was it the people from the coast?

No. According to Chief Louie's story there was a great leader from Kilgard. Either his father or he himself came from Vancouver Island. His name was *Xeyteleq,* Ray Silver carries that name. He's almost a legendary figure. But he really did exist. When you go to Vancouver Island you hear the name *Xeyteleq,* you know Indian names usually aren't shared that much. But I was really glad that I ran into Victor Underwood Sr. you know he was a real important person in the long house [spirit dances]. He was a head speaker and different tribes would hire him to be a speaker at their gatherings. He was asking me to help him identify people by their Indian names so they could be called as witnesses, and I told him that Ray Silver was called *Xeyteleq*. "Oh *Xeyteleq*," he said "That name comes from our country. I'll tell you about it sometime." Then he kept on with his work. Later, I was visiting him and I reminded him "you were going to tell me a story about *Xeyteleq*." "Yeah, Yeah, so you have *Xeyteleq* in the Fraser Valley?" I said "yeah." And he said "well there is a story that goes back to Pat Bay [on the Saanich peninsula near Victoria]. There was a man named *Xeyteleq* there. Today you don't find a *Xeyteleq* at Pat Bay but that's where *Xeyteleq* originated." He said that *Xeyteleq* had four sons. Well, in the old days they'd get a woman but they wouldn't take her home they would live in her village. So he said you go to West Sannich and there is a *Xeyteleq* and you go to Victoria and there is a *Xeyteleq* and you go to LaConner Washington and there is a *Xeyteleq* and you go to Chilliwack in the Fraser Valley there is a *Xeyteleq*. He said "in one of our stories we heard that one of the *Xeyteleq* had moved to the Fraser Valley, but we didn't know where, or from what family." So when you told me about this *Xeyteleq* in the Kilgard longhouse, I thought, "Oh, we found the missing *Xeyteleq*." So that was the story that he told me...

Heather: There was raiding then here amongst the river as well as with groups from Vancouver Island?

History can
Hurt People

I guess there was, but you don't hear it too much, people don't talk about it. You might create friction and family disputes right among our own people, and its past history, its past history. It shouldn't be talked about, and that's the reason I think a lot of these stories about battles was put in the back. You don't bring it up no more or you'll start a

fight again. So they weren't recorded as history. Just certain people knew them – story tellers I guess. But Bert Louie's story, you know, I was really amazed at that one when I heard that.

Heather: We were talking about families

And from families I guess you could go to talking about status or classes. My father used to talk about the different classes: *sí:yá:m* and slaves. And the ordinary regular people that didn't have any title. And in a way he was glad that all that disappeared. If you knew my father, he wanted to be friends with everybody. It didn't matter what class you belonged to. He said, "Maybe classes served a purpose, but I'm glad that we don't have those things today." And he said, "I'm glad the old people who really used to use that cast system strictly are mostly all gone now."

Heather: It was strictly followed?

It was strictly followed by our old people. If you go back just twenty years, it was being brought up on the Longhouse floor. People would say, "That person shouldn't be trying to put himself up there, he's from slave background. You're not supposed to be on the floor talking like that! You're from a slave family." Like I was saying, I don't want a lot of this to be used in the book, you can use it but don't publish names, cause this was *John Doe* our famous Indian Doctor. And there was a split in his community; in the longhouse. When my *friend* was initiated as a winter dancer back in the early 1970's all the leaders of the different families were there, including *Fred Smith* and John Doe and other family leaders. They were all the leaders of the Smoke House, and when my friend was initiated he had all of them working on him; working with him and working for him. But after that it sort of started. I guess you could call it climbing the ladder; trying to be the *siyá:m* [leader]. And if they all worked together the way they did when my friend was in there everything would have been good, but all of them wanted to be the top leader I guess, and Fred Smith was a great, great speaker. When you got him on a good day, boy! My Dad said you can't beat that Fred Smith when he delivers a speech. He's really good and he was a great one for speaking at funeral dinners. You didn't have to tell him what to say, he knew what to say. He knew how to comfort the family and he knew how to respect the person that you were putting away, and there's a certain knack to it. And I guess Fred Smith wanted to take over leadership in the Smoke House. He started correcting his peers; telling them they weren't doing things in the right way, and he got John Doe mad, and John Doe got up and spoke. (I wasn't there at the time, I didn't witness this but it came to me second hand) and John Doe told him, "Fred," he said, "don't be on the floor telling us what to do. We're the leaders here and you have no right being on the floor telling us what to do because you're from a slave family. You shouldn't even be on the floor with us." You know that was twenty or twenty-five years ago, maybe less than twenty, and I was really shocked when I heard that.

And another story: an aunt of Fred Smith used to really promote herself. She liked being the leader of the woman, and she'd decorate the Catholic Church at Christmas time. She'd put everything out and she used to always feed the Oblate priests who camped in the church (you had to feed them supper; you had to feed them breakfast) and my grandmother used to always be mumbling and I didn't understand it, but my friend understood it. He said, "That woman, she shouldn't be doing that – she's from slaves. She's trying to make herself big. She's trying to cover her past by doing things like this, but she'll never do that because she's from slaves." The reason Fred Smith's grandfathers moved out of here was because they were from the slave family. When they got their freedom they moved to the States figuring that they'd get away from that slave stigma, but it followed them. The descendants are all covered with that and it's really hard to get rid of. You can't do that if you're from slaves. Its interesting though, because I don't know whether Fred Smith's sons are considered slaves, because their mother was from an important family. I just don't know whether they inherited that slave stamp? Half their family is from the high class, but if it was up to the Elders they wouldn't have allowed Fred Smith and his wife to get married, but they got married.

Social Status

Legacy of Slavery

Family and Wealth

Heather: What, exactly, are the different classes, then, and what do they mean?

There was the high family. It's mostly like royalty. And the second family? Hmmm, how did my Dad describe it now? I think the second level families were the people that really kept the village together: the hunters and all that. The lower class people were just people who didn't have anybody. They were from small families. Your richness was your extended family in those times. Its like what happened on this reserve; there used to be 5 or 6 families here, but now there's only one. When you got down to being almost by yourself that was the lowest class family, because you didn't have anybody for support. You didn't have anyone to help you with your game or providing for you or anything when you were the lowest class. It didn't mean that you were ignorant, it's just that you didn't have any of the status of wealth, I guess that's what it was. You didn't have the helping people provide for you and the middle class people were the ones that were the foundation of the whole village. They were the workers; the ones that provided, and the higher class people (there wasn't that many of them) they were the descendants from the leaders, but they also married into the middle class. The slaves part, it didn't even count, they didn't count the slaves. I used to think they counted them as the lower of the lowest but they weren't even counted.

Heather: They didn't deserve to be counted?

I guess they didn't deserve to be counted, but my uncle, Bob Joe, used to say that slaves were really treated nice, really treated well; and they were. The only thing you didn't do was bring them to the table to eat with you. They had to eat separately. The way I understand it there was a big round of fire in the longhouse where the families ate, but the slaves had to eat outside or eat in the corner or something. I'm not sure how it was done, but Bob Joe used to describe these things. He explained that a family from near Hope got so rich in slaves that they almost outnumbered the free people in the village. Well, these slaves tied some canoes together and laid planks across them and then put all their possessions on top and their owners said, "You're free. Go back to where you came from." But they never did reach the coast. They settled in another village (I'm not sure which village it is) but Bob Joe said they built another village on the Fraser on their own where they started a village of slaves. But he didn't point out which village it was.

Free Slave Village

Heather: What were the jobs or responsibilities that the slaves had?

I think they mostly did the menial tasks like gathering wood and helping build longhouses or shelters, and gathering plants and berries and even fishing and things like that. When you read the *Chilliwack's and Their Neighbours* I think they talk about one fellow who owned a slave when they were clearing the international boundary line, and that's not too long ago. But they said this fellow got a job for his slave and put him to work and then collected his slave's paycheque. And I guess that was one of the slaves that was well looked after, but his owners just didn't have the money. They bought him clothes and fed him, but he didn't have anything in his pocket – and that's not too long ago.

Heather: When did they stop using slaves?

I really don't know when this was stopped. I guess it sort of just drifted away. But the worse part of it was that families knew; people knew who is descended from slaves. You know, we don't talk about it today because we've lost all that information. People just put it in the back of their mind and it disappears, but some of these things keep popping up like the woman I told you about, and Fred Smith. And then my brother told me, "Yeah, that's the stories we heard a long time ago" He said, my grandmother used to talk about it when Fred Smith's auntie was trying to get up in the social ladder, and "No she doesn't belong there, she's from slaves," That information is in the memory of the old people...

Heather: Which people owned slaves or had slaves?

I'm not sure, but I think it was probably the higher family, the *Siyá:m*. Probably the common people, the workers, too. They all needed help and they probably were in possession of slaves as well. Maybe it depended on who captured them whether a slave was theirs or not.

In the *sí:yá:m* [upper classes] too. They call people chiefs now you know, but my dad said we never had chiefs a long time ago. There was the family leader but you never called him "chief." The main family leader looked after the village. The main leader went down to the village and sort of appointed the other family leaders to do their work and they assumed leadership and those areas. Like the fellow I mentioned earlier, *Tixwelatza,* he was the warrior leader. Anytime Yakweakwioose had a war *Tixwelatza* was the leader and my dad said whenever fishing season came they had a leader in that area too, and he'd take charge of everybody.

Leadership - *Sí:yá:m*

Heather: He'd take charge of the family or the village?

All the working people. All the people that were able to go fishing – he was their leader. He was concerned with the preservation of salmon. And hunting too. The main family leader picked the best hunter – he was a *Si:yá:m* as well – they called the hunting leader *Tewit*. The *Tewit* would take the people out hunting and he was the leader for that period of time – during the hunting season. The same for plant gathering. That was mostly the ladies' work you know. The forest was our garden, and women went out and taught the young people the different uses of all the plants out there.

Winter Dance
Season

There were leaders for the Spirit Dancing too. My dad said, "You young people start singing in October and you go continuously till late February. In the old days we didn't have a continuous season. We'd start singing in November and then during the month of January it got real quiet. Then in February we'd start singing again until the end of February when we finished. Now you young guys go right through January." The way my dad explained it, the power of *Syúwél* [winter dance spirit power] is in the mountains, and in the fall when the snow has come *Syúwél* comes down to the warmer climate and it starts hitting the people. *Syúwél* hits people and then they wake up and start singing; and *Syúwél* goes around the world. And I used to often wonder, "what do you mean it goes around the world? Goes right around to China and comes back?" And then I was looking at a map of the Coast Salish Territory and it sort of goes in a circle: Sechelt,

Nanaimo down to Victoria, across to Neah Bay, you know, and up to Nooksack and it comes back, and its almost like that's the only world the Coast Salish knew. And I was thinking "that's how the Elders described their territory, the Coast Salish territory: around the world." And the Coast Salish are the only people who practise Spirit Dancing. If you go out of the territory to the north they don't practice, they don't have it. You go too far south and they don't have it. So he says, "When *Syúwél* is in the Island there's not much *Syúwél* here, its all over in the Island, and when its coming back and going to the mountains, that's when you wake up again. Then it goes back to the mountains and you're finished – you have to wait for another season. That was the *Syúwél* season, the dancing season." In January we didn't hardly ever sing, because that's when the *Syúwél* was over at the island, and that's when they used to start, in the beginning of January. Now they start in September [laughter].

Heather: Was there movement between different social levels or did you stay in one?

I don't think there was any movement. You were born into your class you know... I guess if you go back in history, well its like Chief Ken Malloway said: "we're the original chiefs of the *Ts'elxéyeqw* people." He meant himself, his uncle, my brother and myself. We trace our history right back to Chilliwack lake. We're the oldest families here, but we don't say we're higher up. Our history says we're from the first families. The names that we carry are from the first family; from the four brothers who started the Chilliwack tribe. Kenny Malloway carries that name *Wili:léq*, and I carry the name *Siyémches*, my son carries the name *Th'eláchiyatel* and my uncle carried the name *Yexwéylem* but now his son Cecil carries that name. So the four names are still in our family and Kenny Malloway always says that if you're looking for chiefs, you look towards our family because we're hereditary chiefs. Even though Kenny Malloway is elected, he's still from the family of chiefs. My dad said that there weren't any 'chiefs' in those days, just *sí:yá:m*. The history of the original four Chilliwack brothers is still in our family and he became very upset when one of the names went to Victoria. He said they never even consulted with us, they just went to see my grandfather and he said, "Yeah go ahead," but he didn't understand what they were doing. When Dad went to talk to him about it grandfather didn't know who the name went to. He said, "Oh, my daughters came over here and said things to me that I didn't understand and I just agreed with them." What they wanted to do was name one of his daughter's grandsons. They wanted her father to share his name with him and so the name *Wili:léq*, is in Victoria, and Kenny was really upset about it. He said, "That's a Chilliwack name and it's a very important part of our history. It should never have left our territory."

Heather: Could you tell me a little about traditional houses and shelters?

When they were planning the *Xá:y:tem* longhouse Interpretive Centre in Mission I said, "I'd like to see somebody build a shed type roof," and that's the way they designed it. Its funny, but a lot of people complained about the shed type roof. They said, "Why don't you build something better? It just looks like a lean-to." But we wanted to teach people. For example, take the Coqualeetza loghouse. People can go there and see its gabled roof, and then they can look at the *Xá:y:tem* longhouse and see the original type of homes we had. If you look at the early paintings of Fort Langley with all the longhouses along the beach, they're all shed type. You won't see any of the gable style roofs or whatever you call it.

Heather: Were the longhouses dug into the ground?

Do you know where the Anglican church is on Higginson Road in Chilliwack? We were always told that was where the Chilliwack people's headquarters were. I'm not sure if it was in Bert Louie's oral history with Oliver Wells, or was it in Bob Joe's oral history too? It's in one of those that they describe the longhouse. They said when you come into it you go down four feet before you get to the floor, it's four feet into the ground, semi-underground, and I didn't read that until I build my longhouse. I wasn't copying anybody's but there used to be an old barn at my place that belong to Chief Louie. I asked my father if I could build my longhouse on that site. The old barn's foundations were still

Hereditary Names

Longhouses

there but they were all covered in blackberry bushes. So he said, "Yeah sure, if you have enough room there, go ahead." So I hired a fellow to come in and excavate, and he hauled away the foundations from the old barn. I told him to level it out, so he pushed all the dirt up until he got everything perfectly level. When I later hired contractors to come and put the foundation in they said that in an eighty foot span there was only inch difference from each end, so that guy did a perfect job...

So after we started building I brought the guy back and he pushed all the dirt back and then when I was levelling out for my doorway I thought, "Holy Smokes, we're way below the surface of the parking lot!" So we had to build our door up to be level with the outside so no water would come in. We ended up two feet below the surface of the parking lot. When you come in, you have to go down and although we didn't realize it at the time it really helped because the soil holds its moisture. By being two feet down it keeps the floor dust-free and the earth packs like concrete when we dance. That was a description of the old building, it was four feet down... I guess it's more or less for warmth and for dust and there's moisture and it stays moist. If you go to the Coqualeetza longhouse there's a lot of dust because the floor is level with the outside. If you go to the Skowkale longhouse it's dusty too because there's very little drop in the floor from the outside.

Heather: Do you know when the last pithouses were used?

Pithouses

My father never really talked about being in one, but at the Coqualeetza Elders's meetings we've heard of some Elders who stayed in pithouses. I think those Elders are gone now, but we did have some Elders who remembered living in one. The only thing my father used to tell me about was the stairs. He would laugh. Each family built the stairs into their pithouse a little different. He said every entrance was a little different, and when woman came down in skirts they didn't know how to cover up or hide their upper legs. He said you'd look up and if it was a stranger you could see thighs [laughter] but if it was somebody that knew how the ladder went you couldn't see thighs. You just saw ankles. [more laughter] We used to joke about that. He said you know when a stranger comes in because they come down the ladder and you can see thighs.

Heather: How big were villages in the past? How many people lived there?

Villages

It's very hard to say because written history only goes back maybe 150 years. The Elders always say that the villages were huge and that they had to spread out because the houses were getting full. You know, a lot of the village sites were left out of the reserves and those people had to be moved. Similar to where Coqualeetza was. There used to be a longhouse on the Coqualeetza properties too. People lived there and they had to move when they cut back on our reserves. I don't know what year it was, they cut back on the reserves and people had to move. Between here and the freeway there was a village, but I'm not sure what its name was. There were a lot of villages left out of the reserves.

Heather: How many people were living in a single longhouse?

Extended Families

Entire extended families – the grandfather and the children and their descendants lived together, but I don't think it went beyond that; if it got too big, they just added on. That's how the longhouses got so long. But Chief Louie, he described a longhouse along here that was a thousand feet long. It housed a huge family and they didn't move because the fish were plentiful. They just stayed out there and when Oliver Wells was asking him to describe where it started and where it ended he said, "Oh, out at Richie Malloway's house, that's where it started and where did it end, over here at Frank's house."

When we were building my longouse we found 2 inches of black soil and it's almost like

ashes, you know, and I was thinking, "There must have been a big fire here sometime ago." And then when Bert Louie said that longhouse burnt down, that's why we're named *Yeqwyeqwi:ws*. "*Yeqw*" means fire. I said, "Boy it couldn't have happened that long ago; the black soil was only two and a half feet down. I'll have to get an archaeologist out here or something." [laughter] There's a lady whose involved with the *X̱á:y:tem* longhouse in Mission. She's a clairvoyant. Do you know who I'm talking about? I used to have 'problems' in the longhouse sometimes. People used to get afraid in my longhouse. They would be walking around in there and hearing things, but I got used to it you know, it didn't bother me. So I told her one day, I said, "When you come down to my longhouse, I want to know where the old longhouse was, the thousand foot longhouse." And she did come here when we had some gathering in the longhouse in the summer time and she was standing in my driveway and I asked, "Can you feel anything? Do you know where the old longhouse was?" She was just standing there and going like this [waving hands], and she said, "There's a real strong 'thing' right through here" – through the orchard. She said, "It goes right through your longhouse and it goes out that way. It's like a trail" So I said, "Maybe they're walking on that trail, maybe that's why people hear people going through the building." I said, "That trail probably went right through here." And she said, "It's really strong, I can feel it." But she never did point out where the old longhouse was, it might have been too far.

Heather: How much were overland routes used: trails, versus waterways?

There was quite a few trails. For example, in my grandfather's time they still used that trail that ran between Cultus Lake and Nooksack, Washington... There's other stories about trails from the Chilliwack Lake area to Skagit Valley. John Wallace talks about how his family history comes from Skagit. He wanted to find out how his grandfathers got to Chilliwack, so he went across Chilliwack Lake and then overland until he got to the Skagit river. He said he went right down to Sedro Woolley, USA, and had to hitch-hike home. I don't know when that was, but he was curious about how his great-grandfather got to Chilliwack and he went through the headwaters of Chilliwack Lake.

Heather: Was there a lot of trading and exchanging that took place?

Trading Fish for Canoes

Yeah, even canoes were traded. It depended on what type of canoe. A lot of the canoes were built in the territory but your ocean-going canoes, they traded for them with salmon, mostly salmon I guess. The west coast canoes (they call them the west coast canoes or "Nootka-type" canoes) they probably got them in Victoria or wherever. They built a lot of canoes here, river canoes and fishing canoes. There's one church in Chilliwack that was moved from Port Douglas. It was brought down on canoes. They latched the canoes together similar to what Samoans do and Hawaiians do, they made a platform between their canoes and they put this church onto that and drifted it down Harrison Lake to Chilliwack. When they came to Chilliwack landing they pulled it in and moved it to where it stands today. Lumber must have been pretty scarce for them to move a church that far. [laughter]

Hard Work and Pride

Also there was something about how people worked so hard, I mean not too long ago. Today you're so used to Department on Indian Affairs looking after you that you don't want to go all-out. For example, if people don't have a house, they wait for someone to build them one. My mother talks about Gordon James. He just died a few years ago and he did some work for somebody and they paid him by giving him that house. But to get it on the reserve Gordon had to take it apart board by board, put it in his canoe, and paddle across the Fraser River to Chilliwack and pack it over and rebuild it. My mother said he brought it over in a canoe board by board and he built that house. He was a World War Two veteran too, and the Government never built him a house. Usually the veterans got homes before anybody else did, but he had to build his own. I was reminded the other day when somebody was making a speech and talking about the young people nowadays. Some are so spoiled they don't like to do things for them-selves. They expect other people to do things for them or supply them things and then my mother's story about Gordon James came into mind about how he hauled that house over by canoe, board by board.

Heather: What time period did people start switching over from canoes to different modes of transportation?

I think when they brought the out the Model T Ford [laughter]. The horse and buggy came into effect when they started damming and blocking the sloughs and putting in drainage ditches. It was when our waterways began vanishing that we switched transportation. My dad talked about how a lot of times they just walked the trails and then when they made roads they switched over to horse and buggies. I think it was as settlement came in that different things began to change slowly – in 1860's, 1870's. There's a story in Tracey Joe's family and my wife's family, about my wife's grandmother – she was half Chinese. Her mother was Chief Louie's sister, and her grandfather was *Tixwelatsa*. Her mother took her to Ashcroft but her father decided to go back to China, and he took two sons and the oldest daughter (which is my wife's grandmother) with him. He was taking them to China. He left the two smaller girls with his wife. She was travelling by train and they had to stop at Mission to take on water, (it was still steam trains in those days). When they stopped she jumped off the train and ran back along the tracks until she reached Scowlitz where she talked to an old man and asked him to help her get to her uncle's place. The old man said, "I'll take you there," and he brought her across the river in a canoe. He probably paddled her part way up

Canoes into Cars

the Chilliwack River and then walked the rest of the way to this site right here. When she got older I guess they arranged a marriage for her and old Chief Louie gave her a lot up Bailey Road. He also gave another niece a lot (that's the Roberts family). Chief Louie owned a lot of land. So you know, they still used the canoes for transportation when they brought her over to Chilliwack after she ran away from the train.

You know, one of the things we didn't touch on when we were discussion the methods of travelling with the canoes was the sail. They used to use a sail and Lawrence James (from Union Bar and American Bar near Yale) he use to come down to Hope by canoe do his shopping. When I was on my way fishing, I used to see him sitting in the park and he'd say, "Oh, I'm going home in a while. I'm just waiting for the wind." "Waiting for the wind?" I'd ask. "Yeah, I came down in the canoe, and I've got to wait for the wind before I put my sail up and go back up the river." So he used to go all the way up Fraser and the wind would carry him up with the sail. I never knew how those worked, I never did. I used to see canoes with the board across the top, you know, with a hole in them and another board in the bottom with a hole in it and that's where you put the sail mast. The sail was like a sheet of silk – like parachute material. Those sails really moved your canoe. Lawrence used to travel all over with the canoe, and go all the way down to Fort Langley and come back. James Charlie, Jimmy Charlie, used to take a canoe load of fish down to Fort Langley by canoe. He said, "It didn't take us long to get down there, but it took us two to three days to get back." They'd have a load of fish and go and sell it to the buyers down there and it took them two to three days to get back to the Harrison River. I don't know how they used to get back; whether they used sails or not, or if they poled up the river or what, but it would take them a while.

"Sailing" the Fraser

Heather: Perhaps we could change subjects now and you could explain how marriages were arranged in the past?

I really don't know *how* they were arranged, but I know most of them were arranged. Nancy Phillips talked about her marriage being arranged. She was still in school when they brought William there; William's parents came there. I don't know whether they knew her before or whether he's the one that told them he wanted her for his wife, but they just accepted it. She said, "Well I really didn't know him, the family came to talk to me and then my father came to talk to me, and he said that these people want you to be their son's wife, and I agreed." I'm not sure, but it must have been done through her father, her father William. I'm not sure whether they had prior knowledge of each other. I'm not sure whether she came home or went right to Chehalis. Norman Francis, who is really close to death right now, both him and his wife are almost at the end of their lives and theirs was one of the last arranged marriages that I know of.

Arranged Marriages

My dad talked about it in a different way. He said there were some other things that happened before that. Norman Frances told me himself that his family used to bring him over to Chilliwack in a canoe. He said, "There was just board sidewalks in those days, like a western town, and I used to see Sadie walking on the other side so I'd really rush across the street and just walk down the sidewalk so I'd meet her. And I'd say 'hi' to her and she wouldn't say anything. She just kept going." But I guess he choose her and he talked to his family. He must have told them, "That's the girl I want."

My dad remembered the Easter celebration at Chilliwack Landing, (the Skwah reserve). It was a hub of activity there you know. They used to always have an Easter celebration and he said the people came up the slough and they had that little skinny guy. [laughter] That's the way he described Norman: tall and skinny. Dad said they had Norman on their canoe and the family came forward and they wanted to see the chief. So they came over and Norma's family said they wanted Sadie for their son. My dad remembers that because he was down there playing lacrosse when they came over. But what he didn't know was the things that happened prior to that. Norman explained these things to me when I went to Chehalis and I asked him, "Wasn't your marriage arranged?" and he said "Yeah, it was." "We had the old people talk for us," he said. "But I knew her before. I used to go over to Chilliwack just to see her walking in the street." Sadie was a jockey, you know. Harry Stewart had a string of race horses and she was a jockey.

Proposing the
Traditional Way

There's other different ways that people used to propose to one another that Elders used to laugh about. I think they were telling Louise Bolan. There was Henry Thomas, he's gone now just a few years ago, but Louise used to stay in Agassiz, and Henry would always come and sit downstairs. When she got home from shopping he'd be sitting downstairs and never say anything. Then she'd go up to her room – she had to climb a flight of stairs. Then the next week and he'd be sitting there again and she'd ask him, "Are you waiting for somebody?" and he'd just look at her and smile. Then she said "Well you've been sitting here all the time, you better come in and have some coffee." So she invited him upstairs and they had coffee. She was telling this to the Elders and they started laughing at her and they said, "You know what Henry was doing, he was there kind of proposing, but in a silent way – the traditional way. He was sitting there and the minute you invited him up, you accepted his proposal." [laughter] She didn't know this, you know, and, "Yep, you accepted his proposal." That was one of the old ways of doing things. Then they started telling stories about these young people. If they were stuck on a girl, they'd go there and they'd pack wood. They'd bring wood into the house and then they'd go outside and sit and wait and if the parents accepted him, they'd keep the wood and burn it, but if they packed the wood out and put it on the steps, they were saying your proposal is not accepted. Different things like that, you hear different stories in different places about being accepted and rejected. It was mostly up to the parents that accepted or rejected, it wasn't up to the girls.

Tracey: Did they ever talk about families bringing gifts when somebody wanted to marry somebody else's daughter. Did they bring them stuff? Did they talk about that?

Puberty Training for
Girls

I think the family would bring something if they were looking for a wife for the boy. They'd probably bring blankets; woven blankets were the money in those days. But I'm trying to think of something else. One of the other things I learned about were the puberty rites they used when girls entered womanhood. An Elder explained to us the way she was when she had her first menstrual period. They dug a hole in the back about three feet deep and they lined it with cedar boughs and they treated her almost like a "new Spirit Dancer." But all day she had to sit in that pit. They had a tent over the top and she was only brought out to sleep at night and to eat. They used to bring her these fir boughs and they told her, "You pick all the needles out of them, one at a time." That was what she had to do all day, pick the needles out. Then they'd bring her inside and they'd cook for her and feed her; they'd bathe her and comb her hair and wash it. She wasn't allowed to do anything for herself until her period was over. I guess that only happened for the first menstrual period, after that she was able to do things for herself, but that was the rite she had to go through.

Heather: Was that standard practice for all girls, throughout the years?

Yeah, but it's very seldom practiced now.

Heather: When did they stop practicing that?

I don't know; when they sent them all to residential school I guess. I don't know what the men went through. I was never told about what the men went through when they reached a certain age. All they used to say was, "When the young man was around twelve and thirteen – when he was entering his teen years – you had to keep him very busy, keep him working all day." If you didn't the boys would be lazy the rest of their lives. They had to work hard entering teens. You had to keep them busy and keep them working. If you didn't do that, they'd be lazy people. Being lazy was something people looked down on.

Heather: What age did they actually start getting married?

I don't really know. A lot of youth mature early, a lot of them don't mature at all. I guess it all depended on how good a provider they were, probably different ages.

Heather: What kind of training did kids and adolescents go through as they were growing up?

Well, the girls I think received more training then the boys. You hear about it because most of our Elders were ladies, and they's describe all the things that they were taught, but we had very few male Elders in the original Coqualeetza Elder's Group [in the early 1970's] so we really didn't hear too much about it. My father never really talked to me about his training when he was becoming a man. He just said that he had to work all the time and that time you were in a transition period where you couldn't live like the old people. My dad grew up in the transition period and so did my grandfather, but my great grandfather, *Tixwelatza,* lived the old way, the good years. So my dad never talked about any training, my dad never even knew how to fish. I had to learn my fishing skills from somebody else. He couldn't tell fish apart. I'd bring a fish home and he'd ask, "What kind is it?" He knew a dog salmon and that was about all.

Heather: Did many Stó:lō people go into farming?

Yeah, in this area there was a lot of farmers. They even had their own association: the "Native Farmers Association." I used to go to their meetings. They had about 13 or 14 farmers there. Tzeachten had quite a few farmers. There was Tracey's great-grandfather Alex Joe, Saul *Wili:léq,* Fred *Wili:léq,* Frances Roberts, George Mathison, John Hall, Earl Campbell, everybody who had farms here. My father, Dan Milo, Harry Uslick, and Billy Sepass they were the farmers here. They were dairy farmers, and I guess my dad was the last one. He used to have a hard time keeping up to regulations. A lot of his money was put right back into the farm, and they had stricter controls of milk then. He eventually got a big bulk coolers, and they cost him a lot of money. And so did the compressor to keep the milk cool. When he was shipping by cans they used to pick up in the morning and the evening. After they got the cooler in there you only had to pick up every other

Stó:lō Farmers

day, and so he was able to keep up. But one of the things my father never really learned was the strict control of the cattle itself: the amount of milk they gave and the bloodlines in the cattle. He was sentimental. I went to the Coqualeetza Hospital when I was twelve years old, and when I got out when I was fifteen he still had one of those old jersey cows that hardly gave any milk, but it was like a family member. She should have been killed three years before, but he kept her just because he liked Old Nellie. Every cow had a name. [laughter] That was one of the things he would have done better, made more money, if he didn't get so close to his cattle. The younger ones he didn't bother with, but the older ones he kept for years even though they only gave milk for three or four years and then they'd dry up. He should have killed them, but that was one of his problems. And the calves that were good producers, he didn't' mark them, he mixed them up with the others, he didn't know which cow they came from.

Heather: What were some of the popular crops that the farmers planted?

Mostly corn. For income, for cash crops, mostly corn and on some farms it was peas, but some of the farms didn't have enough land, they just had enough land to make hay for their cattle to survive. We have some communal reserve property up at Bantford and Prairie Central that belongs to the nine bands [the Grass Reserve]. It wasn't until 1951 that they turned that land over for the first time. It used to be just pasture land and then they started ploughing it for crops. My father used to put corn there. Mostly corn was all he grew there, and he tried beans for a while but he had to pick them every other day and it was too hard getting pickers. There was no money to be made when you could only offer two or three cents a pound or something like that. If as the farmer you got three cents a pound, and you had to pay your pickers one cent a pound or two cents a pound, you'd only make a penny a pound at it. I think those were the only crops I'd seen our farmers raise; they needed more land. My dad used to plant about ten acres of corn every year. He never did raise peas, but Robbie Sepass over here, he had his land in peas, Wilfred Charlie had corn and peas. One *Stó:lō* farmer I knew used to make cash crops because he became an alcoholic and so he could never look after his herd of cows. He ended up selling them all and he just used his land for cash crops. When he couldn't look after it, he leased the land, he still leases that land today. Alex Joe, he never did raise any cash crops because it's kind of gravelly soil up there and he just had enough land for pasture and hay. His son was a log-

You Are Asked To Witness

ger and after Alex Joe got killed his son kept the herd for only two years and eventually sold them one by one until he didn't have any left.

Heather: Did many people have cows?

Like I said, all those families I mentioned had cows. I guess beside my dad was Duncan Wealick, Saul Wealick and when he died he didn't have any sons to carry on. Fred Wealick, I'm not sure how successful he was farming. He was a dairy farmer, but I'm not sure how successful he was in that area. George Mathison was a good farmer and so was Earl Campbell. George Mathison was a Haida and he married into *Stó:lō* territory. Art Hall, he took over from his father shipping milk. At the Chilliwack Landing reserve they have a lot of land but they didn't have a lot of farmers. Harry Stewart was into race horses. Gordon James owned some land up in Rosedale but he never did get into farming. He tried to raise cash crops, but in those days it was single ploughs, horse drawn ploughs and it was a lot of land to turn over with a horse. He tried it for a couple of years and said it wasn't worth it. That was when he first got out of the army. I don't remember anybody having a farm on the Squiala reserve, but Dave Pat-Joe was a farmer from Kwaw kwaw apilt.

Heather: What were some of the effects of the draining of Sumas Lake on the different farmers in that area?

It didn't really effect the farms, but it really impacted the food that was taken out of Sumas Lake. There was a lot of sturgeon, there was sturgeon spawning grounds, coho spawning grounds and it affected the food supply of the *Stó:lō* people from Sumas and Kilgard. It really didn't have an effect on their farms, just the food supply. I don't think I can really touch on any more subjects.

Heather: I think we've covered a lot in every topic area.

I'm not too knowledgable in a lot of it, just what I've learned from working with our Elders and teachings from my father and a little bit of early experiences. There's not too much I can remember about the early times. You were talking earlier about dispute resolution and something about who settled everything and like today we have Steven Point as our chief spokesperson. In

Traditional Dispute Resolution

the old days when I was a child, we had either Billy Sepass or Harry Stewart as our spokesperson for the chiefs. I remember an incident, I was describing before when I was talking to Dr. Bruce Miller from UBC. I told him about the time when Dan Milo first returned (Dan was Roy Point's step-grandfather). Dad didn't really know Dan because he was travelling. When he got out of school he travelled all over and Dad didn't really know him until he moved home with the old lady and went to this father's homestead (which wasn't very much, just a few acres). One day Dan began repairing his fence. I guess Harry Uslick was probably using his land while he was away and he was putting a fence up to fence his lot, and Harry came out there and told him, "Your fence is too far over, you're taking my land." They had a big dispute so my dad and Bert Louie told him, "You better get Harry Stewart out here and see what he has to say about it." I remember stopping over there with my dad when I was just a little kid, I remember walking back, those people looked huge in my memory. Old Harry Stewart used two canes for walking. He went right down to the end to where Dan Milo built his fence and I don't remember the discussion, but my dad talked about it later. He said Dan Milo was into Harry Uslick's lot, but Harry Stewart said, "Well you're this far with the fence. I'm not going to tell you to take it all down and start over, what you can do is just go across to Paul Charlie's lot; just go across and join up with Paul Tommy's, then Harry can have that." So that's why the fence is the way it is today. You can see where it cuts off, it goes out so far and then heads this way. So that was Harry Stewart, he came in and settled that dispute and when he made his decision, people respected it.

Chiefs

So those are the chiefs that were not really from chief's families but they were appointed by the Department of Indian Affairs because of their knowledge; their education. Billy Hall was well educated, Joe Hall's great-grandfather, he could read and write and that's what the Indian agents were looking for – people to write letters to them and report to them. So Billy Hall was appointed chief of Tzeachten. On this reserve there was a choice between Billy Sepass (a well spoken person), and Chief Louie, but Chief Louie wasn't educated, he was Indian educated, not through the school system, so Billy Sepass was chosen by Department of Indian Affairs to be a spokesperson. Harry Stewart, they all say he was half-breed, he had green eyes or something and he was a spokesperson for all the Chilliwack people.

So, it's noon time. What do you say we call it a day?

Heather: Oh, it is too! Well, thank you very much for sharing with us.

Tracey: Yes, thank you .

You're welcome.

Siyémches (Frank Malloway)

CHAPTER 2

FIRST CONTACT:

Smallpox

"a sickness that no medicine could cure, and no person escape"[1]

Keith Thor Carlson

INTRODUCTION

The subject of "contact" provides an avenue for discussing a broad range of *Stó:lō-Xwelítem* relations in the pre-settlement years. This chapter diverges from the traditional approach that views contact as an aspect of the *Xwelítem* exploration process, instead focusing on the complex and controversial issues of depopulation and disease. Smallpox reached the traditional territory of the *Stó:lō* people at least a generation before the arrival of the first Euroamerican (*Xwelítem* in the *Halq'eméylem* language). To better appreciate the physical and social impact of smallpox on *Stó:lō* communities this chapter documents the clinical features of the disease, and then places the discussion within a broad historical context. The cultural survival of the *Stó:lō* people in the wake of such devastation serves as an indicator of the strength of their cultural traditions and their ability to adapt in the face of adversity.

1 FIRST CONTACT WAS PASSIVE – NOT ACTIVE, BUT IT WAS DEVASTATING ∎

When people ask "when did first 'contact' occur between the *Stó:lō* and Euroamericans," a common response is "in 1808, when Simon Fraser travelled down the Fraser River." This answer is probably satisfactory if we think of "contact" as simply being the first "face-to-face" meeting of people from different cultures. Scholars suggest that we also consider the likelihood that at least a few *Stó:lō* must have briefly met European maritime fur traders and explorers like Captain George Vancouver in the Strait of Georgia, almost sixteen years before Simon Fraser arrived.[2]

In many ways the "face-to-face" definition is too limiting. Perhaps a better way to define "contact" is to try and determine when meaningful or significant exchange occurred between the *Stó:lō* and *Xwelítem*.

Stó:lō communities had been "contacted" by European society a generation before Simon Fraser travelled along the lower Fraser River in 1808.

Fraser only spent a few short days in the region, and therefore one might conclude that "contact" did not really occur until years after his arrival, perhaps at the time Fort Langley was established in 1827 by the Hudson's Bay Company. However, when using the definition "meaningful exchange" it is more useful to look back, rather than forward, into history to the year 1782 – twenty-six years before Simon Fraser arrived. In that year, a devastating disease called "smallpox" was introduced into *Stó:lō* territory from Mexico through an extensive network of Aboriginal trade routes.[3]

It is estimated that within weeks of contracting smallpox in 1782, roughly two thirds of the *Stó:lō* population died horrible, painful deaths. By comparison, the kind of "contact" represented by the arrival of Simon Fraser had a relatively small impact upon *Stó:lō* society. This is interesting, because Fraser's contact was "active," in the sense that he made a conscious effort to meet the *Stó:lō*. Ironically, the devastating 1782 smallpox epidemic was a passive form of "contact," because no one from either culture intended it to happen. In fact, Europeans were unaware that the smallpox disease had travelled into *Stó:lō* territory until a decade later. Similarly, because no Europeans were in *Stó:lō* territory when the epidemic broke out, the *Stó:lō* did not immediately associate the disease with its European source.

Two generations of *Stó:lō* people had been exposed to aspects of "contact" before the Hudson's Bay Company establishe[d] Fort Langley in 1827 along the lower Fraser River.

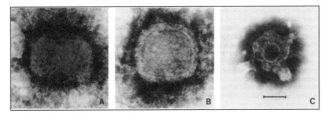

Variola Virus – The first ambassador of European society to the *Stó:lō*. Virions of variola virus (A and B) and varicella virus (C) as seen in negatively stained preparations submitted for diagnosis to the WHO Collaborating Centre at the Centres for Disease Control, Atlanta Georgia. Bar = 100nm.

2 WHAT IS SMALLPOX? ∎

Smallpox is caused by a parasitic virus called variola. It is classified as a parasitic disease because the virus is destructive to its host (the person who catches it). Smallpox is also considered a "crowd disease" because it only spreads between humans and requires a large densely populated community in order for it to survive. Like other crowd diseases, smallpox spreads from urban centres outwards into non-immune populations until it eventually reaches areas where the population is too thin to allow it to spread further. Once smallpox runs out of new host bodies, it dies out.

Biologists believe that approximately 3000 years ago (in either Egypt or India), a virus which originally effected only cattle, mutated, creating the smallpox virus. This follows the trend of the world's extremely lethal "crowd" diseases, most of which originated after the domestication of animals. Because large scale animal domestication

never occurred in North or South America this region essentially escaped such viruses until they were introduced by Europeans.[4]

Smallpox is spread by "droplet infection." Droplets are body fluid, such as the moisture which escapes when a person sneezes. A single human sneeze releases up to 5000 droplets, each of which has the potential to carry viruses. During a sneeze droplets are expelled from a person's mouth at up to 160 km/hr, and travel over four metres. Smallpox can also be transmitted by other forms of physical contact. The smallpox virus remains active on corpses for up to three weeks, and can therefore spread from a dead host to a living host though body fluids. If the smallpox virus is deposited onto warm damp items, such as clothing or blankets, it can remain infectious for up to one year.

3 IMMUNIZATION/ VACCINATION ∎

If a person catches smallpox and lives, they develop an immunity to the disease and can never catch it again. People in Europe and Asia accidentally discovered that people who became infected with smallpox through a scratch on the skin suffered a less severe form of the disease than those who contracted it through their respiratory tract. By the early 1700's, some European doctors began storing samples of smallpox pus and scabs in jars. If an epidemic broke out, doctors made a small cut in a person's arm and smeared some of the pus or scab into the wound. Intentionally infecting people in this manner was called "inoculation." Inoculated patients became sick with

Immunization Guide

TOTS NEED THEIR SHOTS!

PreventionCare
B.C. MINISTRY OF HEALTH

Originally people were inoculated against smallpox by having the vaccine smeared into an open cut on their arm. More recently, hypodermic syringes have been used to inject vaccines into a person's system.

a mild form of smallpox, but was spared any future risk of contracting the more deadly version.

In 1797, a scientist named Edward Jenner improved upon the inoculation/variolation method. He discovered that by intentionally injecting a vaccine made from cowpox into a healthy person their system developed a resistance or immunity to the smallpox disease through the creation of antibodies. After being vaccinated people could be exposed to the smallpox virus without fear of catching the disease. This process was called "vaccination," and did not result in the patient developing the terrible side effects of mild smallpox associated with the earlier inoculation process.

In the mid-nineteenth century, government officials and Christian missionaries began attempting to vaccinate Aboriginal people whenever a smallpox outbreak occurred. During one devastating smallpox epidemic, in 1862, Catholic and Methodist missionaries vaccinated hundreds of *Stó:lō* people, thereby preventing their communities from being as badly impacted by the disease as more northern Aboriginal people who had no access to the vaccine.

By the early twentieth century, most Canadians were being routinely vaccinated as children. This process was so successful, that by the 1970's smallpox had been essentially eliminated, and the government began to phase out their vaccination program. Until the early 1980's the smallpox vaccine was available upon request for Canadian travellers visiting isolated countries. The world's last immunization occurred in 1983.[5] In that year the World Health Organization (WHO) declared that due to the success of the immunization process there was no longer any chance of smallpox occurring naturally – the virus had been eliminated. To prevent future outbreaks, scientists with WHO destroyed all existing samples of smallpox, locking a single flask containing the last known

Charles Desbordes' painting "La Vaccine," 1822, illustrates arm-to-arm vaccination, as practiced in Europe in the 1800's.

sample of the variola virus in a vault at the offices of the U.S. Centre for Disease Control in Atlanta, Georgia. WHO plans to destroy this sample on June 30, 1999. But before doing so, they want to be absolutely certain the disease has been truly eradicated in the natural environment, and that no samples are held by terrorist organizations. Today, you can identify a person who has been vaccinated or immunized by the presence of a small round "pox scar" on their shoulder or hip. People born in British Columbia after the late 1970's do not have this scar, because they were not vaccinated.

نحن أعضاء اللجنة العالمية للإشهاد الرسمي باستئصال
الجدري نشهد بأنه قد تم إستئصال الجدري من العالم .

WE, THE MEMBERS OF THE GLOBAL COMMISSION FOR THE
CERTIFICATION OF SMALLPOX ERADICATION, CERTIFY
THAT SMALLPOX HAS BEEN ERADICATED FROM THE WORLD.

NOUS, MEMBRES DE LA
COMMISSION MONDIALE
POUR LA CERTIFICATION
DE L'ERADICATION DE
LA VARIOLE, CERTIFIONS
QUE L'ERADICATION
DE LA VARIOLE A ÉTÉ RÉA-
LISÉE DANS LE MONDE
ENTIER.

我们，全球扑灭天花证实委员会委员，
证实扑灭天花已经在全世界实现。

МЫ, ЧЛЕНЫ
ГЛОБАЛЬНОЙ
КОМИССИИ ПО
СЕРТИФИКАЦИИ ОСПЫ,
НАСТОЯЩИМ
ПОДТВЕРЖДАЕМ, ЧТО
ОСПЫ В МИРЕ БОЛЬШЕ
НЕТ.

NOSOTROS, MIEMBROS DE LA COMISION MUNDIAL PARA LA CERTI-
FICACION DE LA ERRADICACION DE LA VIRUELA, CERTIFICAMOS
QUE LA VIRUELA HA SIDO ERRADICADA EN TODO EL MUNDO.

The official parchment certifying the global eradication of smallpox, December 9, 1979.

4 THE SMALLPOX DISEASE ■

Imagine what would happen if a terrorist broke into the vault at the Centre for Disease Control and stole the flask containing the only remaining sample of the variola smallpox virus and in their escape they dropped the flask and became infected. Imagine further, that person visited your home town and sneezed on you as you walked down the street. The "sneeze droplets" would immediately be sucked into your respiratory tract, infecting you, and making you infectious to others. For the next seven to eighteen days the virus would incubate within you, yet there would be no symptoms to indicate to you or anyone else that you had caught the virus. After the incubation period had ended, you would begin to show outward signs of being sick. First, you would develop a fever, headache, and body pains. The head and body aches would last two days, but the fever would remain throughout the duration of the sickness. After two weeks, you would develop a rash. Red spots would appear on your face, hands, and feet, and then slowly spread over your entire body. These spots would soon become raised lesions which would fill with a watery pus similar to a blister. The lesions would grow to approximately the size of a dime and would quickly transform into pustules as hard crusty scabs formed over their surface.

All of the symptoms described above are standard responses for anyone contracting the smallpox disease. If you were lucky, and survived to this stage, the dried scabs covering your body would slowly fall off, leaving deep permanent scars called pockmarks. Once the scabs had disappeared, you would no longer be contagious. If you were not as lucky, the sores would move from your outer skin and spread to the inside of your mouth or throat. Once this occurred, you would be unable to eat and could only swallow liquids with a great deal of pain. Such sores sometimes became so large, they would grow together into giant hemorrhaging lesions. If this happened, it would not be unusual for all the skin on your arm, leg, or face to simply slip off, exposing raw muscle and bone.

If the disease reached this point there is essentially no chance of your survival. It would take only one month from the time the terrorist, or someone he infected, sneezed on you until either the scabs fell off or you died. The death rate increases substantially if other factors combine to complicate the situation. For example, people who are exposed to smallpox often developed pneumonia, pleurisy, and blindness caused by scarring of the cornea. Death rates are also higher for infants, children, elderly people, and pregnant women.

Today, even with modern medicine there is no cure for smallpox. If you become infected,

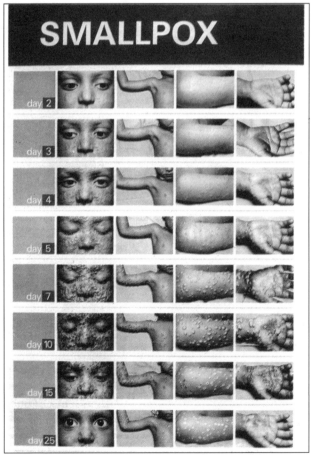

The above United Nations poster provides a visual depiction of smallpox rashes on four areas of the body following the incubation period.

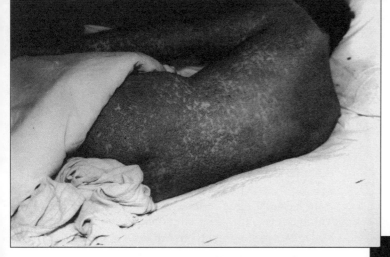
Mr. F.D., age 28, suffering from smallpox
in Vancouver General Hospital, 1932.

at the Vancouver General Hospital. These rare archival photographs and notes are currently stored at the University of British Columbia. The following are copies of a few of the actual photos and records kept by Dr. Mathewson.

Mrs. E.S.:
– (Symptoms) onset January 28th with insomnia, headache, nausea and fever. January 30th macular rash appeared on forehead and face.
– Patient admitted to the hospital at once. Temperature

absolutely nothing can be done to stop the disease from running its full course and there is little doctors can do to alleviate the painful symptoms. Once you are exposed to smallpox you have smallpox.[6] A minimum of one third, or 33%, of all people exposed to smallpox die from the disease.

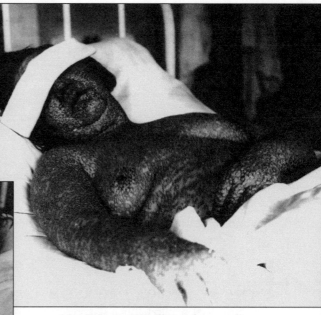
Mrs. E.S., age 37, suffering from smallpox
in Vancouver General Hospital, 1932.

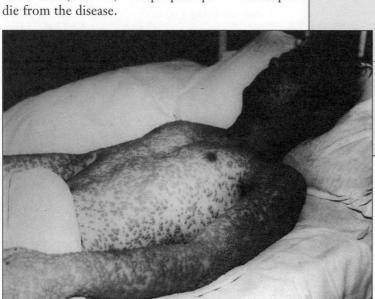
Mr. L.P. age 21, suffering from smallpox
in Vancouver General Hospital, 1932.

of 104 degrees Fahrenheit (40 degrees Celsius). Rash rapidly spread to involve whole body and showed early tendency to become confluent (merge). Many spots in mouth and pharynx (mouth, nose, and upper throat).
– February 3rd much oedema (swelling) of throat.
– Patient died February 7th.

Mr. L.P.:
– (Symptoms began on) February 1st when patient developed headache and backache. The following day he was nauseated and felt chilly. February 3rd (patient) started to develop muscular rash on forehead, face and arms.
– Admitted to the hospital February 4th. Temperature 103.2 degrees Fahrenheit (39.6 degrees Celsius). On admission erythema- redness typical in character and distribution. Very severe lobster red crythoma on face. General adenopathy (enlargement of lymph glands). February 7th patient developed toxic psychosis.
– Died February 14th.

5 BRITISH COLUMBIA'S LAST SMALLPOX EPIDEMIC ■

For a variety of reasons, in the early twentieth century some British Columbian residents refused to allow doctors to vaccinate them against smallpox. In January of 1932, approximately 100 people in the Vancouver region became sick, suffering from fever, headaches, and rashes. Doctors became horrified when, upon admitting the patients to the Vancouver General Hospital they learn that the people had contracted smallpox. Tragically, nearly all died within a month.

As the disease progressed, detailed notes, records, and some photos of the patients were kept by Dr. Mathewson

Dentalia shells originating from the deep waters off the west coast of Vancouver Island, recently excavated in *Stó:lō* territory by UBC archaeologists working with the *Stó:lō* Nation.

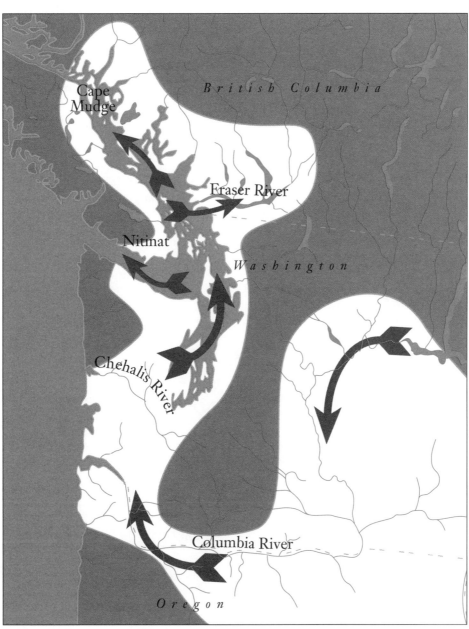

Map showing the route taken by the smallpox virus as it travelled to *Stó:lō* territory in 1782.

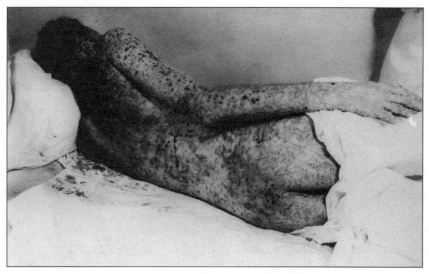
Mr. F.D., age 28, case 52, lying on his back.

Mr. F.D.
– Temperature 96 degree Fahrenheit
(35.6 degree Celsius).
– Severe confluent smallpox with intrapockal hemorrhages (bleeding within pocks just below surface).
– Admitted to hospital on November 27th, 1931 for treatment of fractured right femur (leg bone) and synovitis of the right knee.
– On February 8th, 1932, had incision on right ostermyeritis abscess (collection of puss) of the right thigh.
– Wound well healed on March 1st.
– On March 7th in Ward F had sudden onset of abdominal cramps and vomiting, accompanied by moderate headache.
– On March 8th, a macular rash appeared over the chest, back and on left leg. Later appeared on axillae (underarm).
– On the 6th of March temperature was 101 Fahrenheit (38.3 degrees Celsius).
– On the 8th of March rash well out; temperature 103 degrees Fahrenheit (39.4 degrees Celsius).
– On 10th of March, temperature 100 degrees Fahrenheit (37.8 degrees Celsius). There are occasional haemorrhages (bleeding) into some of the vesicles (small sac containing liquid). Outcome of this case was considered doubtful.
– April 8th, 1932. Patient is making an astonishing recovery. At the present time practically all the scabs have separated, leaving him badly scarred. His recovery is complicated by a few scattered boils and a foot drop (foot "drops" due to paralysis of muscles on front leg) on the left side.
– Confluent haemorrhagic smallpox. (Severe and highly fatal type) Bleeding occurs in skin and mucus membranes (moist live cells, eg: lips, tongue, cheeks, eyelids, etc.) before onset of rash or after rash appears.
– Vaccinated on March 6th after exposure to patient in the next bed Mr. R. D. who had mild smallpox. Has been conscientious objector (and therefore was not vaccinated during WWI).

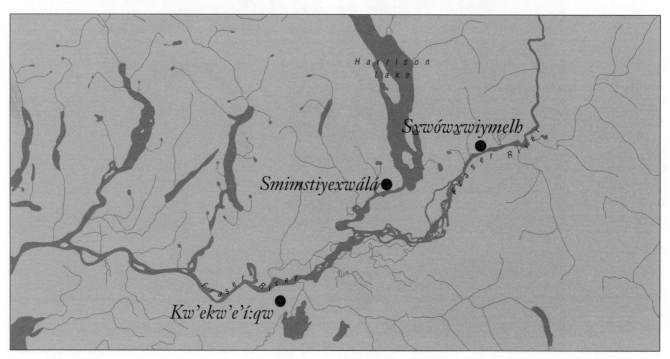
Map showing the location for some *Stó:lō* place names which refer to epidemic disease and stories of population decline.

6 THE SMALLPOX EPIDEMIC OF 1782 ■

European explorers such as Captain Vancouver reported seeing Aboriginal people in Puget Sound in 1792 who had "suffered very much from the smallpox." He reported that

> This deplorable disease is not only common, but it is greatly to be apprehended is very fatal amongst them as its indelible marks were seen on many; and several had lost the sight of one eye, which was remarked to be generally the left, owing most likely to the virulent effects of this baneful disorder.[7]

When Vancouver's ship neared the Fraser River, one of his crew reported that most of the Aboriginal people were covered with pock marks, "and most terribly pitted they are; indeed many have lost their eyes and no doubt it has raged with uncommon inveteracy among them..."[8] As well as the pockmarked survivors, Captain Vancouver

Drying racks were used by the *Stó:lō* to "wind dry" salmon for winter consumption.

also witnessed the devastating mortality the disease had caused. Along the sea-shore he observed human skeletons "promiscuously scattered about the beach, in great numbers." What were once large populated villages had now "fallen into decay... overrun with weeds."[9]

As mentioned, the arrival of the smallpox virus to *Stó:lō* communities in 1782 was not due to direct person-to-person contact with Europeans, but was spread in large part through existing Aboriginal exchange and trade networks. Such wide-reaching networks had been in existence within North American Aboriginal societies for thousands of years. This is demonstrated in the archaeological record through the analysis of artifacts. For example, dentalia shells found in the Fraser Valley come from the west coast of Vancouver Island. Artifacts manufactured from obsidian, a black volcanic glass, and found in *Stó:lō* archaeological sites are manufactured with obsidian that can be sourced from sites in southern Oregon.

A few competing theories exist regarding how the first smallpox epidemic reached *Stó:lō* communities. One suggests it spread along Aboriginal exchange networks from Alaska where it had been introduced by Russian fur traders after the Kamchatka Siberian epidemic of 1769. A second and more likely theory argues that the disease spread to the Fraser River all the way from Mexico. According to this interpretation, smallpox was contracted by an Aboriginal community in Mexico from a Spaniard in 1779. The disease then spread to another neighbouring Aboriginal community to the north which in turn gave it to the next community and so on. In a few short months the disease had spread as far north as the present day state of Idaho. From Idaho, it travelled down the Snake River from one Aboriginal community to the next, and then along the Columbia River. The Chinook people living near the mouth of the Columbia had extensive trading networks with the southern Coast Salish people of Puget Sound. These people in turn had family and trade connections with the *Stó:lō* on the lower Fraser River. Thus, through indigenous exchange networks – networks which connected densely populated communities – smallpox travelled all the way from Mexico to the Fraser Valley. This happened despite the fact that the Europeans who actually introduced the disease were never closer than 3,600 km to the Fraser River.

7 *STÓ:LŌ* ORAL TRADITIONS OF SMALLPOX ■

Stó:lō Elders provide their own knowledge about the devastating smallpox epidemics. They are remembered in place names as well as oral traditions. Throughout the Fraser Valley there are many sites with names that tell part of the story of the various smallpox epidemics that impacted *Stó:lō* communities. These place names create a cultural geography that keep the story of smallpox alive. For example, the place name "*Sxwóxwiymelh*" means "a lot of people died at once." *Stó:lō* Elder Evangeline Pete of Chawathil (near Hope), explains the name's meaning by relating how during the smallpox epidemic twenty-five to thirty people died at *Sxwóxwiymelh* each day. Their bodies were placed in one of the larger pit houses and set on fire.[10] Another site is called "*Smimstiyexwálá*" which means "people container." *Stó:lō* Elder Jimmie Charlie of Chehalis explains that this name refers to a mass grave site where survivors of the smallpox epidemic buried the bodies of relatives and neighbours.[11]

Other *Stó:lō* Elders also spoke of the ravages of smallpox. Albert Louie of *Yeqwyeqwi:ws* (Yakweakwioose) in Sardis explained that smallpox "killed, oh, half the Indians all around the Fraser River there."[12] Dan Milo of Skowkale related that after the epidemic everyone at the village of *Kw'ekw'í:qw* (just east of Abbotsford) died except one boy who "settled down with a girl who was the only survivor from a village nearby."[13]

In 1936, *Stó:lō* Elder Peter Pierre of Katzie (near Maple Ridge) told what is probably the most detailed oral history account of the smallpox epidemic of 1782.

Stó:lō Elder Peter Pierre.

The news reached them from the east that a great sickness was travelling over the land, a sickness that no medicine could cure, and no person escape. Terrified, they held council with one another and decided to send their wives, with half the children, to their parents' homes, so that every adult might die in the place where he or she was raised. Then the wind carried the smallpox sickness among them. Some crawled away into the woods to die; many died in their homes. Altogether about three-quarters of the Indians perished.

My great-grandfather happened to be roaming in the mountains at this period, for his wife had recently given birth to twins, and according to custom, both parents and children had to remain in isolation for several months. The children were just beginning to walk when he returned to the village at the entrance to Pitt Lake, knowing nothing of the calamity that had overtaken its inhabitants. All his kinsmen and relatives lay dead inside their homes; only in one house did there survive a baby boy, who was vainly sucking at his dead mother's breast. They rescued the child, burned all the houses, together with the corpses that lay inside them, and built a new home for themselves several miles away. If you dig today on the site of any of the old villages you will uncover countless bones, the remains of the Indians who perished during this epidemic of smallpox. Not many years later Europeans appeared on the Fraser, and their coming ushered in a new era.[14]

Stó:lō men standing beneath their elevated fish caches. These caches were used as storage containers to hold wind dried salmon throughout the winter months. If food was not put away people suffered throughout the winter, as likely happened during the smallpox epidemic.

8 DEVASTATION ACCOMPANYING SMALLPOX ■

The *Stó:lō* procured and preserved food at seasonally prescribed times of the year when the salmon were "running" and berries and other plant resources were ripe. If they were unable to collect berries when they ripened there was no second chance. If the berries were not dried and stored the *Stó:lō* would not only

The emotional, psychological, and spiritual legacy of smallpox was horrific. Many Aboriginal people suffered from profound "despondency" as they tried to deal with their losses.

lack variety in their winter diet, they would also lack an essential source of Vitamin C. The same was true for salmon. If a family failed to catch and dry hundreds of salmon in the late summer for winter consumption they would go hungry.

Researchers believe the smallpox epidemic of 1782-83 likely struck *Stó:lō* communities in the late summer or early autumn. One reason to suspect this is the high number of survivors who suffered from blindness. Blindness was a common complication among smallpox victims who were malnourished. If smallpox did arrive in late summer of early autumn the entire community would have been seriously ill and unable to hunt, fish or gather food. Moreover, the surviving population would have been in mourning, depressed, and fearful about what had occurred. Many of *Stó:lō* undoubtedly developed pneumonia and other sicknesses. The devastating effects of smallpox were thus compounded by many other factors.

Many Waves of Introduced Diseases

The epidemic of 1782 was only the first in a series of devastating European diseases to impact the *Stó:lō*. They were also effected over the course of the next century by

at least three other major epidemics (smallpox or measles in 1824; measles in 1848; and smallpox in 1862). In addition, *Stó:lō* communities were effected by outbreaks of mumps, tuberculosis (T.B.), venereal disease (gonorrhea, syphilis etc.) colds, influenza (flu), and alcoholism. With each epidemic and every outbreak of disease people were impacted. Scholars estimate that 62% of the population died in the 1782 smallpox epidemic. In subsequent epidemics, the figures may have been lower because survivors of previous epidemics would have been immune, and missionaries and government officials began vaccinating the *Stó:lō* against smallpox in the 1860's.

Mumps and influenza outbreaks took the lives of approximately 10% of population each time there was an outbreak. Alcoholism has since deprived many *Stó:lō* of their lives and dignity (See Appendix 1 for a comparative list of introduced and indigenous diseases).

Traditional Medicinal Responses to Smallpox

Some traditional *Stó:lō* medical practices may have compounded the smallpox death rate. The medical problems *Stó:lō* people dealt with prior to "contact" were of a different nature. Their traditional health care practices were not designed to deal with this type of illness. For example, some traditional healing practices involved community members gathering around the sick person's bed singing, praying, among other things, to provide spiritual assistance. While this demonstration of community support was beneficial for many pre-contact diseases, with smallpox it simply ensured everyone was exposed to the infected person. Other medical practices included cleansing "sweats" and cold morning baths in rivers or lakes. Again, while appropriate for many pre-contact illnesses such techniques sent smallpox sufferers into a state of shock sometimes killing them instantly.

We should not be surprised that traditional *Stó:lō* medical practises did not work against smallpox. Nor should we categorize them as ineffective simply because they were not designed to deal with a non-indigenous, introduced, parasitic crowd disease. In the past, people in Europe used to believe the "Black Plague" was spread by smell and they were encouraged to carry fragrant flowers to protect themselves from the disease. The nursery rhyme "Ring Around the Rosy" refers to people trying to avoid falling "down" dead with the plague by stuffing their pockets with sweet smelling "posies." Similarly, in Europe, doctors used to place live leaches on sick people to draw out what was considered "bad blood." In many instances this practise actually lowered blood pressure in already weakened people and increased the likelihood of death. Similar inappropriate medical practices have also occurred in contemporary times. For example, only a few

Because of their sacred nature, contemporary *Stó:lō* people do not allow photographs to be taken of masked *sxwó:yxwey* dancers. They have graciously consented to allowing use of this photo of a carving of a masked *sxwó:yxwey* dancer found on the house post at Skowkale Hall.

decades ago doctors were prescribing a drug called "thalidomide" to pregnant women, thinking it would simply relieve the symptoms of nausea and vomiting. In reality the medication also affected the development of the fetus causing children to be born without hands and feet.

The problems associated with treating unknown or poorly understood diseases are clearly formidable. While many traditional *Stó:lō* medical practises would not have been effective against smallpox, *Stó:lō* oral traditions provide examples of traditional medicine being able to cure people of introduced diseases. One such story, told by Mrs. Robert Joe to the anthropologist Wilson Duff in 1949, describes the arrival in *Stó:lō* territory of a terrible disease. Based upon the genealogical evidence provided by Mrs. Joe, Duff estimated that she was describing events "roughly about 1780."

In Mrs. Joe's story the disease causes a wealthy young man's skin to "break and rot," and his flesh to "stink." The young man "spent all his wealth trying to cure (himself), but failed." In desperation he left the village to "hide himself somewhere and die." Arriving at the edge of a bluff at Kawakawa Lake near Hope the man fell into the water, but he did not drown. Upon reaching the bottom of the lake he met a community of people who were covered in sores similar to his own. One of them asked the young man to cure the people, to which he replied "I'll cure them if you cure me." The man from the lake then took shredded cedar-bark and "wiped away the sores on the young man's body and he was cured." The young man then observed that the sick water people's sores were caused by "human spit which had fallen from the surface of the lake."

He cured them by using cedar-bark to wipe away the spit. The lake people asked the young man what he wanted in payment for curing them. They offered him many valuable things, but in the end he asked for and received a special mask and regalia which was called the "*sxwó:yxwey*."[15] (The root of the word *sxwó:yxwey* means many peopled all died at once.[16]) Another version of this story, recorded by turn of the century ethnographer Charles Hill-Tout explains that after the man returned to his community he was able to cure other people of their sickness.[17] Today the hereditary *sxwó:yxwey* mask continues to be used by *Stó:lō* people during celebrations and certain healing or purification ceremonies.

Other *Stó:lō* oral histories explain that spiritual healers used songs to cure people of smallpox and other sicknesses. While *Stó:lō* people today make full use of modern medical facilities and technology, they still rely heavily upon spiritual healing power. In the 1920's a well know *Stó:lō* spiritual healer named Tasalt (or Catholic Tommy) agreed to allow some of his healing songs to be recorded by a researcher from the Smithsonian Institute. Tasalt explained that these songs were not passed down to him by his mother, who was also a spiritual healer. Rather he received all of his songs from spirits. While singing the songs he "gets the sickness and throws it away." After the "sickness had been taken out" Tasalt's patients reportedly regained their strength rapidly. Tasalt had different songs for each illness. Among his healing songs were ones that treated "smallpox, fever, palsy, hemorrhage for the lungs, and pneumonia," among other sicknesses.[18] Tasalt's song for treating smallpox is as follows:

Free translation.—I am curing you. I am going to take you and cure you.

Other stories of people being healed of smallpox describe someone acquiring special "spirit power" which made them strong enough to withstand the deadly disease. Sometimes through special spiritual intervention people were able to escape some of the subsequent smallpox epidemics which revisited *Stó:lō* communities in the nineteenth century. For example, Gwen Point relates a story that she learned from her grandmother Dolly Felix of Chehalis (near Harrison Hotsprings). The story is an excellent example of the blending of traditional *Stó:lō* and Christian healing traditions:

You Are Asked To Witness

All that I remember is my grandmother Dolly Felix talking to us about the smallpox epidemic that went through and why Chehalis survived the smallpox. And what she said is that her grand uncle (Ey:iá) was like that man who took care of the people all his life and after he died the creator said that where that man is buried will grow a cedar tree. He didn't take a family for himself, you know he just lived and worked with the people in the longhouse. He helped all the different families in the community. They knew when the smallpox was coming soon, this disease was coming up the river like that. Anyway this man, he knew that he has it and he told the one family that he was sick and the women in the longhouse just started crying because they didn't want to lose him... He knew that he was going to die so he called two young men over and told them "tie my canoe up and take me across the river. I want you to dig a hole so that when I die I'll fall in the hole and you can just cover me up. Burn my canoe, burn everything. Don't touch nothing." ...In those days they didn't normally bury the people in the ground, they put them up in the trees. ...So it was like an insult to go in the ground. Only the bad people went into the ground. But he was worried about the other people, if this disease spread. He was covered with sores, so they brought him across the river and left him there. He sat there right at the head of the hole that they had dug, the grave, facing the river with a blanket over him... Early the next morning all they heard is "ooooooh, oooooh, ooooh, ooooh" four times like that. All the women started to cry again. "He's dead, he's gone." They were feeling really bad. But they sent the same two young men "you go over there and bury him, that's what he wanted, and you burn his canoe, everything..." So the same two boys got on the canoe and started to go across the river... They could see him sitting there yet with the blanket over and the two young boys were getting a little bit scared, thinking that maybe that was his ghost talking in the language... Then they really got scared, you know, and they wanted to leave. Then he called them in "don't be afraid, come

The continuance and survival of *Stó:lō* oral traditions and culture today.

in."... Just when they were getting close to him, he took the blanket off. He was clean and he didn't have a mark on him. ...He said "I was getting ready to die and I prepared myself to die and I thought that my time came and he looked up like that and he could see coming over the mountain, coming like if it came from over the mountain, a light. The light got closer." He said that there was a man inside this light. The man standing there with his hands open. He said that my name is Jesus. He said that I'm going to help you and then I want you to go back and help your people. So that's what he did. He went back across the river and helped the people that were sick. That's why they say the smallpox didn't kill as many of the families in Chehalis.[19]

9 CONCLUSION: SOCIAL AND CULTURAL IMPACT OF SMALLPOX – CULTURAL CONTINUITY AND SURVIVAL ■

It would have been impossible for *Stó:lō* life to continue as normal after the 1782 epidemic suddenly wiped out two thirds of their population. Understanding the physical impact of smallpox allows us to speculate about the social and cultural legacy of the disease. Without books or computers, one of the greatest impacts upon *Stó:lō* society would have been the terrible effects of "culture loss." *Stó:lō* Elders possessed a large proportion of the community's cultural knowledge. In traditional *Stó:lō* society there were no books or computers to store information. Knowledge could only be passed on by word of mouth. While the analogy is imperfect and in no way captures the rich and complex importance of Elders within *Stó:lō* society, people might find it useful to think of Elders playing a role in *Stó:lō* society that was somewhat analogous to the position of a hard drive in a computer system. The variola smallpox virus was like a computer virus that erases information off hard drives. The smallpox epidemics killed most of the Elders which therefore resulted in a loss of their knowledge and a gap in learning. Some people refer to this as "culture loss." *Stó:lō* survivors also suffered from severe depression. In addition, economic hardships were encountered, which resulted in poverty and feelings of despair. While some aspects of *Stó:lō* society were necessarily altered, the striking feature was not the changes, but the amazing degree of cultural continuity. This cultural survival is a testimony to the strength, endurance and innovative nature of *Stó:lō* cultural traditions.

Appendix 1

LIST OF INDIGENOUS AND INTRODUCED DISEASES[20]

Indigenous North/South American Diseases
1. dysentery (bacillary, amoebic)
2. viral pneumonia
3. non-ventral syphilis + pinta
4. American leishmaniasis (Forest Yaws)
5. American trypanosomiasis (Chagas)
6. localized rickettsial diseases (Rocky Mtn. Spotted Fever)
7. streptococcus + staphylococcus (Strep throat, Rheumatic Fever. etc.)
8. salmonella + other food poisons
9. tuberculosis
10. trachoma (Chlamydia) (?)

Diseases Introduced to North/South America
1. smallpox
2. malaria
3. viral influenza
4. yellow fever
5. measles
6. typhus
7. bubonic plague
8. typhoid fever
9. cholera
10. pertussis (Whooping Cough)
11. diphtheria
12. scarlatina (Scarlet Fever)
13. polio
14. colds (?)
15. venereal syphilis (?)
16. herpes zoster (?)

Recommended Further Readings

Jenness, Diamond, *The Faith of a Coast Salish Indian,* Victoria: Anthropology in British Columbia, Memoirs 3, 1955.

Harris, Cole, "Voices of Disaster: Smallpox around the Strait of Georgia in 1782," *Ethnohistory, Winter 1994.*

Wells, Oliver, *The Chilliwacks and Their Neighbours,* Vancouver: Talonbooks, 1987

Footnotes

1 Peter Pierre of Katzie, as quoted in Wayne Suttles, *Katzie Ethnographic Notes,* (containing Diamond Jenness, *Faith of A Coast Salish Indian*), (Victoria: Provincial Museum, 1955), p.34.

2 Historians continue to debate whether or not Juan De Fuca (aka Apostolos Valerianos, a Greek sea captain working for the Spanish Crown) sailed as far north as the straights between Vancouver Island and the mainland that now bare his name in the year 1592.

3 Cole Harris, "Voices of Disaster: Smallpox Around the Strait of Georgia in 1782." In *Ethnohistory* 41:4 (fall 1994).

4 Robert T. Boyd, *The Introduction of Infectious Diseases Among the Indians of the Pacific Northwest, 1774-1874,* (Unpublished Ph.D. Dissertation, University of Washington, 1985), Chapters 1&2.

5 Personal communication with Dr. Rick Mathius, Epidemiologist, University of British Columbia, June 14, 1995.

6 See Boyd, Chapter 2.

7 W. Kaye Lamb, ed., *A Voyage of Discovery to the North Pacific Ocean and Around the World, 1791-1795,* (London: Hakluyt Society, 1984), p.540.

8 Peter Puget, *Log of the Discovery, June 12-August 19, 1792,* (Manuscript Admiralty, 55/27, Public Record Office, London; Microfilm No. 274 in Suzzallo Library, University of Washington, Seattle), p.34.

9 Lamb, p.516, 538.

10 Reuban Ware, *Stó:lō History Field Notes,* (Unpublished manuscript, Stó:lō Nation Archives, 1978).

11 Jimmie Charlie in conversation with Keith Carlson, January 16, 1993.

12 Albert Louie in conversation with Oliver Wells, (Copy on file at Stó:lō Nation Archives), July 28, 1965.

13 Oliver Wells, *The Chilliwack and Neighbours,* (Vancouver: Talonbooks, 1987), p.40.

14 Jenness, p.34.

15 For the full story as told by Mrs. Robert Joe see Wilson Duff, *The Upper Stalo Indians,* (Victoria: British Columbia Provincial Museum, 1952), pp.123-125.

16 Brent Galloway, *A Grammar of Upriver Halkomelem,* (Los Angeles: University of California Press, 1984), p.585.

17 Charles Hill-Tout, "Ethnological Studies of the Mainland Halkomelem, A Division of the Salish of British Columbia," in Ralph Maud, ed., *The Salish People,* Vol.III, (Vancouver: Talonbooks, 1978), pp. 63-65.

18 Frances Densmore, *Music of the Indians of British Columbia,* (New York: Da Capo Press, 1972), p.20.

19 Conversation between Gwen Point and Keith Carlson, (Transcript on File at Stó:lō Nation Archives), October, 1995.

20 See Boyd and Merck, *Manual of Diagnosis and Therapy.*

CHAPTER 3

Stó:lō-Xwelítem
Relations
during the Fur
and Salmon
Trade *Era*

Keith Thor Carlson

INTRODUCTION

For *Xwelítem* people the fur trade is probably the aspect of Aboriginal history they feel most familiar with. Indeed, too often the fur trade is seen as synonymous with all Aboriginal history. This chapter revisits the history of the fur trade along the lower Fraser River and in doing so challenges many commonly held assumptions. Until recently historians viewed the fur trade as a relationship between technologically superior people (the Europeans) and "primitive" Aboriginal people. The latter allegedly being "duped" by the former. More

European ships visiting the Pacific Northwest Coast.

thorough studies have now shown that the *Xwelítem* traders adapted more to Aboriginal ways of life than vice versa, and that Aboriginal people were not dependent upon the newcomers or the newly introduced goods and technologies. This chapter seeks to set the groundwork for those which follow. Aboriginal history is not simply fur trade history, and Aboriginal contributions to British Columbian culture, economy, and society did not end with the fur trade era. Moreover, for the *Stó:lō*, it was "salmon trading" and not "fur trading" which characterized their relationship with the *Xwelítem* during this period.

1 MARITIME FUR TRADE ■

When did the fur trade era begin and end in *Stó:lō* territory? Those who are aware of the relationship between the *Stó:lō* and the *Xwelítem* at Fort Langley will know this is a trick question. In western Canada, the "fur trade era" began when maritime fur traders from Boston, Massachusetts, and London, England arrived off the shores of what is now British Columbia in the 1780's. However, it was not until the establishment of Fort Langley in 1827 that a land based "direct" fur trade really got underway. An "indirect" fur trade had begun previous to the establishment of Fort Langley, as European goods were traded among Aboriginal people within established Aboriginal trade networks. What we refer to as the "the fur trade era" came to a close when the Fraser River gold rush began in 1858, ushering in a new era of *Xwelítem* settlement and land and resource use. But the term "fur trade" is somewhat misleading, because the *Stó:lō* traded

few furs during this period. Along the lower Fraser River, the fur trade era in many ways can be better understood as the "salmon trade era."

After returning from the Northwest Coast the British explorer Captain James Cook published accounts of his voyage describing the thousands of golden haired sea otters he had seen along the shores of British Columbia and how people in China were willing to pay great prices for their pelts. American and English businessmen responded to this news by sending ships to the Northwest Coast loaded with European manufactured items to exchange or trade with Aboriginal people for sea otter pelts. The "Boston men" (as the Americans were known to the Aboriginal people) and the "King George men" (as the Englishmen were called), then took the pelts to China and exchanged them for silk, spices and other items unavailable in America or Europe. They then travelled back to London or Boston and exchanged the silk and spices for items which they hoped Northwest Coast Aboriginal people would be interested in trading for.

TABLE 1
Fur Imports by American Vessels at Canton, 1804 – '34 and 1836 – 37
(Gibson)

Season	Beaver	Fox	Fur Seal	Land Otter	Sea Otter	Others	Total
1804-05	8,756	000	183,000	000	11,003	67,000	269,759
1809-10	20,000	3,500	000	15,000	11,003	000	49,503
1815-16	168	12,533	109,000	14,364	4,300	000	140,365
1820-21	2,870	8,967	13,887	5,927	3,575	9,254	44,480
1825-26	4,886	10,188	32,521	14,833	2,250	930	65,608
1830-31	000	5,263	6,022	6,454	329	000	18,068
1836-37	1,465	1,198	000	6,773	560	000	9,996

Following this exchange, the traders headed back to the B.C. coast to start the process over again. Thus, they formed a "triangle of trade" which covered the globe.

Between 1785 and 1830 an average of ten to fifteen ships visited the Northwest Coast annually. On high years, such as 1792, there were twenty-one ships, and in 1801 there were twenty five. When the maritime traders embarked for the Northwest Coast they initially anticipated being able to trade any kind of European item to Aboriginal people for great profits. However, they immediately found otherwise. The maritime trader's journals show that the Aboriginal people not only set the prices, they also determined which items were marketable. For example, if an American ship arrived with steel files and attempted to trade them at excessively high rates the Aboriginal people simply kept their furs and waited. They knew that other ships would soon arrive and that it was to their advantage to play off the various traders to obtain the best prices. Likewise, when it was found that steel files were popular among Aboriginal people one year it resulted in many ships arriving the following season with their holds full of steel files.[1] To the trader's chagrin, by that time the

The triangle of trade (R. Ross, 1995).

Aboriginal people had decided they did not want any more steel files, but instead desired calico cotton cloth and glass window panes. As a result, the "Boston men" and "King George men" found themselves either trading their steel files at a great financial loss, or facing the prospect of sailing back to their home ports loaded with unsold files. As one English maritime trader explained, "we had the sorrow to see valuable furs escape us... for want of suitable objects to exchange."[2]

Some American and British traders found the Aboriginal control of the trade more than inconvenient. Some voyages were financial failures. In the words of the American trader John Mears, Aboriginal people showed great "judgment and sagacity" when selecting items.[3] Moreover, the Aboriginal people were very concerned with quality. If a ship arrived with cheap wool, brittle files, or muskets with poor quality firing mechanisms, they were not accepted.

When describing Aboriginal people's astute trading skills, American Captain Richard Cleveland remarked that,

The Indians are sufficiently cunning to derive all possible advantage from the competition, and will go from one vessel to another, and back again, with assertions of offers made to them, which have no foundation in truth, and showing themselves to be as well versed in the tricks of the trade as the greatest adept.[4]

British traders at Clayoquot Sound became frustrated in their efforts to trade bolts of cloth. Cloth was measured "by the fathom" (an arm span), and the Clayoquot people insisted that Chief Wickaninish's tall brother be the

TABLE 2
Prices in Spanish dollars of Prime Sea-Otter Skins at Canton for Various Years from 1779-1832
(Gibson)

Season	Price[2]	Season	Price[2]
1799 - 80	$50 - 70.00	1810 - 11	21.50
1785 - 86	37 - 43.00	1815 - 13	35.00
1790 - 91	15 - 25.00	1819 - 20	35 - 50.00
1795 - 96	9 - 17.00	1824 - 25	30.00
1800 - 01	18 - 22.00	1829 - 30	64.00
1805 - 06	17 - 19.00		

TABLE 3
Value of American Exports to the Northwest Coast, 1789 – 1817
(Gibson)

Year	Dollar Value	Year	Dollar Value
1789 - 90	$ 10,362	1804 - 05	$302,859
1794 - 95	44,063	1809 - 10	145,918
1799 - 1800	756,153	1814 - 15	170,985

one to measure the fathom. His arm span was well over six feet, at least a foot longer than the average British ship's captain's.

Likewise, among some of the more northern coastal people, trading was the exclusive prerogative of women who were specially trained in the art of barter. Knowing this, the ship's captains searched for canoes of men on sealing or whaling expeditions and tried to coax them into trading without the guidance of their shrewd female partners.

The written observations of American and British maritime explorers and traders provide many insights into the trading relationships between Europeans and Aboriginal people. However, while these written documents provide clues about Aboriginal culture they do not tell the whole story. To more fully appreciate the nature of Aboriginal trade and exchange it is necessary to consult the ethnographic records created by anthropologists working with Aboriginal Elders.

The ethnographic record shows that the *Stó:lō* were experienced traders long before the arrival of Europeans.[5] It also shows that *Stó:lō* society shared certain characteristics with European cultures. The *Stó:lō* valued things because they were either useful or prestigious. These concepts had their equivalents in European society. For example, nineteenth century European society valued coal because it was useful – it made locomotives operate. Nineteenth centu-

ry *Stó:lō* society valued canoes because they were similarly useful. Prestige items in European society included diamond jewellery which had no practical function other than to look good and show the wealth of the owner. In traditional *Stó:lō* society jewellery made from indigenous copper was valued for essentially the same reason.

The traditional *Stó:lō* economy differed from the European market economy in that it focused on resource re-distribution (including food, tools, prestige objects, slaves, house boards, canoes, etc.). Leaders of extended families, called *sí:yá:m*, were expected to both share and accumulate family resources. Wealth was exchanged for wealth or, in the case of Fraser canyon fishing sites, wealth was also exchanged for the right to access family owned fishing spots.

Unlike in contemporary mainstream society the principles of *Stó:lō* economics were seldom isolated from family social obligations and rituals. The most well understood form of traditional exchange occurred among related extended families and co-parent-in-laws (the parents of married children).[6] For example, families living on the Harrison River caught and smoked large amounts of "spring" salmon, some of which they brought to exchange with their children's in-laws at other villages where people did not smoke fish as often (such as the mouth of the Fraser River). After receiving the Harrison River smoked salmon the hosting

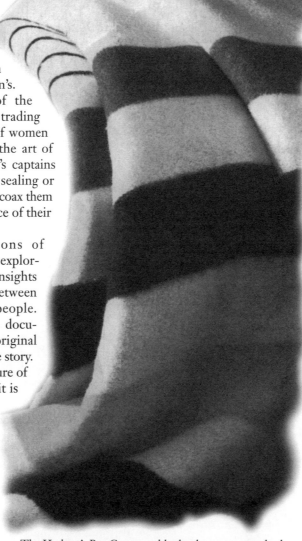

The Hudson's Bay Company blanket became a standard measure of wealth. Its adoption by Aboriginal people undermined the indigenous weaving industry.

TABLE 4
Salmon Cured at Fort Langley, 1870 - 73
(Cullen)

Year	Amount Cured	Year	Amount Cured	Year	Amount Cured
1830	200 barrels		salmon	1847	1835 barrels
1831	300 barrels	1837	450 barrels	1848	1703 barrels
1832	No Record	1838	597 barrels	1849	2610 barrels
1833	220 barrels	1839	400 barrels	1850	1600 barrels
	100 half barrels	1840	300 barrels	1851	950 barrels
1834	30 barrels		1500 pcs dried	1852	1757 barrels
	55 half barrels		salmon		150 half barrels
	669 pcs dried	1841	540 barrels	1853	2000 barrels
	salmon	1842	No Record	1854	2000 barrels
1835	605 barrels	1843	No Record	1855	No Record
	112 half barrels	1844	890 barrels	1856	510 barrels
1836	200 barrels	1845	800 barrels	1857	No Record
	350 pcs dried	1846	1600 barrels		

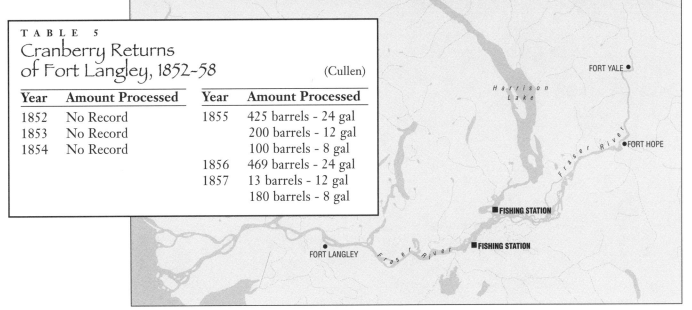

TABLE 5
Cranberry Returns
of Fort Langley, 1852-58
(Cullen)

Year	Amount Processed	Year	Amount Processed
1852	No Record	1855	425 barrels - 24 gal
1853	No Record		200 barrels - 12 gal
1854	No Record		100 barrels - 8 gal
		1856	469 barrels - 24 gal
		1857	13 barrels - 12 gal
			180 barrels - 8 gal

Map of HBC posts established on the lower Fraser River.

TABLE 6
Fur Returns, Fort Langley, 1827-65
(Cullen)

Beaver	1827	1828	1829	1830	1831	1832	1833	1834	
Large	683	823	1277	417	1477	944	2062	873	
Small	228	303	421	228	517	449	725	585	
Coating - lbs	19	3	16	9	20	23	36	23-1/2	

Beaver	1835	1836	1837	1838	1839	1840	1841	1842	1843
Large	951	823	659	444	803	568	419	520	529
Small	413	352	324	183	222	245	173	242	302
Coating - lbs.	13	7-1/2	16	6	5-3/4	12	12-1/4	2-3/4	19-1/2

Beaver	1844	1845	1846	1847	1848	1849	1850	1851	
Large	428	202	267	195	150	67	36	42	
Small	161	84	96	118	100	45	24	11	
Coating - lbs	4	6-1/4	8	3-3/4	3-1/4	1-1/4	—	—	

Beaver	1852	1853	1854	1855	1856	1857	1864	1865	
Large	69	189	294	801	842	699	170	217	
Small	54	100	129	99	246	186	50	46	
Coating - lbs.	—	6-1/2	5-3/4	6	6-1/2	6-1/4	5-1/4	1/2	

An early photo of Fort Langley.

A Coast Salish potlatch feast where the hosts
distributed items to their guests.

in-laws organized a feast, inviting their entire community. At this feast, the Harrison River people received gifts such as dried clams and woven bull-rush mats, (things which were readily available at the mouth of the Fraser River, but not on the Harrison River), in appreciation for the salmon.

It was expected that these "appreciation" gifts would be at least of equal value to the original salmon gift. If the family did not have appropriate gifts immediately available they were expected to present them during future gatherings. Those families who did not quickly fulfill their social obligations risked being ostracised and thereby losing their access rights to distant resources. In addition the *Stó:lō* were also familiar with the technique of trading for profit with strangers. Expert canoe makers and jewellers sold their creations to the highest bidder long before the arrival of the *Xwelítem* traders.

Both the journals of the maritime traders and the ethnographic record demonstrate that Aboriginal people were experienced traders. They also paint a picture of the relationship which existed between the two cultures. European items such as steel files and axe blades, calico cloth, muskets, and window panes were new, interesting and nice to have, but they were neither indispensable nor necessary. Such items were quickly adopted for their utilitarian function or their prestige value. If the Aboriginal

The *Stó:lō* have always had firm concepts of resource ownership.
"Fishing spots" are controlled by extended families.

You Are Asked To Witness

Stó:lō women married HBC employees at Fort Langley. They brought many of their customs with them into the fort. Here, high status women "shape" the head of a high status infant.

people decided not to trade (as they sometimes did), the Europeans suffered financial losses. If the Europeans had decided not to trade, (which they never did), Aboriginal life could have been relatively unaffected.

However, the fur trade had other affects on Aboriginal communities. Unwittingly, fur traders often exposed their Aboriginal trading partners to European diseases which deci-

Salmon were so plentiful it was said you could almost walk across the river on their backs.

2 LAND-BASED FUR TRADE ■

Lasting only until the 1830's, the maritime fur trade involving the *Stó:lō*, the "King George men" and "Boston men" was relatively short lived. Each spring the *Xwelítem* ships arrived off the mouth of the Fraser River to trade throughout the summer and then they left. Aside from their desire to exchange manufactured products for animal pelts the maritime traders were not interested in establishing long-term relationships with the Aboriginal people. And while Aboriginal people were not exploited victims in this relationship, the maritime traders did impact Aboriginal people. The establishment of permanent land-based fur trading posts changed aspects of this relationship, but not its fundamental nature.

Fort Langley, 1858 *Harpers Weekly*

Women were primarily responsible for food gathering.

mated their populations. Increased emphasis on capitalist style commercial exchange also had the effect of undermining certain traditional Aboriginal social structures. Some astute Aboriginal traders from what were previously lower class families were able to increase their status through trade. Conversely, some high ranking families's status diminished depending on their adaptation to the new economic conditions.[7]

Stó:lō men standing beneath their elevated fish caches.
These containers were used to store wind dried salmon throughout the winter months.

night). As a means of protection, the HBC employees quickly constructed a palisade and mounted small cannons in the fort's bastions. However, the men within the fort also developed a more favourable means of ensuring *Stó:lō* acceptance of their presence. Their solution was to establish lasting and meaningful relations with the *Stó:lō* community by marrying into *Stó:lō* families. As a result, the *Xwelítem* fur traders became family members, not enemies.

Governor Simpson of the HBC advocated cementing social ties with the leaders of the Aboriginal communities as "the best security we can have of the goodwill of the Natives." Responding to this, the fort's Chief Trader, Archibald McDonald, noted in the post's journal that the matter of marrying his men into the high ranking *Stó:lō* families was "a subject on which much stress is laid." Within the first year nearly all the fort's men married into *Stó:lō* families.

For the Hudson's Bay Company these marriages helped encourage the *Stó:lō* to trade their furs at Fort Langley, rather than with the "Boston men" who were

In the 1820's the Hudson's Bay Company (HBC), a giant fur trading corporation based in London, England, decided to expand its operations and open a permanent trading post on the lower Fraser River. The HBC had slowly been extending its network of forts westward from Hudson Bay in central Canada for over one hundred years. They now wanted to secure British claims to the territory on the Northwest coast and at the same time drive away American maritime traders who were regarded as cutting into potential HBC profits.

In July 1827 the Hudson's Bay Company established Fort Langley. This was the first time *Xwelítem* had settled permanently in *Stó:lō* territory. Judging from records left by the HBC officers who built Fort Langley, the initial *Stó:lō* response appears to have been cautious acceptance. Apparently, the *Stó:lō* decided not to destroy the fort because it posed no immediate threat. Over time they appear to have come to value Fort Langley much the same way they valued and protected family owned resources like Fraser canyon fishing sites.

Even though the *Stó:lō* showed no explicit outward hostility towards the fort and its inhabitants, the dozen or so men behind the fort's walls were extremely vulnerable. They recognized that the *Stó:lō* had the power to destroy the fort at any time. (This became very apparent when an accidental fire destroyed the entire fort in one

The *Stó:lō* moved to temporary summer camping sites to be closer to the resources they were gathering. Note the preparation of food and shelter resources.

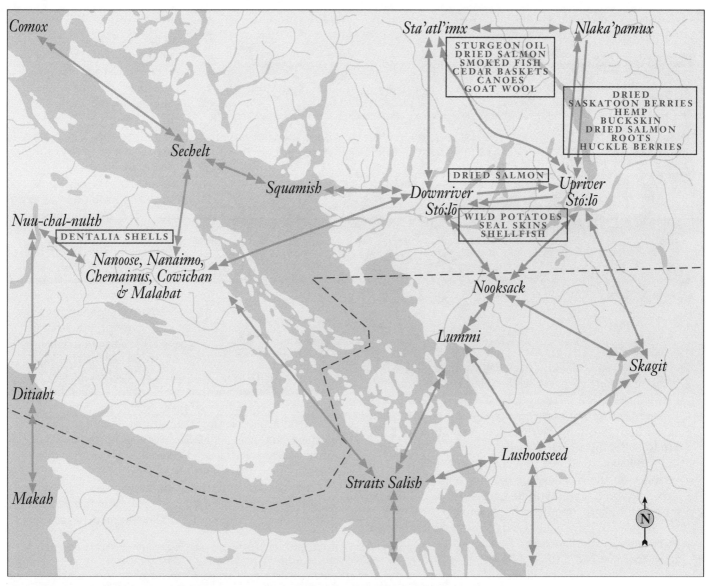

STURGEON OIL
DRIED SALMON
SMOKED FISH
CEDAR BASKETS
CANOES
GOAT WOOL

DRIED
SASKATOON BERRIES
HEMP
BUCKSKIN
DRIED SALMON
ROOTS
HUCKLE BERRIES

DRIED SALMON

WILD POTATOES
SEAL SKINS
SHELLFISH

DENTALIA SHELLS

Comox
Sta'atl'imx
Nlaka'pamux
Sechelt
Squamish
Downriver Stó:lō
Upriver Stó:lō
Nuu-chal-nulth
Nanoose, Nanaimo, Chemainus, Cowichan & Malahat
Nooksack
Lummi
Skagit
Ditiaht
Lushootseed
Makah
Straits Salish

Schematic illustrating a few of the trade relationships between the *Stó:lō* and their neighbours.

still visiting the mouth of the Fraser in their ships each summer. These alliances also provided the HBC with interpreters.

For the *Stó:lō*, these marriages meant something different. They did not view ownership in the same way as did the *Xwelítem*. Most *Stó:lō* resources were communally held, and access to them was controlled by *sí:yá:m* (leaders of extended families). For example, the *Stó:lō* believed that everyone (except slaves) had a right to access salmon. However, they also believed particularly good fishing sites were owned by individual families. The more prosperous a family's fishing site, the faster and more easily they could catch fish. To access new sites, upper class families arranged marriages among their children.

Leg hold traps were introduced as trade items by the HBC.

The *Stó:lō* likely saw Fort Langley as a resource similar to a family-owned fishing rock. HBC employees at the fort were likely viewed as representatives of the families who controlled the fort's resources. The fort was full of useful and prestigious European items such as wool blankets, rope, and steel axe blades and fish hooks. To obtain preferred access to these things, the *Stó:lō* forged marriage alliances with the men at the fort. People from the nearby Kwantlen community were so eager to control access to the fort's resources that they actually relocated themselves so their new village was situated adjacent to the fort.

One Kwantlen woman who married an officer of the fort was the daughter of the influential leader *Ni-ca-meus*. After the marriage, *Ni-ca-meus* felt so strongly about his family's ownership of the

You Are Asked To Witness

fort, that when Aboriginal people from Vancouver Island or other places wanted to trade with Fort Langley, *Ni-ca-meus* demanded they go through him, and not deal directly with the *Xwelítem*. When Aboriginal people arrived who did not have family ties with the fort, *Ni-ca-meus* insisted that they give their furs to him so he could trade on their behalf. Much to the chagrin of the Chief Trader at Fort Langley, once *Ni-ca-meus* finished trading he always kept a small share of the profit for himself – in recognition of his family's special relationship with the HBC and the fort.[8]

Chief Trader Archibald McDonald became concerned with the way local *Stó:lō* like *Ni-ca-meus* were controlling the fur trade. In 1829 he wrote in the fort's journal that the local "leaders of the villages now attempt to secure all trade with the fort for themselves." When McDonald attempted to stop an Aboriginal leader known as "Joe" from forcing all other Aboriginal people from his community to trade through him, Joe became upset and told McDonald not to interfere. He explained that the fort would not lose anything by him acting as a middleman, saying "if I have a great advantage from the trade I will naturally see that the furs are not... [traded to the American maritime traders] by them that give them to me now."[9] Joe's comments reminded McDonald that unless he accepted *Stó:lō* customs he might lose valuable trade profits.

With the land-based fur trade, as with the maritime trade, Aboriginal people were in control. Not only did they continue to drive hard bargains and set high standards for the type and quality of European goods they would accept, they also transformed Fort Langley from a fur trading post into a salmon trading post.

3 SALMON NOT FURS ■

The most important aspect of the *Stó:lō* economy was the harvesting, processing, and trading of salmon. They also hunted, gathered berries and roots, and collected shell fish. When the HBC established Fort Langley, they expected the *Stó:lō* to begin trapping large numbers of beavers for the Fort. Yet, while the Fort's European trade goods were interesting, these items were not crucial to the *Stó:lō* economy, and therefore limited time was spent trapping beaver. The sea, river, and forests were so plentiful that the *Stó:lō* needed little from the fort, and therefore saw no reason to alter their lifestyle to accommodate the HBC.

This frustrated the officers at Fort Langley. In an attempt to encourage the *Stó:lō* to catch more beaver, the company offered a variety of new and different trade items. For example, they gave one *Stó:lō* man a valuable steel "leg hold" trap. Unfortunately for the HBC officers the majority of the *Stó:lō* were indifferent to these sorts of new trade goods and incentives. Some even laughed at Chief Trader McDonald when he asked them to spend more time trapping beaver.[10] All of this frustrated the Hudson's Bay Company. Directors back in London threatened to close Fort Langley. The fort's survival was only secured after McDonald proposed that rather than try to force the *Stó:lō* to change their ways, it would be easier for the Europeans to change the way they traded. McDonald had seen the phenomenal catches of salmon the *Stó:lō* brought back from the Fraser Canyon during the summer spawning runs. He suggested to his superiors that Fort Langley re-focus its activities on exporting salmon rather than furs. The company liked his idea, and apparently, so did many of the *Stó:lō*. In the month of August in 1829, the *Stó:lō* supplied Fort Langley with 7000 salmon.

Over the next few decades, the trade relationship between the *Stó:lō* and the men at Fort Langley grew. Along with the millions of salmon that were being traded to the fort for exportation to the HBC supply post in Hawaii, some *Stó:lō* also began trading hazelnuts and cranberries to the fort for export. In this way, the *Stó:lō* integrated Fort Langley into their traditional economy. They had a long tradition of trading salmon and other items with Aboriginal people from neighbouring communities. The men at Fort Langley simply became another trading partner.

Ultimately, the Hudson's Bay Company became a major broker of *Stó:lō* salmon and other food items. This consumption reflected the earlier relationship that was established between the *Stó:lō* and explorers like Simon Fraser. When Fraser became the first *Xwelítem* to visit *Stó:lō* territory in 1808 he was forced to leave most of his supplies upriver of Hell's Gate in the Fraser Canyon. As such, he relied upon the generosity of his *Stó:lō* hosts for food. Later, during the 1858 gold rush, thousands of hungry miners were dependent upon the *Stó:lō* to fulfill their nutritional needs. This historic dependency may explain the origins of the *Halq'eméylem* expression "*Xwelítem*" which *Stó:lō* people use to this day when referring to people of European ancestry. *Xwelítem* translates as "hungry people" or "starving people."

4 CONCLUSION ■

The arrival of *Xwelítem* explorers and traders on the Northwest Coast modified local Aboriginal societies, but cultural adaptations worked both ways. In the Fraser Valley region the establishment of Fort Langley certainly did not result in the *Stó:lō* radically altering their lifestyles to suit the Hudson Bay Company. On the contrary, the officers and men at the fort were quick to adopt *Stó:lō* cultural traditions, including those associated with inter-family marriage ties. These indigenous customs so heavily imprinted themselves on the HBC, that the *Xwelítem* were forced to accept *Stó:lō* in-laws as middlemen in their trade with the broader Aboriginal communities. Indeed, the fort's primary economic activities soon shifted from fur trading to salmon trading in order to accommodate the traditional *Stó:lō* salmon economy.

Recommended Further Readings:

Cullen, Mary K., *The History of Fort Langley,* 1827-96, Ottawa: Canadian Historic Sites, Occasional Papers in Archaeology and History, No. 20, 1979.

Gibson, James, *Boston Ships, Otter Skins & China Goods.*

Newell, Diane, *Tangled Webs of History,* (Toronto: University of Toronto Press, 1994).

Footnotes

1. Aboriginal people transformed steel files into knives that could be sharpened more easily and retain their sharp edge longer than Indigenous stone knives and adzes.
2. Robin Fisher, *Contact and Conflict* (Vancouver: UBC Press, 1977), p.8.
3. Ibid, 7.
4. Ibid, 9.
5. See Keith T. Carlson, "*Stó:lō* Trade Dynamics," forthcoming in the *Native Studies Review.*
6. Wayne Suttles, "Affinal Ties, Subsistence, and Prestige among the Coast Salish", in *Coast Salish Essays* (Vancouver: Talonbooks, 1987).
7. For more information on the economic and cultural changes that ensued from the fur trade see Steven R. Acheson, "In the Wake of the Iron People: A Case for Changing Settlement Strategies Among the Kunghit Haida," *Journal of the Royal Anthropological Institute* (N.S.), Vol.1, No.2 (June 1995), pp.273-299, or Richard Inglis and James C. Haggarty, "Cook to Jewitt: Three Decades of Change in Nootka Sound," in Bruce G. Trigger, Toby Morantz and Louise Dechéne, editors, *Le Castor Fait Tout: Selected Papers of the Fifth North American Fur Trade Conference,* 1985, (Montreal: Lake St. Louis Historical Society, 1987), pp.193-222.
8. Fort Langley Journal.
9. Fort Langley Journal.
10. Mary K. Cullen, *The History of Fort Langley,* 1827-96, (Ottawa: Canadian Historic Sites, Occasional Papers in Archaeology and History No. 20, 1979).

A Legacy of Broken Promises:

The *Xwelítem* Exploration and Settlement of *Solh Temexw* (Our Land)

Keith Thor Carlson

INTRODUCTION

In the *Halq'eméylem* language the word for people of European decent is *Xwelítem*. *Stó:lō* Elders explain that *Xwelítem* translates as "hungry people" or "starving people." No one remembers exactly when the *Stó:lō* adopted this term to describe the immigrants who came to their land, but Elder Dan Milo was of the opinion that it dates back at least as far as the 1858 gold rush when thousands of poorly provisioned miners arrived in *Stó:lō* territory. The term continues to be used today and when asked most *Stó:lō* say it refers to the *Xwelítem's* insatiable appetite for land and resources. Elder Tilly Guiterrez says that the *Xwelítem* hunger has even motivated them to explore space and visit the moon: "They want the moon!" Such metaphorical definitions ultimately provide this chapter with its focus. As the *Xwelítem* arrived in *Stó:lō* territory they began taking possession of *Stó:lō* land and resources, squeezing the *Stó:lō* onto ever smaller plots of reserve land. Conflicting *Stó:lō* and *Xwelítem* land use patterns, and the political marginalization of the *Stó:lō* in the nineteenth century have left a haunting legacy as yet unresolved. The history behind these processes provide an introduction to the issues of contemporary land claims, Aboriginal rights and title, and the current treaty process.

A Coast Salish leader addressing the 1913 Royal Commission. *Stó:lō* leaders were insistent that their title to the land be recognized, as promised by Governor Douglas.

1 *STÓ:LŌ* CONCEPTS OF LAND OWNERSHIP ■

There are at least two ways of appreciating the moral dilemmas arising out of the non-Aboriginal settlement process – an Aboriginal perspective and a *Xwelítem*, or mainstream Canadian society perspective. Contrary to what one might think, these perspectives are not contradictory. However, they often appear so when people allow prejudice and suspicion to cloud their thinking or refuse to accept that other people have different ways of relating to the environment. In the 1960's, *Stó:lō* Elder Joe Louis explained this difference in these terms.

The white people stop to pray; we stop to respect – the same thing you know. We respect the woods, the living trees in the woods. We drink the water, it's alive. We breathe the air, it's alive too – Respect it! And it seems like everything you respect helps you along in life, what your gonna try and accomplish see. That's the teaching of our old peoples here.[1]

The *Stó:lō* have a very clear understanding of their Aboriginal title and rights. It is based upon countless generations of occupation, use and management of their territories' resources, and self-government. *Yewal Sí:yá:m* (respected community leader[2]) Albert "Sonny" McHalsie of *Shxw'ōwhámél*, explains how he understands *Stó:lō* Aboriginal title and rights:

Over 100 years ago the artist Paul Kane travelled across the Canadian west capturing scenes of Aboriginal life on canvas. He thought he was witnessing the last expressions of a soon to be extinct culture. In this painting he illustrates aspects of Coast Salish family life.

Archaeologists tell us that we have been here for at least 9,000 years. Our Elders tell us we have been here since time immemorial. They also tell us through *sxwōxwiyámx* (stories and legends) that many of our resources were at one time our ancestors. Many of our people have stories about a particular resource which at one time may have been their own people. For instance, people at a village near Hope claim the sturgeon as their ancestor; others from a village near Chilliwack and Agassiz claim the mountain goat as their ancestor. One legend common to all *Stó:lō* tells the story of the origin of the cedar tree. It goes like this: At one time there was a very good man who was always helping others. He was always sharing whatever he had. When X̱eX̱à:ls (the transformers) saw this they transformed him into a cedar tree so he would always continue helping the people. And so to this day he continues to give and share many things with the people – cedar roots for baskets, bark for clothing, and wood for shelter.

So our resources are more than just resources, they are our extended family. They are our ancestors, our *shxweli* (spirit or life force). Our *shxweli* includes our parents, grandparents, great grandparents, cedar tree, salmon, sturgeon and transformer rocks… Our Elders tell us that everything has a spirit. So when we use a resource, like a sturgeon or cedar tree, we have to thank our ancestors who were transformed into these things. We don't like to think that our ancestors came over the Bering Land Bridge. We have always been here.[3]

Family is very important to the *Stó:lō*. Their family relations extend beyond people to include the natural environment. Here members of the McHalsie family enjoy spending time together.

The *Stó:lō* have a complex personal relationship with the environment which includes family ties. They believe that in the distant past the world was very different than it is today. "There were many evil spirits, people with power, animal people, deformed men and other creatures."[4] To "arrange the earth as it is today," *XeXà:ls*, the transformers, arrived and made order out of chaos – transforming things into their permanent forms.[5] As Elder Tilly Gutierrez explains, *XeXà:ls* transformed some people into animals and stones."[6] Others he turned into plants. The salmon which return to the Fraser River to spawn

The cedar tree is believed to have once been a very kind and generous man. He was transformed into a cedar tree in order for him to continue giving to his people.

each year are believed to be the descendants of early *Stó:lō* who were transformed into fish. Certain rocks, such as *Xá:ytem*" situated in Mission, are believed to have once been living people, and the "*shxweli*" of these people are still considered to be active within the rock. The mountains themselves have personalities and specific stories attached to them. Mt. Cheam (or "*Lhílheqey*" in *Halq'eméylem*) is Mt. Baker's spouse, and the mother of "*Séyowòt*," "*Óyewòt*," and "*Xomó:th'ìya*" (smaller mountains below her). She and her husband moved to the Fraser Valley from the south. *XeXà:ls* changed her into a mountain and gave her the responsibility to look after *Stó:lō* people, the river, and the salmon.[7]

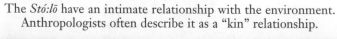

The *Stó:lō* have an intimate relationship with the environment. Anthropologists often describe it as a "kin" relationship.

The Mountain goat is considered to be a member of the extended family. People from a village near Hope claim the mountain goat as their ancestor.

You Are Asked To Witness

2 BRITISH/CANADIAN CONCEPTS OF ABORIGINAL LAND OWNERSHIP ■

Current Canadian concepts and legal definitions of land title and ownership are derived from earlier British laws – laws which both reflect and shape public opinion. While not necessarily contradictory, these mainstream, Canadian concepts differ from those of *Stó:lō* people.

By the 1700's, Britain and other European nations were engaged in a fierce competition over North American land. For most Europeans, the fact that North America was densely populated with Aboriginal people did not stop them from viewing the continent as a vacant "New World."

In order for a European government to be recognized by its European neighbours as the legitimate claimant to a new territory, its representatives were required to perform a "claiming ceremony." Upon their arrival, they were required to raise their nation's flag and official-

Rocks are also believed to have a *shxwelí* or life force. Elder Jimmy Charlie of Chehalis tells the story of how *XeXà:ls* transformed a man into a stone figure of *chítmexw* the great horned owl.

THE FIRST SUCCESSFUL LAND CLAIM

A contemporary newspaper cartoon spoof of a British "claiming ceremony".

ly claim the land in the name of their sovereign King or Queen. For the British, (as will be explained in detail later), this ceremony was not intended to extinguish Aboriginal title to the land and resources. Rather, it implicitly recognized Aboriginal title as existing along-

side British sovereignty. When the ceremony was performed properly, other European nations usually recognized them as legitimate. Of course, Aboriginal people were never consulted in this process. Typically, they were unaware that such ceremonies had ever taken place; nor did they understand their European significance.

In their race to lay claim to all of the "New World," the European powers constantly stretched the boundaries of the territory they had claimed. It was not unusual for them to include areas that were hundreds, if not thousands of kilometres from the location where the actual "claiming" ceremony had occurred, in regions they never even visited. For example, in the late 1700's Spain claimed all land that drained into the Mississippi River (the "Louisiana Territory"), despite the fact that no Spaniard had ever travelled to the headwaters of the river. When Spain ceded the Louisiana Territory to France, the French government accepted the Spanish boundary, even though the French had never undertaken any serious explorations of the area. In 1804 when France "sold" the Louisiana Territory to the United States, the Americans also initially accepted the old Spanish territorial boundaries. However, U.S. President Thomas Jefferson was quick to stretch the Louisiana Territory's boundary all the way to the Pacific Ocean after the successful exploration of the Columbia River by Meriwether

The New World

GREENLAND

CANADA

Louisiana
Territory

UNITED STATES

MEXICO

SOUTH
AMERICA

The vast "Louisiana Territory" was claimed by the Spanish even though no Spaniard had ever visited more than a fraction of it.

Lewis and William Clark in 1805.

Because the territories claimed by various European governments were so expansive, it was not unusual for them to overlap. For example, in the 1763, the British King issued a "Royal Proclamation" declaring that their North American territory extended from Hudson's Bay in what is now central Canada, all the way to the Pacific Ocean. This claim was made to ensure the expansion of the extensive and profitable fur trading activities of large corporate resource extraction companies like the Hudson's Bay Company. The English wanted to restrict other European powers from making use of British claimed lands and resources. The amount of land included in the claim was huge, especially considering that the British were unaware of the distance from Hudson's Bay to the coast of what is now called British Columbia. From their position in Mexico the Spanish also claimed the Pacific Northwest Coast, as did the Russians in Alaska. Later, based upon the explorations and "discoveries" of Lewis and Clark, the Americans also claimed this vast area as part of the Louisiana Territory. Such claims were made without the knowledge, consent, or understanding of the

Family controlled fishing sites are one expression of the intimate relationship the *Stó:lō* have with the land and its resources. It also demonstrates *Stó:lō* concepts of ownership to the land.

Aboriginal population. Indeed, at this time no relationship of any kind had been established between the Europeans and the vast majority of Aboriginal people living within the claimed territories.

Eventually the competing European powers came to recognize and acknowledge British sovereignty to the Northwest Coast. This recognition did not stem from the original British "Royal Proclamation of 1763" which claimed all the land stretching from the shores of Hudson's Bay to the Northwest Coast. Rather, the British emphasized a subsequent ceremony performed in 1778 by Captain James Cook on the shore of Vancouver Island. Initially Spain disputed the British position, citing the 1774 voyage of Captain Juan Perez to the Northwest Coast as their claim. In reality, all such claims of discovery were weak arguments in international law, and were typically disregarded in favour of actual acts of conquest or effective occupation. Ultimately, it was the British government's ability to convince Spanish diplomats that they would back up their claim with military might that compelled others to accept the British claim as legitimate.

3 BRITISH SOVEREIGNTY AND ABORIGINAL RIGHTS ■

By the late 1700's the British government claimed undisputed sovereignty over most of northern North America. At the same time, British common law still recognized that Aboriginal peoples, as the original occupiers of the territory, had special rights to the land and its resources. The British recognized that to ensure peaceful and profitable relations between Aboriginal people and the new settlers, these rights had to be protected. As mentioned earlier, to clarify the extent of these rights, and to affirm their continued existence, the British monarch

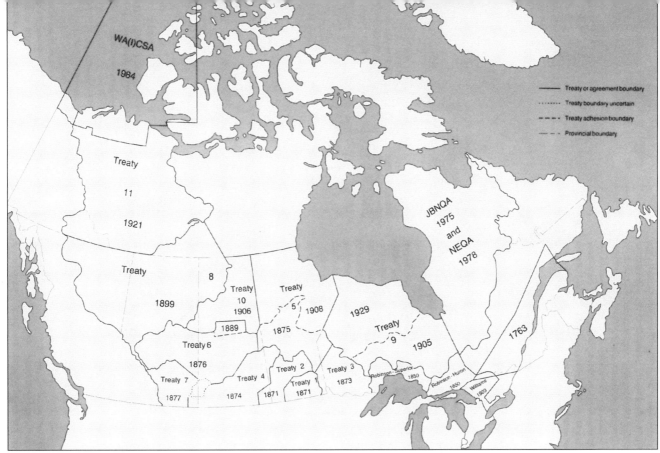

Map showing the "Indian Treaties in Canada".

issued a special proclamation known as the "Royal Proclamation of 1763." In this document the British crown proclaimed that it was

> R eserving... under British Sovereignty, Protection and Dominion for the use of the said Indians, all Lands and Territories not included within... (existing Crown colonies or those lands set aside for the Hudson's Bay Company in central Canada).[8]

It also clarified that the

> S everal Nations or Tribes of Indians with whom we are connected, and who live under our Protection, should not be molested or disturbed in the Possession of such Parts of Our Dominions and territories as, not having been ceded to or purchased by Us, are reserved to them... as their Hunting Grounds...[9]

In short, the "Royal Proclamation" clarified that Aboriginal people had pre-existing rights to the land and its resources. It gave expression to the fact that Aboriginal land could not be purchased from Aboriginal peoples, unless they voluntarily surrendered their rights in the form of treaties, and then only to the British crown.[10] Therefore, before a British settler or company could move into Aboriginal territory, formal "nation to nation" treaties had to be concluded between Aboriginal communities and the British government. Until such time, the government was obliged to "protect" Aboriginal land rights by preventing European settlers and companies from moving into Aboriginal territory. As legal historian Brian Slattery has observed, the "aboriginal interest constitutes a legal burden on the (British) crown's ultimate title until (voluntarily) surrendered."[11]

The British common law encoded in the "Royal Proclamation" was applied in most regions of Canada east of the Rocky Mountains with the notable exceptions of Quebec, Newfoundland and the Maritimes. In Ontario and the Prairies, Aboriginal people signed treaties surrendering their land in exchange for specific compensation packages. However, as shall be demonstrated, the principals articulated in the Royal Proclamation were never applied in the province of British Columbia (except for a few minor treaties negotiated on Vancouver Island). Until 1990, the British Columbia government refused to consider the possibility that Aboriginal rights needed to be extinguished by treaty. Only now are the federal and provincial governments beginning to negotiate with the Aboriginal people of British Columbia by participating in the B.C. Treaty Commission.

4 THE ABORIGINAL LAND QUESTION IN BRITISH COLUMBIA ■

In the 80 years between Captain James Cook's arrival at Vancouver Island in 1778, and the establishment of a British colony on the mainland of British Columbia in 1858, *Xwelítem* (Europeans) did very little which can be considered a threat or challenge to Aboriginal title. In the Fraser Valley, the arrival of Simon Fraser in 1808, and the

Illustration of Fort Langley, circa 1862.

subsequent establishment of Fort Langley by the Hudson's Bay Company in 1827, did not usher in an era of *Xwelítem* domination of *Stó:lō* people. Instead, *Xwelítem* explorers and fur traders were far more dependent upon the *Stó:lō*. This was evident in the way fur traders adapted to *Stó:lō* social and economic patterns.[12]

In the Spring of 1858 word reached San Francisco that gold was in the sandbars of the Fraser River. This news sparked off a massive migration and set in motion a series of events which profoundly affected the *Stó:lō* people's ability to interact with their natural environment. When word reached Puget Sound in March 1858 it caused American "mills to shut down, soldiers to desert their posts and sailors to abandon ship."[13] By April, news had spread to California, precipitating a mass convoy of ships northward to the Fraser River. Between May 19 and July 1, 1858, nineteen steam ships, nine sailing vessels and fourteen decked vessels transported 6,133 men from San Francisco to Victoria, while thousands more trekked northward along the coast on foot or in small private vessels. On a single day in July over 2,800 miners arrived on two steamers in Victoria harbour looking for smaller vessels to take them to the Fraser.[14] According to the estimates of the American consular agent, in the months of May, June and July at least 23,000 men had travelled from San Francisco to Victoria by sea and another eight thousand reached the Fraser River through Puget Sound or overland.[15] Thus, in the space of a few short months over 30,000 *Xwelítem* gold miners (and the usual compliment of opportunists who follow miners) arrived in the lower Fraser canyon looking for instant wealth. The legacy of the gold rush has provided a consistent focus for *Stó:lō* political activism on the "land question" up to the present era.

Unlike the men at Fort Langley who realized that they needed to develop positive relationships with the *Stó:lō* in order to prosper, the gold miners sought to pursue their dreams of fortune *despite* the *Stó:lō*. Except as guides, packers and occasionally labourers, the miners had no use for the *Stó:lō*. To them the *Stó:lō* were essentially impediments. *Stó:lō* villages, berry patches, and fishing sites often sat upon the most promising gold bars. Self-serving stereotypes of "Indian savages" were transported from California – where extermination of the Aboriginal population had been a semi-official objective – and made it easy for the miners to treat the *Stó:lō* as people without rights.[16]

The *Stó:lō*, like their up-river Aboriginal neighbours the N'lakapamux, considered the river, land and resources as their property, and resented the miners' arrogance and assumption that the resources were open for exploitation. Governor James Douglas understood the Aboriginal perspective and relayed it to his superiors in London in early April 1858:

> The search for gold and prospecting of the country had, up to the last dates from the interior been carried on by the Native Indian population, who are extremely jealous of the whites and strongly opposed to their digging the soil for gold. It is, however, worthy of remark and a circumstance highly honourable to the character of those savages that have on all occasions scrupulously respected the persons and property of the white visitors, at the same time that they have expressed a determination to reserve the gold for their own benefit...[17]

By July 1858, Governor Douglas was reporting to the London Colonial Office that the Aboriginal people near the present day town of Lytton

Have lately taken the high-handed, though probably not unwise course, of expelling all the parties of gold diggers, composed chiefly of persons from the American territories, who had forced an entrance into their country. They have also openly expressed a determination to resist all attempts at working gold in any of the streams flowing into the Thompson's River, both from a desire to monopolize the precious metal for their own benefit, and from a well-founded impression that the shoals of salmon which annually ascend those rivers and furnish the principal food of the inhabitants, will be driven off, and prevented from making their annual migrations from the sea.[18]

In June 1858, *Stó:lō* resentment over *Xwelítem* insensitivity to what they considered their property rights threatened to turn violent. A small city had sprung up at Hill's Bar (between Hope and Yale) and 4000 miners were squeezing the *Stó:lō* from the river bed and digging up the gravel and soil.[19] Describing the situation, James Douglas reported that:

On the arrival of our party at 'Hill's Bar', the white miners were in a state of great alarm on account of a serious affray which had just occurred with the native Indians, whom mustered under arms in a tumultuous manner, and threatened to make a clean sweep of the whole body of miners assembled there.

The quarrel arose out of a series of provocations on both sides, and from the jealousy of the savages, who naturally felt annoyed at the large quantities of gold taken from their country by the white miners.

I lectured them soundly about their conduct on that occasion, and took the leader in the affray, an Indian highly connected in their way, and of great influence, resolution, and energy of character, into the Government service, and found him exceedingly useful in settling other Indian difficulties.

Douglas did not reserve his lectures for just the *Stó:lō*. He also spoke sternly to the *Xwelítem*, clarifying that "no abuses would be tolerated; and that the laws would protect the rights of the Indian no less than those of the white man."[20]

As Douglas explained, the miner's occupation of the river bank around Hill's Bar resulted in a "series of provocations" which offended the *Stó:lō*. While not found among papers in *Xwelítems'* archives, accounts of these provocations have been passed down through *Stó:lō* oral narratives. One of these narratives explains that the region around Hill's Bar was known to the *Stó:lō* as *Hemhemetheqw*, which means "good place to make sockeye salmon oil." Countless seasons of oil processing had

resulted in many of the large boulders in the vicinity having been turned into "pecked pots" for the collection of salmon oil. After a relatively short time out under the sun and laying in a pecked pot, the oil escaped the freshly caught sockeye and was easily collected from the rock bowl. It was essential that the oil be collected during the brief window of opportunity which occurred in late summer. Conditions had to be perfect: sockeye running in numbers, hot sun to melt the oil, and a strong wind to keep off the flies. With the miners occupying the shoreline and overturning rocks in their haste to find gold, *Stó:lō* people were understandably anxious over their inability to secure access to their pots.[21]

Douglas further addressed *Stó:lō* concerns over the miner's disregard for their well defined property rights when he met delegations of *Stó:lō* leaders at Hope. Recalling this meeting in a letter to his superiors in London, Douglas wrote:

The Indians were assembled, and made no secret of their dislike of the white visitors. They had many complaints of maltreatment, and in all cases where redress was possible it was granted without delay. One small party of those natives laid claim to a particular part of the river, which they wished to be reserved for their own purposes, a request which was immediately granted, the space staked off, and the miners who had made the claims were immediately removed, and public notice given that the place was reserved for the Indians, and that no one would be allowed to occupy it without their consent.[22]

Accounts of a particular promise made by Governor Douglas to the *Stó:lō* regarding specific tracts of land along the river near Hope are also recalled by contemporary *Stó:lō* people. Sonny McHalsie shared the following story which he explained had been passed on to him by Chawathil Elder Gilbert Ewen who in turn sited an Elder from the previous generation, Oscar Dennis Peters, as his source. Mr. Ewen explained that

In the past Governor Douglas had come and stood on that point, right there on the corner of Park St. and the Highway in downtown Hope, and he faced over to Qemqemó – or Mt. Ogalvie – and said... "all the land on the north side of that line, right up to where its bounded by the Fraser River and the Coquihalla and that straight line, would be made into Indian Reserve. And all the land south of that line would become the town of Hope."

Now I had heard that before. Peter Dennis Peters talked about that, and also I read it in that report that was made by James Teit, I think it was 1922, where he was interviewing

The "City of Yale" was created in a few short months to accommodate the thousands of miners entering *Stó:lō* territory in 1858 during the Fraser River gold rush.

my great grandfather Dennis Peters, and Dennis Peters told him basically the same story...[23]

Many disputes stemmed from the *Xwelítem* desire for land. When the miners arrived they were issued 25 square foot claims upon application to the Colonial government. While this may seem like an insignificant amount of land, it becomes less so when one considers the thousands of people involved, and that all the land considered valuable was along the banks of the river and streams and therefore was among the most heavily used lands by the *Stó:lō*. Furthermore, beyond the individual mining claims, entire towns sprang up overnight, complete with court houses, post offices, hotels and supply stores. Trees were cleared and *Stó:lō* settlements and land use patterns marginalized.

The loss of land was more complex than a discussion about the issuance of mining permits would lead one to believe. Land was also physically removed. Elder Harold Wells of Union Bar (near Hope) remembers his grandmother telling him that Chinese gold miners arrived and started panning the gravel on the river bank near their family home just as the family prepared to leave to visit relatives farther down river. When his family returned they found that the miners had relocated from the actual river bank "back 200 feet onto a flat field" where his family home had been. Over the month that Harold's family had been away the miners had removed a large section of the land leaving a permanent scar: a twelve foot deep quarry.[24]

Halq'eméylem place names from the area of the most intense mining activities between Hope and Yale also reflect aspects of the relationship between the *Stó:lō* and the *Xwelítem* miners. Elders Susan Peters and Amelia Douglas explained that the *Halq'eméylem* name for one of the gold rush Bar's translates into English as "cleared away." This term describes the rocks that had been stripped of moss through the mining process.[25]

Stó:lō-Xwelítem relations steadily deteriorated as more miners arrived in the valley and lower canyon. By mid-summer, 1858, a British journalist with the *London Times* reported from the gold fields near Yale that the "Indians complain that the whites abuse them sadly, take their squaws away, shoot their children, and take their salmon by force." In the opinion of the reporter, "some of the 'whites' are sad dogs."[26] Six years later, a Quamichan leader (a relative of the *Stó:lō* from Vancouver Island who spoke the same language and could access Fraser Canyon fishing sites through his *Stó:lō* family connections) outlined his feelings about the newcomers to the explorer Robert Brown. The Quamichan speaker said: "You came to our country. We did not resist you - you got our women with children & then left them upon us - or put them away when they could have no children to keep up our race (a fact, or nearly amounting to as much). You brought diseases amongst us which are killing us. You took our lands and did not pay us for them. You drove away our deer & salmon & all this you did & now if we wish to buy a glass of firewater to keep our hearts up you will not allow us. What do you white men wish?"[27]

Taking the issues raised by the Quamichan leader in the order presented we learn that the *Xwelítem* gold min-

You Are Asked To Witness

ers were desirous of female companionship, but not typically within a consensual relationship. Historical documents indicate that miners became involved in short term sexual relations with some *Stó:lō* women.[28] Thus, the relationship the miners wished to form was, for the most part, fundamentally different from that forged between the Hudson's Bay fur traders at Fort Langley and the *Stó:lō* women of an earlier generation. Whereas the HBC employees were trying to establish long term, family ties between themselves and the *Stó:lō*, most *Xwelítem* miners had no intention of spending any longer in *Stó:lō* territory than it took to extract the gold from the sand bars.

In the mid-summer of 1858, *Xwelítem* miner's disrespect for *Stó:lō* women frequently resulted in violence. The most well documented conflict broke out in the lower canyon just upriver from Yale. The *London Times* journalist reported that large scale violence erupted after two French miners "stole away and deforced (raped) an Indian girl." In retaliation, men from the girl's family executed and decapitated the miners responsible, throwing their headless bodies into the river.

When other miners discovered their comrade's bodies floating in an eddy – which to this day is referred to as "deadman's eddy" – they organized themselves into formal military regiments and prepared to fight a war of extermination. Some accounts of the ensuing conflict paint a rather pitiful picture of the Aboriginal people, and argue that the Frenchmen were actually killed in a last ditch desperate attempt to frighten the miners who were "make(ing) inroads into the Indian country."[29] According to the reminiscences of some of the American miners involved in the incident, in the battles that followed the miners quickly "bettered the Indians" by burning their villages and forcibly preventing them from accessing their fishing rocks during the summer salmon runs. These self-serving accounts maintain that the Aboriginal people quickly accepted defeat at the hands of the miners and sued for peace, "offering young women as brides to the miners."[30]

The British journalist provides a second perspective on this conflict. He recorded that the Aboriginal people had not been "bettered," in battle. Rather, after suffering atrocities at the miner's hands during the initial days of the campaign, the Aboriginal forces were regrouping and preparing to launch a counter attack. Many of the casualties suffered by the American expedition resulted not from ambush, (as the miners maintained) but from their own gun fire after they began "shooting at shadows" during the night. According to the British correspondent, the frightened and humiliated miners retreated to Yale in the hopes of reorganizing. However, before any further bloodshed could occur Governor Douglas and a contingent of British Marines arrived to enforce a peace.[31]

Early *Xwelítem* settlements began springing up throughout the Fraser Valley after the 1858 Fraser River gold rush had concluded.

DELTA

NEW
WESTMINSTER

PORT MOODY

SURREY

WHITE
ROCK

PORT
COQUITLAM

BLAINE

LANGLEY

HANEY

Pitt Lake

FORT
LANGLEY

LYNDEN

WHONNOCK

ALDERGROVE

Alouette
Lake

Nooksack River

MISSION

Stave
Lake

ABBOTSFORD

SUMAS

DEWDNEY

Só:lō Reserves
Past & Present

Sumas Lake
(to 1924)

CHILLIWACK

SARDIS

■ **Present Day Reserves**
■ **Douglas Reserves**
■ **Sproat Reserves**
(recommended)

MAPLE
FALLS

Cultus
Lake

AGASSIZ

Harrison
Lake

MOUNT
BAKER

CANADA / US BORDER

W A S H I N G T O N   B R I T I S H   C O L U M B I A

YALE

HOPE

Chilliwack
Lake

Coquihalla River

Despite the tension which existed between the *Stó:lō* and the *Xwelítem*, instances of friendly interaction did occur. Most miners were obsessed with finding the "mother load" and becoming rich overnight. Little time, apparently, had been spent planning and provisioning. From the diary of Otis Parsons, a miner who arrived in *Stó:lō* territory in the summer of 1858, we learn that the *Stó:lō* supplied many miners with fresh and dried salmon.[32] The British journalist recorded on December 17, 1858, that "winter has set in and some miners would have starved had the Indians not provided provisions."[33] The *Stó:lō* have never forgotten the pathetic state of the miners in the Autumn of 1858. Elder Dan Milo, at age 99 in 1963 related the following piece of oral history to a CBC reporter:

> . . . Xwelítem, that's what the Indians call the white man, because in them days those white people travelling on the way to the gold rush, they were starving. Xwelítem, that means "starving." Well, the Indians began to feed them, feed them till they get alright. They say the Indians here in this valley, the Chilliwack, are about the kindest Indians that's living – that's what the white people said.[34] 😊

Over thirty years later, Elder Tilly Guiterrez echoes Dan Milo, stating that the gold miners were so hungry they began to "suffer from scurvy." She tells us that her "granny explained that the miner's scurvy became so bad that their skin broke out in open sores." In her words, "we had to feed them; they were starving."[35]

Following in the miners' wake were an assortment of enterprising social parasites who planned to grow rich selling cheap whiskey to the local Aboriginal populations. Many *Stó:lō* had accumulated a fair amount of gold during the years 1858-1860. Aside from providing miners with provisions many mined the gold bars themselves. Others acted as labourers for American miners, and a good number acted as ferrymen, canoeing miners across the river at Hope and Yale, or piloting paddle wheelers. This Aboriginal wealth was a tempting bonanza for enterprising *Xwelítem* whiskey pedlars. As Robert Brown's quote of the Quamichan speaker illustrates, "fire water" quickly became a serious problem. Commenting on the matter at Hope as he announced a new law outlawing the sale of

Racist Interpretation of Heirarchies of Civilization

A common European assumption of the mid-to-late nineteenth century, which has now been dismissed, was that all "civilizations" were hierarchically arranged, and European society occupied the uppermost position.

alcohol to Aboriginal people, Governor James Douglas explained, "Spirituous and other intoxicating Liquors have been sold to the Native Indians of the Fraser River and elsewhere, to the great injury and demoralization of the said Indians; and also thereby endangering the Public Peace and the lives and property of Her Majesty's subjects and others in the said Districts.[36] Sadly, the alcohol introduced during the gold rush has taken a tragic and heavy toll on *Stó:lō* families.

By 1860, most of the more than 30,000 original miners had given up and returned home. However, the arrival of the gold miners had opened a door to migration which could not be closed. While the miners were primarily single American men, the first permanent immigrants to the Fraser Valley tended to be British farming families. Colonial authorities had encouraged these people to come to British Columbia, in part to help offset the influence of the American mining population. It was anticipated that the settlers would provide a stable agrarian economy and loyal British tax base. Yet, as previously noted, Aboriginal rights were still protected by British common law as articulated in the Royal Proclamation. Therefore, as no treaties had been negotiated, the occupation of the Fraser Valley by immigrant settlers was technically illegal.

In the decade prior to the gold rush, the process of negotiating and signing treaties extinguishing Aboriginal title had begun in limited form in what was then the independent British colony of Vancouver Island. Governor James Douglas had signed treaties with Aboriginal people living around the *Xwelítem* communities of Fort Victoria, Nanaimo, and Fort Rupert. However, this process was never completed on the rest of Vancouver Island, or even initiated on the mainland. Understanding why treaties were never signed on the mainland provides an opportunity for better understanding the current legacy of unsettled land claims and related issues in British Columbia. To accomplish this, it is essential to investigate British archival documents as well as corresponding *Stó:lō* oral traditions, both of which describe the government's intentions towards the *Stó:lō*. Such an investigation provides multiple perspectives of how things happened, and allows us to form a richer more balanced view of the past. The degree to which these two diverse forms of historical evidence correspond and complement one another is particularly reassuring.

5 TREATIES OR JUST RESERVES? ■

In the mid-nineteenth century, official British policy towards Aboriginal people underwent a significant change, reflected by shifts in mainstream public opinion. Earlier in the century, British policy had been directed towards "protecting" Aboriginal people, both through the negotiation of treaties, and restricting them to reserves, thus segregating them from the new immigrants. The government policy intended that Aboriginal people be allowed to pursue their traditional lifestyles in isolation from settler communities.

By the time the colony of British Columbia was officially proclaimed in 1858, the idea of signing potentially expensive treaties and then placing Aboriginal people on large isolated reserves appears to have been losing favour among both the British government and the public. Most *Xwelítem* observers shared the opinion that time was drawing to a close for Aboriginal people. Traditional lifestyles based upon fishing and hunting were seen as incompatible with the agricultural/industrial immigrant society. This belief appeared to be supported by the rapid decline in Aboriginal populations resulting from exposure to European diseases. Likewise, many *Xwelítem* of this era viewed Aboriginal people as capable only of absorbing *Xwelítem* vices, not virtues.

Europeans and Americans felt that agricultural and industrial development signified the culmination of human social evolution. Mid-nineteenth century American concepts of their country's "Manifest Destiny" held that the United States represented the culmination of human social-political evolution. Americans regarded themselves as a chosen race, predestined to dominate and conquer not only the resources of the continent, but also its indigenous people. Likewise, the British were fond of viewing their massive expanding Empire as evidence of their superiority over the peoples and cultures they colonized. Such views held that all races or civilizations were hierarchically arranged. North American Aboriginal societies were seen as being near the bottom of this hierarchy, along with the African peoples.

These interpretations of the world held that "civilized" people exploited natural resources and manipulated the environment to serve their purposes, by cutting down trees, planting crops, mining the earth, and constructing factories. In contrast, "primitive" or "savage" people, situated at the bottom of the hierarchy, were seen as being dominated by nature. They appeared to modify their lives in order to accommodate nature. Only those who made agricultural use of the soil were considered to have real rights to the land. Nineteenth century interpretations of the Biblical "Book of Genesis" supported this view of the world. The Bible stated that God had given humankind dominion over the plants and animals of the earth. In the nineteenth century, the planet's natural resources were seen as limitless, and "dominion" was understood to mean that God gave people not only the right, but an obligation to transform and harness nature. Viewed from this perspective, Aboriginal people had not only demonstrated to the settlers the inferiority of their civilization; they had also turned their back on God's mission. Responding to these changes in attitudes, officials began developing new "Indian policies." In the case of British Columbia, this improvisation was initially described as "benevolent assimilation."

Stó:lō people's concept of land and land ownership clearly differed from that of nineteenth century *Xwelítem* immigrants. The settlers regarded the environment from a utilitarian perspective – it contained resources which could be exploited. The land and resources were inanimate objects which needed to be consumed or marketed before they became "valuable." In contrast, the *Stó:lō* did not see nature as a force to overcome. Rather, they saw themselves as an integral part of the natural environment. They viewed the environment as part of their family. Everything in it had a spirit, and was therefore alive, and had a right to exist in its natural state for its own sake.

6 GOVERNOR DOUGLAS: "BENEVOLENT ASSIMILATION" AND TREATY PROMISES ■

British Columbia Colonial Governor, James Douglas, shared the commonly held opinion that traditional Aboriginal culture was incompatible with the modern European immigrant society. He felt that traditional *Stó:lō* culture could not co-exist along side European culture. However, unlike most of the prominent government officials who succeeded him, Douglas did not appear to believe that certain racial groups were innately superior to others. Rather, from his writings, it would seem that he thought that one's environment and upbringing were more important than genetic racial factors in determining a person's potential and ability. This belief was relatively progressive for the time, and probably stemmed from his personal background and experience. He was part African-American (his mother was from the British West Indies), and his wife was half Aboriginal. If "proper" education and European cultural cultivation could transform his own wife from a "humble half-breed" into "Lady Douglas," the respected matriarch of colonial British Columbian society, it is not difficult to imagine that Douglas thought other Aboriginal people held the same "potential."[37] For Douglas, all that was needed was a standardized process to facilitate their transformation from "savage" to "civilized."

The racial tensions produced by the sudden influx of gold miners in 1858 provided Douglas with the necessary motivation to formally establish a "civilization and assimilation" process. He decided that the Aboriginal people inhabiting British Columbia needed to be encouraged and coaxed into rejecting their traditional culture, and replacing it with *Xwelítem* social, political, economic, and religious beliefs and activities. They would, as a result, become assimilated. Writing to his superiors in London England, Governor Douglas explained how his proposed policy of benevolent assimilation would,

> Result in the moral elevation of the native Indian races, in rescuing them from degradation, and protecting them from oppression and rapid decay... Provided we succeed in devising means of rendering the Indian as comfortable and independent in regard to physical wants in improving his condition, as he was when a wandering denizen of the forests, there can be little doubt of the ultimate success of our experiment... Anticipatory reserves of land for the benefit and support of the Indian races will be made for that purpose in all districts of British Columbia inhabited by native tribes. Those reserves should in all cases include their cultivated fields and village sites, for which from habit and association they invariably conceive a strong attachment, and prize more, for that reason, than for the extent or value of the land.[38]

Douglas expounded the theory that the only way *Stó:lō* people could escape physical extinction was to embrace the notion of their own cultural extinction. He anticipated that, with the assistance of Christian missionaries and by being treated as equals under the law with people of European decent, *Stó:lō* people would become farmers and adopt the *Xwelítem* culture. He wanted to "rescue" *Stó:lō* people from the "degrading" influence of the *Xwelítem* gold miners and whiskey pedlars by creating "Indian reserves," which would be set aside for their exclusive use. The remaining land would be made available to *Stó:lō* farmers and immigrant settlers alike for agricultural purposes and urban development. Encouraging the *Stó:lō* to pre-empt land off reserve as freely as the *Xwelítem* settlers was central to the success of Douglas' vision. Douglas hoped this would entice *Stó:lō* people to give up their traditional lifestyles of fishing, hunting, and gathering to become settled Christian farmers.

Douglas also hoped that as the *Stó:lō* became assimilated they would gradually "be trained to habits of self-government and self-reliance."[39] Of course, *Stó:lō* people had been self-governing and self-reliant for thousands of years before the colony of British Columbia was proclaimed. What Douglas meant was a self-governing and self-reliant "European style" community integrated into the expanding new Euroamerican society. He anticipated that one way for the *Stó:lō* to become self-supporting would be to lease parts of their "Indian reserves" to non-Aboriginal farmers.

However, Douglas also seemed to realize that the *Stó:lō* and other Aboriginal people required specific financial compensation for the loss of their land and resources. This money would be essential if long term European style economic development and sustainability were to become a reality for future generations of *Stó:lō* people. According to *Stó:lō* oral history records, Douglas repeatedly explained that he intended to compensate them for

their land. However, for a variety of reasons, Douglas and *Stó:lō* people never negotiated treaties. It appears that the major impediment was the fact that settlement had occurred too rapidly as a result of the 1858 gold rush in the Fraser River. Most of the gold miners were veterans of the California gold rush of 1849. The treatment of California's Aboriginal population at the hands of the miners shows that these men cared little about Aboriginal rights, or treaties, on either side of the border. As such, the colony was suddenly populated by people who were not necessarily loyal to the British crown. While these Americans were begrudgingly open to the idea of paying taxes to open a road to upriver gold fields, they were unwilling to pay taxes to a British government in order to finance the creation of Indian treaties. In light of this, it would seem that Governor Douglas may have decided to wait until British Columbia had a larger more loyal tax base before negotiating treaties. In the meantime, he determined to create generous Indian reserves of at least 40 hectares (100 acres) per family, to help facilitate the assimilation process. Douglas appears to have reasoned that if his "benevolent assimilation" policy worked, treaties might even become unnecessary.[40]

7 WHAT WERE GOVERNOR DOUGLAS' INTENTIONS?

Historians have expended a great deal of time reviewing and re-reviewing Douglas' papers attempting to determine if he ever truly intended to sign treaties and legally extinguish aboriginal rights to the land, as required by British common law and the "Royal Proclamation of 1763." While the archival documentation on this specific question may be fragmentary and somewhat inconclusive, *Stó:lō* oral history is clear. Unfortunately, there are few instances from the Colonial period where *Stó:lō* oral history was recorded on paper. For that reason it is necessary to depart from our chronological treatment of this subject and jump ahead briefly to the year 1913. In that year, after over half a century of Aboriginal complaints about the inadequate size of reserves and the fact that Aboriginal people had never given up their title to the land, the federal and provincial governments established a Royal Commission with the hopes of putting forever to rest the Aboriginal land question. Commissioners travelled throughout the province listening to the grievances of Aboriginal people. While the commission ultimately did little to address Aboriginal concerns, it did create an opportunity for *Stó:lō* oral histories to be recorded and documented.

One of the most prominent *Stó:lō* leaders of the early twentieth century was Chief James of Yale. By 1913 Chief James was an old man, but he remembered clearly the promises Governor Douglas had made to him over fifty years earlier. The legacy of successive governments' unwillingness to make good on Douglas' promises weighed heavily upon Chief James. He said very few words to the Commissioners, and the frustration of half a century of waiting was impossible to hide: "He (Douglas) said that white men would not take land away from the Indians, unless White men will buy it before they take it away – that's what he said. I remember it in my heart!"[41]

Chief James was not the only one to testify to the promises Douglas had made. Another eloquent spokesman for his people was Chief William Sepass of Skowkale. Chief Sepass was one of the most respected leaders in *Stó:lō* society, and he spoke with the authority bestowed upon him through his ancestors. For Chief Sepass there was no room for doubt as to Governor Douglas' intentions:

Sir James Douglas was the one that surveyed this property for us. The grievances which I am laying before you is what I have already said. After this reserve was surveyed for me by Sir James Douglas, from then I came to learn that there would be compensation made to us Indians for all the land in the province.[42]

Chief Charlie of Matsqui began his testimony discussing the difficult time his people were having accessing their traditional resources off of their reserves:

I have been waiting a long time to see you. I want to see you because I am a poor man. We have no facilities for doing anything... Often I start away from my home with my gun on my shoulder and I try to get a deer, and some of the white people will see me and they want to have me arrested right away. This is all that we have been living on before and it is the same thing today. We live on wild fowl and deer...

Chief Charlie made it clear that he was speaking on behalf of the 50 people living on the Matsqui reserve who were living under very trying conditions – "A lot of our people here are dying." For Chief Charlie the answer to

Chief William Sepass and his wife Rose of Skowkale, about 20 years before he testified at the 1913 Royal Commission.

the problem lay in great part in securing a greater land and resource base.

...We are the real owners of the land from time immemorial as God created us Indians in this territory, so God created the white people and other nations in their own territories in Europe; therefore we claim a permanent compensation for the

You Are Asked To Witness

Stó:lō people gathered with their leaders in Sardis to discuss the "land question" before appearing before the 1913-15 Royal Commission.

enormous body of land known as the province of British Columbia, which was taken by the British Columbia Government and sold to our white brothers and occupied by them. In the time of the late Sir James Douglas, he made a lasting promise to us Indians, as all the Indians deserve a lasting support and benefit by the name of Queen Victoria. Also Governor Seymour, the second Governor, he made a lasting promise to us Indians in New Westminster that we will receive, or are deserving, one fourth from all taxes this money for our support and to improve our land. These promises were never kept. If those promises was kept up by the British Columbia government the Indians would be all rich, and they would be all living comfortably; be as happy as our white brothers today...[43]

Chief Harry Stewart was another highly respected and influential *Stó:lō* leader from Chilliwack. When the commissioners asked him what the chief occupation of the Chilliwack Indians was, Chief Stewart answered, "improving the land" – farming. As a farmer Chief Stewart and his people were regarded by their *Xwelítem* neighbours as "good Indians," well on the road to being assimilated. The Chief himself had cleared a great deal of land, planted crops and orchards, and was raising fifteen horses. Yet, Chief Stewart's adoption of aspects of the *Xwelítem* society did not mean that he had abandoned his traditional

culture, or given up on pursuing what he regarded as his people's justified and legitimate land claims. The commissioners seemed surprised when Chief Stewart emphasised that:

In the early days we use to hold more land than we are holding today. Yes, this bargain which has been made by the first Chief, and the first Governor, Sir James Douglas, and this land in Chilliwack which has been surveyed by Sir James Douglas and surveyed a second time, and now it has been surveyed over for the third time and it has left us with very little land which now shows on the map. That is why we say today that the B.C. government has taken our land away from us – that is why our land is too small for us today, and furthermore the Provincial government says that is has an interest on the present reserves today... That is why we say that the two Governments (federal and provincial) today should give us compensation for all the land that they have taken away.[44]

The sentiments and recollections of the *Stó:lō* leaders recorded during their testimony before the 1913 Royal Commission continue to be echoed by contemporary *Stó:lō*, and passed on to succeeding generations. The late Chief P.D. Peters of Chawathil, near Hope, was one of the most visible *Stó:lō* political leaders in recent memory. An articulate advocate of *Stó:lō* rights, Chief

Governor Douglas deferred the treaty making process indefinitely.

Douglas... he had good intentions, the way I hear... [my grandfather] interpret this Douglas. He tried to buy land, you see, started in Victoria, somewhere around there, that's the way he used to tell (the story), you know. This Governor (Douglas) tried to buy land until he ran out of money, so he wrote to... England, to the Queen. "The only way," the Queen told him, "is to charge taxes," something like that. Split every dollar four ways, I forgot which, the other three, but there's $0.25 went to the Indians, supposed to be... That's what he was supposed to have done. Then they put... the Indians onto reservations, you see, then they lost their land. A different government [came to power], you see. So that's the way I heard him talk about it.[45]

Stó:lō oral histories describing Governor Douglas' intentions have remained clear and consistent for over 150 years. They leave little doubt that Douglas did indeed intend to recognize the legitimate *Stó:lō* claims to their traditional land. The *Stó:lō* permitted *Xwelítem* to settle peacefully in their territory in part because because Governor James Douglas guaranteed that *Stó:lō* people would receive sufficient reserve lands in order to remain a self-supporting community. They were led to believe that they would receive fair compensation for lands and resources outside of their reserves which were occupied and used by settlers.

Thus, by combining the archival records with *Stó:lō* oral history we gain a much richer sense of British Columbia's history. We learn that although Governor Douglas recognized Aboriginal title, he was apparently unable or unwilling to raise the necessary funds to negotiate treaties. Instead, he pushed ahead with his policy of "benevolent assimilation." One of his most significant aspects of this policy was his decision to allow *Stó:lō* leaders to establish the size of their Indian reserves. Once these reserves were established, Douglas intended to open the areas outside the reserves to development by *Xwelítem* immigrants. Compensation was apparently to be provided to *Stó:lō* people at a later date, when the colony could better afford treaties.

Peters was respected within both *Stó:lō* and mainstream Canadian society. In recognition of his life long dedication to preserving *Stó:lō* cultural knowledge and serving his community, he was given the honourary title of Grand Chief in 1989 – a prestigious honour bestowed on very few *Stó:lō* leaders. In 1985, Grand Chief P.D. Peters of Chawathil explained how his grandfather Dennis S. Peters had passed on to him the oral history behind Governor Douglas' promises:

You Are Asked To Witness

8 SETBACKS AND BROKEN PROMISES ■

Douglas' reserve policy specified that Aboriginal leaders would determine the size of their reserves. Col. Moody of the Royal Engineers (the military corps responsible for conducting most of the surveys) understood this: "the rule is that the Indians in all cases state the bounds they claim and their statement defines the boundary provided it is within reason – say 300 acres to a village on average – ...The justice of the claim is to be recognized."[46] Moody's second in command, Captain Parsons, in turn, communicated the following orders to the actual surveyors: "Stake all Indian villages, Burial Places, reserves etc... as they may be pointed out to you by the Indians themselves."[47] This policy remained consistent throughout Douglas' tenure as governor. In April of 1864, surveyors were instructed to mark out as reserve "whatsoever land the Indians claim as theirs." [48]

Significantly, government officials also recognized that the reserves needed to include *Stó:lō* people's "isolated provisioning-grounds." The colonial government acknowledged that such sites were important to the *Stó:lō*. They were "often" located "in hidden spots, and the Indians (possibly distrusting our statements) are loath to show them."[49] This illustrates that land well beyond the restrictive boundaries of villages, potato patches, and cemetaries was vitally important to the *Stó:lō*. Yet, because the *Stó:lō* were "loath to show them" few such places were included in the original Douglas reserves. The *Stó:lō* knew that most *Xwelítem* did not understand or respect their indigenous spiritual beliefs. As explained earlier, the *Stó:lō* regarded the natural environment differently than nineteenth century Europeans did. Special locations were also associated with powerful spirits. These places were sacred and had to be treated with respect otherwise harm could come to people or the spirits of their ancestors. Contemporary Elder Evangeline Pete recently explained that these beliefs continue to be adhered to: "these places are special. They were put here for a reason. *XeXà:ls* meant for these places to last for all time. They were not meant to be destroyed. But white men don't understand this."[50]

Contemporary *Stó:lō* Elder Jimmie Peters echoes Mrs. Pete's sentiments, explaining that

Some places are sacred. Your not supposed to go there and touch anything. Even the lakes way up the mountain... and parts of the river... You can't just go there and do as you like... Certain things (were) done to it by the old timers... People used to carve on these big rocks, and that's sacred too. Your not supposed to touch them or do anything wrong with them... It was so sacred... Well, that's the native ways, you know.[51] 😊

Sacred spirit quest sites and transformer rocks like "*Xá:ytem*" near Mission needed to be protected from people who might destroy or desecrate them. The most expedient means of protecting such sites was to keep their locations secret, and hope that the *Xwelítem* settlers would leave them alone. Albert Phillips recently explained that secrecy is still regarded as the most effective means of preserving the spiritual integrity of sacred sites. In explaining his feelings to an archaeologist who was working for the *Stó:lō* Nation, Albert Phillips explained:

I'm reluctant to tell you of these spots because the last time a logging company tried to take the "head of the dog" (a transformer site made by *XeXà:ls*) and destroyed the whole thing... . You know, I'm a proud man, and these places are sacred to me. I was taught all of this by four Elder Chiefs. If I tell you about these places and they are recorded, then people will go there and destroy what is there. So I'm reluctant to tell you. Enough damage has been done.[52] 😊

Not disclosing the location of sacred sites ultimately proved a more effective means of preserving a site's spiritual integrity than naively identifying a site for government officials and hoping that a reserve might one day be established. Douglas' policy sought to ensure the *Stó:lō* had sufficient territory to continue their traditional spiritual and subsistence activities as well as enough agricultural land to facilitate the gradual process of assimilation. *Stó:lō* cultural practises concerning protection through secrecy conflicted, therefore, with Governor Douglas' intentions. However, as will be demonstrated, *Stó:lō* suspicion and fears over *Xwelítem* land use plans and disregard for their spirituality ultimately proved well founded.

Just before he retired in the spring of 1864, Governor Douglas directed Sergeant William McColl to create reserves for the *Stó:lō* communities of the central Fraser Valley (present-day Abbotsford, Mission, and Chilliwack). The surveys were completed on May 16. McColl then returned to Victoria with a map outlining 14 Indian reserves covering 15,760 hectares (39,400 acres). The largest *Stó:lō* reserve surveyed was at Matsqui, 3,840 hectares (9,600 acres), and the smallest was Skway in Chilliwack, 120 hectares (300 acres). Even though these initial reserve were considered "generous" by the standards of the day, they were still small in relation to the land available to *Xwelítem* settlers. For example, McColl's survey listed 885 *Stó:lō* inhabitants living within the area he surveyed – 18 hectares (45 acres) per person. By comparison, an immigrant settler family arriving in the Fraser Valley could pre-empt 64 hectare (160 acre) farms, and were eligible to purchase an additional 180 hectares (450 acres).

After completing the preliminary surveys, McColl

began the process of officially registering the *Stó:lō* reserves – an essentially bureaucratic procedure. Once registered, carefully detailed surveys were to be completed, accurately marking the exact boundary of each reserve. However, McColl died before completing this task, and no one was assigned to replace him to finish the work. The decision not to complete McColl's project was made by the man who assumed responsibility for "Indian Matters" after Governor Douglas retired. He was the Chief Commissioner of Lands and Works, and held very different ideas about Aboriginal rights and title than his predecessor. His name was Joseph Trutch.

Xwelitem immigrant settlers moved into the Fraser Valley and established farms before reserves were secured for the *Stó:lō*.

9 JOSEPH TRUTCH AND THE EMERGING SETTLER MENTALITY ■

Trutch did not recognize Aboriginal rights and title, moreover, he viewed Aboriginal culture with contempt. He saw society as evolutionary; on an unstoppable and irreversible progression towards an agrarian, and ultimately industrial state. A farmer and surveyor by trade, Trutch was a British citizen who had lived in the United States before moving to British Columbia in 1859. Arriving in the wake of the Fraser River gold rush, Trutch anticipated that he could make his fortune building bridges and roads and developing new townships. Historian Robin Fisher writes that, to Trutch, "the colony was an area of land requiring development and

consequently anything, or more importantly anyone, who stood in the way of that development had to be moved."[53] In Trutch's view, Aboriginal people were the single largest impediment to the development of the colony. Whereas Douglas typically referred to Aboriginal people as "Native Indians," Trutch preferred to use the expression "savages."[54]

Trutch did share some of Douglas' views about Aboriginal people. His attitudes were simply less accommodating and more extreme. Like Douglas, Trutch believed that traditional Aboriginal society was incompatible with European agricultural and industrial life. The 1782 smallpox epidemic killed an estimated 64% of the *Stó:lō* population. Subsequent outbreaks of other introduced diseases like mumps, measles, influenza, and chickenpox further reduced *Stó:lō* numbers.[55] Trutch and other government officials were on the scene to witness the smallpox epidemic of 1862 in which roughly one third of all Aboriginal people in British Columbia died. To Trutch, and other like minded individuals, this was further evidence that Aboriginal people were destined for extinction. Whereas Douglas had paternalistically thought that Aboriginal people could be "saved" through assimilation, Trutch was convinced they were incapable of integrating into the introduced European culture.

When Sgt. William McColl consulted with *Stó:lō* leaders in the Spring of 1864 to determine the size of their reserves, fewer than one dozen *Xwelítem* settler families were living in the central Fraser Valley. These immigrants had built small houses and started planting crops on opened pasture land. They had not purchased the land from the *Stó:lō* or the Colonial government, nor had they officially registered pre-emptions with the Colonial authorities. Rather, they had simply moved into the area on their own accord. Upon discovering the extent of the *Stó:lō* reserves mapped by McColl, these farmers became upset. They petitioned Trutch, demanding that their farms be excluded from the *Stó:lō* reserves. Failing this, the settlers demanded compensation for the loss of their "developed land." They felt their rights superseded the *Stó:lō* people's claim because they had built their homes before the reserves were registered. The issue of pre-existing *Stó:lō* ownership of the land was never considered by the settlers.

Trutch sympathized with the settlers. He stated that because the *Stó:lō* were neither clearing land nor farming, they actually had "no right to the lands they claim, nor are... (the lands) of any actual value or utility to them."

He expressed that "the extent of some of the reserves staked out by McColl is out of all proportion to the numbers or requirements of the tribes to which they were assigned."[56] If the *Stó:lō* did not cultivate the soil, as far as Trutch was concerned they had "really no right to or use for the land."[57]

If the local newspaper can be regarded as reflective of public opinion, Trutch's attitudes would appear to have been widely shared. In December 1865, the New Westminster British Columbian sensationally reported on the reserves laid out by McColl, stating that: "several millions of acres of the choicest prairie land... in Matsqui and Chilliwack... were laid off as the greed and caprice of the wandering Indians suggested."[58] The paper claimed that it was ludicrous "under the color of an imaginary right, to see large districts of our most valuable lands locked up, and good settlers discouraged and driven from the country in disgust. Let the Indians have all the land they can make good use of and nothing more."[59] The idea of Aboriginal title to the soil was "nonsensical and ludicrous" because

Colonization necessarily involves the contact, and practically the collision, of two races of men – one superior, and one inferior – the latter being in possession of the soil, the former gradually supplanting it. The history of every civilized country illustrates the truth of this proposition... The Indian who was once the lord of the soil – monarch of all he surveyed, is to be found retreating back into the jungle, as though seeking to conceal himself from the bright rays of civilization. There is no denying that the Indians have disappeared, and are disappearing, and will continue to disappear, until finally the race will become utterly extinct... The rights of the Indian we have always defended, and we always will defend them. But these rights we do not conceive to be to hold large tracts of valuable agricultural and pastoral land which they do not use, and cannot use.[60]

The newspaper article shows that the settlers' concepts of land ownership and the value they place on land use were vastly different from those of the *Stó:lō*. Apparently, they could not appreciate that *Stó:lō* land use activities could be different from their own and still be valuable. Obviously the *Stó:lō* utilized the land and it was of value to them. The use they made, and the values they placed on it were simply different. Instead of cutting down trees and farming, the *Stó:lō* utilized the forests in their natural state, for hunting, gathering and spiritual purposes.

In redefining British Columbia's Aboriginal land policy in 1865, Trutch sent the Chief of the Colonial Police force, Chartres Brew, and a second surveyor, to meet separately with the *Stó:lō* leaders and immigrant settlers. Brew reported back to Trutch that he was "decidedly of the opinion that these settlers are entitled to have their land surveyed. They pre-empted their lands long before the Indian Reserves were staked out..." Demonstrating his utter lack of appreciation for how the

Stó:lō occupied and utilized the land, Brew assumed that because the reserves were "mostly timbered... they were absolutely worthless to the Indians." He concluded that it was "a pity that so much fine land... should be shut out from settlement by being reserved for Indians to whom it is useless."[61]

In light of prevailing anti-aboriginal public sentiments and Brew's report, Trutch had no difficulty justifying the reduction of the *Stó:lō* reserves established under *Stó:lō* direction by Douglas and McColl. However, he was faced with one additional problem. According to the government's own regulations, pre-emptions had to be "rectangular, with the shortest side of the rectangle about two thirds of the long side – except where the land is bounded in whole or in part by natural boundaries." Trutch acknowledged that the longer side of the settler's pre-emptions in the central Fraser Valley were often "four times longer than the length of the shorter sides." He recognized that the Fraser Valley pre-emptions represented a "departure from the strict requirements" and threatened to establish a dangerous "precedent... which must rule in all other surveys."[62] Yet, despite this additional point in favour of the *Stó:lō*, Trutch boldly chose to recognize the settlers illegal and irregular pre-emptions.

Under Joseph Trutch's direction, all central Fraser Valley *Stó:lō* reserves were officially resurveyed and "reduced" in 1867. With the stroke of a pen, 91% of the *Stó:lō* reserve land base (which was only a fraction of their traditional territory) was alienated from their control. Over the following decades further "alterations" periodically occurred (some increasing the reserve's acreage) as the government and industry continued to act in accordance with the policy of "agricultural or industrial land use is good land use." The following table graphically illustrates the extent of the reductions.

In stripping the *Stó:lō* of the land and resources they required for their traditional life style, Trutch also erased most of the legacy of Douglas' policy of "benevolent assimilation." Under Douglas, Aboriginal people had been:
1) appointed government magistrates;
2) able to acquire private farm lands;
3) and encouraged to engage in the *Xwelítem* economy.

Under Trutch, the *Stó:lō* were effectively denied the rights of a British colonist. Not only were the reduced *Stó:lō* reserves too small to support agricultural activities and to allow them to continue with their traditional lifestyles, but in 1866 the pre-emption law was amended in order to deny Aboriginal people the right to pre-empt off-reserve land (an essential aspect of Douglas' policy).[63]

11 THE 1870'S: *STÓ:LŌ* PETITIONS, GOVERNMENT INTIMIDATION AND INACTION ■

In the decades following the "Trutch reductions," *Stó:lō* leaders continually expressed their dissatisfaction with the Colonial government's Indian land policies. When the colony of British Columbia joined Canada in 1871, jurisdiction over "Indian matters" transferred to the federal government. *Stó:lō* leaders seized the opportunity to try and reverse the policies of Douglas' successors. In 1874, two *Stó:lō* leaders, Chief Peter (Pierre) Ayessick of Hope, and Chief Alexis of Cheam (near Chilliwack), organized a meeting with 23 other *Stó:lō* leaders and 31 other Aboriginal leaders from neighbouring communities at St. Mary's Mission. There, with the assistance of the Catholic Oblate priests, they drafted a petition to Ottawa asking that their land base be increased (See Appendix 1).

Alexis and Ayessick both came from high status *Stó:lō* families – they were *Sí:yá:m* – and as such they took their leadership responsibilities seriously. They recognized that

Reserve	Size in 1864		Trutch's 1868 Reductions		Current size in 1996	
	(ACRES)	(HECTARES)	(ACRES)	(HECTARES)	(ACRES)	(HECTARES)
Aitchelitz	400	162	45	18	52	21
Kawakwawapilt	400	162	175	71	155	63
Lakahamen	6,400	2,591	109	44	1,210	490
Matsqui	9,600	3,887	148	60	1,038	420
Skowkale/Yakweakwioose/Tzeachten						
	2,500	1,012	200	81	914	370
Skwah	3,200	1,296	720	291	844	341
Skway	300	121	490	198	538	218
Soowahlie	4,000	1,619	690	279	1,140	461
Squiala	1,000	405	160	65	315	127
Sumas	7,600	3,077	515	209	579	234
Tlalt whaas	2,000	810	86	35	0	0
Whonnock	2,000	810	92	25	1,358	550
Saamoqua	500	202	0	0	0	0
TOTAL	**39,900**	**16,154**	**3,430**	**1,376**	**8,143**	**3,295**

You Are Asked To Witness

The *Stó:lō* protested their inadequate land base in front of the government buildings in New Westminster in 1874.

the world was changing, and that the *Xwelítem* were in the Fraser Valley to stay. Their people's future was uncertain and potentially perilous. Given the choice between Douglas' vision for the *Stó:lō*, and that advocated by Trutch, the choice was obvious. *Stó:lō* leaders like Alexis and Ayessick determined to accept those things from the *Xwelítem* culture which were useful, while rejecting those which ran contrary to their traditional values and beliefs. Both men were instrumental in working with the Catholic missionaries to fight the persistent whiskey traders by establishing "Temperance Societies." They encouraged their people to become vaccinated by the Oblate and Methodist missionaries, and as a result the *Stó:lō* escaped much of the devastation of B.C.'s last province wide smallpox epidemic in 1862. Chief Alexis enrolled his children in St. Mary's school where his daughter became one of the first *Stó:lō* to learn to read and write. These new skills enabled residential school graduates like Alexis' daughter to advise their Elders about *Xwelítem* ways and effectively enter into written communications with the government.

In the 1874 petition to Ottawa, Chiefs Ayessick and Alexis stated that they were aware that Aboriginal people in other parts of Canada had been treated more fairly and liberally with regard to reserve land – a fact they probably learned from the Oblates. They expressed that they were taking steps to adopt aspects of the new *Xwelítem* society, but that the B.C. government was thwarting them:

Our hearts have been wounded by the arbitrary way the Government of B.C. has dealt with us in allocating and dividing our reserves... For many years we have been complaining of the land left us being too small... We have felt like men trampled on, and are commencing to believe that the aim of the Whitemen is to exterminate us as soon as they can, although we have always been quiet, obedient, kind and friendly to the Whites. Discouragement and Depression have come upon our people. Many of them have given up cultivation of the land because our gardens have not been protected against the encroachment of the Whites... We are not lazy and roaming people... We have worked hard and for a long time to spare money to buy agricultural implements, Cattle, Horses etc., as nobody has given us any assistance.[64]

Ayessick and Alexis looked to the federal government to assist them in their transition to an agricultural economy, and to defend their Aboriginal rights. But the *Stó:lō* leaders did not speak from a position of helplessness. In a thinly veiled threat they warned the federal officials that if their request for an increased land base was not met there would be "ill feelings (and) irritation amongst our people, and we cannot say what will be the consequence."[65]

According to official correspondence, Canadian officials appear to have been surprised to learn that treaties had never been signed in British Columbia, and that groups like the *Stó:lō* were so exasperated at their dealings with B.C. officials. Yet they did little to address the issue. While most federal officials might have been shocked to learn that the *Stó:lō* believed the White men aimed to quickly exterminate the Aboriginal people, no doubt many Canadian officials did share the view that Aboriginal peo-

Stó:lō leaders, with the assistance of Catholic missionaries (seen in the centre back row), gather in New Westminster to petition the governor and express their dissatisfaction over their inadequate land base.

Reserve Commissioner G.M. Sproat was thwarted by the provincial government when he tried to have *Stó:lō* title to the land officially recognized.

ple were destined for extinction. Whatever their reasoning, the federal government chose not to respond to the 1874 *Stó:lō* petition until a related crisis in the B.C. interior threatened to escalate into a full scale race war.

By the mid-1870's, violent conflicts between Aboriginal people and the American government in what is now Washington and Idaho States had become a major concern for officials on the Canadian side of the border. In pre-colonial times, Aboriginal communities had not been divided along the 49th parallel, and therefore many of people fighting the Americans considered the Canadian side of the Okanagan Valley just as much their home as the American side. Federal and provincial authorities became concerned that local Aboriginal grievances over land rights and reserve size appeared to be becoming inflamed by the American situation. To avert this possibility, a special federal/provincial commission was established in 1876 to listen to Aboriginal concerns. The commissioners were given jurisdiction to resolve issues

relating to reserve size "on the spot." While the original motivation for forming the commission stemmed from events in the Okanagan, the 1874 *Stó:lō* petition and similar complaints by other Aboriginal groups highlighting their unhappiness with their current land base convinced the governments to expand the commission's mandate to include all of British Columbia.

Clarifying his opinion on the matter the federal Minister of the Interior, David Laird, wrote to the B.C. Superintendent of Indian Affairs, Dr. Israel Wood Powell, noting that,

> The present state of the Indian Land question in...
> [British Columbia] is most unsatisfactory, and...
> is the occasion, not only of great discontent among
> the Aboriginal Tribes, but also of serious alarm to the
> white settlers.
>
> To the Indian, the land question far transcends
> the importance of all others, and its satisfactory
> adjustment in British Columbia will be the first step
> towards allaying the wide-spread and growing
> discontent now existing among the native tribes of
> that province.
>
> ...The policy heretofore
> pursued by the Local
> Government of British
> Columbia toward the red
> men in that Province, and
> the recently expressed views
> of that Government in the
> correspondence herewith
> submitted, fall far short of
> the estimate entertained by
> the Dominion Government
> of the reasonable claims of
> the Indians.[66]

The camps of the "Indian Commissioners" c.1878.

In a letter, the Minister acknowledged to Powell that, the "Indian rights to the soil

One of the conditions when British Columbia joined confederation was the promise of a transcontinental railroad. The construction of the CPR resulted in the creation of a "federal railway belt" which Commissioner Sproat believed should have protected *Stó:lō* lands from provincial and private development projects.

in British Columbia have never been extinguished. Should any difficulty occur, steps will be taken to maintain the Indian claims to the country where rights have not been extinguished by treaty."[67] The Minister's choice of words indicates that officials in Ottawa wanted to ensure that the commissioners dealt fairly and adequately with Aboriginal demands. They also indicate while the federal government did not necessarily want to enter into full scale treaty negotiations, they were willing to consider the issue of Aboriginal title in the event that the reserve allocation process broke down.

12 STRONG PROVINCIAL OPPOSITION, WEAK FEDERAL SUPPORT:
THE *STÓ:LŌ* FIND A SYMPATHETIC ADVOCATE IN COMMISSIONER GILBERT MALCOLM SPROAT ■

When British Columbia joined Confederation in 1871, Joseph Trutch was promoted from Chief Commissioner of Lands and Works to the powerful position of Lt. Governor. There he was able to continue shaping "Indian Policy" for the province. His impact on the activities of the Joint Reserve Commission resulted in the Commissioners focusing the first two years of their activities on the crisis in the Okanagan. Throughout that period *Stó:lō* leaders continually requested that the Commissioners visit them to address their longstanding grievances. However, as soon as the threat of an "Indian

war" in the interior subsided, the provincial government lost all interest and suggested that the commission be reduced from three members to one, to which the federal government agreed. This indicates that neither government was as serious about dealing with peacefully presented Aboriginal grievances as they were in placating Aboriginal leaders who resorted to more drastic actions. From 1878 until 1880 the jointly appointed commissioner, Gilbert Malcolm Sproat, was left to single handedly try and resolve British Columbia's "Indian land question." He did this with minimal support from the Ottawa, and in the face of blatant resentment and animosity from Victoria.

Sproat arrived in British Columbia from Scotland in 1860 and established a saw mill on the west coast of Vancouver Island at Alberni. Surrounded, as he was, by Aboriginal people he quickly came to develop a respect for Aboriginal society that was not shared by most subsequent *Xwelítem* immigrants. Before being appointed to the Reserve Commission Sproat had already established a reputation as a respected amateur ethnographer. He was considered by the government as a man capable of establishing relationships with Aboriginal leaders.

Like the missionaries and James Douglas, Sproat's actions also appear to have been inspired to a great extent by humanitarian impulses. However, also like Douglas and the missionaries, Sproat shared their aversion to the idea that Aboriginal people might try and retain their traditional lifestyle unaltered in the face of the new immigrant society. He wanted Aboriginal people to make a transition to European culture, but he recognized that this could not be accomplished overnight, and that the Aboriginal population required both time and a land base to make the assimilation process less jarring.

One of the conditions agreed to by the federal government when British Columbia joined Confederation was the construction of a rail link to the new province. This agreement involved the transfer to the federal government of a 520 kilometres (200 mile) wide swath of land along the railroad route. The rest of the crown land

This is the dredge "Col. Tobin" about ½ way up the Vedder Canal, Marsh Construction Co was the contractor Sumas Prairie E W Carlson 1921

The Sumas Dyking Project of 1878 was merely a prelude for the more extensive activities associated with the Sumas Lake Reclamation Project of 1924. In this photo the dredge "The Col. Tobin" works to dig the Vedder Canal.

remained under provincial control. The federal railway belt was intended to provide the federal government with sufficient saleable land to enable them to fund the construction of the Canadian Pacific Railway. Once the Terms of Union were finalized, land within the railway belt became, in theory, frozen to provincial development. The railway belt included all of the public land within the entire Fraser Canyon and Valley. In Sproat's opinion, these lands were therefore available to the federal government to allocate as Indian reserves. After meeting with "most of the Lower Fraser Chiefs" (some of whom travelled fifty miles in canoes to speak with the Commissioner in New Westminster) and learning first hand how disappointed they were with the size of their reserves, Sproat advised the provincial government "to reserve from pre-emption all lands near (*Stó:lō*) Reserves until I have examined them."[68] He believed that for the "Yale, Hope and Cheam (near Chilliwack) Indians" the reserved land should include:

> The land on the left bank of the Fraser from the point or bluff opposite Marianville Island (three miles below Hope) down to Scowlitz Reservation with a width of two miles back from the river.
>
> The land on the right bank of the Fraser River from Gordon Ranch (1 1/2 miles below Yale) to American Bar with a width of 2 miles back from the river.
>
> The land on both sides of [the] Fraser River from the first little canyon about 1 mile beyond the toll house above Yale, up to the 4 mile post with a width of 100 yards on the left bank and the whole space between the wagon road and the River on the right.[69]

Sproat also wanted a strip of land "two miles long" and "a mile wide" excluded from pre-emption for the *Stó:lō* along the Fraser River below Mission.[70]

As mentioned, the initial three member Reserve Commission had been originally granted the authority to resolve Indian reserve issues "on the spot" as they worked in the sparsely settled interior and arid upper Fraser Canyon near Lytton. However, when the Commission's membership was reduced to just one member, and when Sproat's work brought him to the fertile farm lands of the Fraser Valley, the provincial government refused to acknowledge that Sproat was entitled to these same powers. The provincial motivation in this regard may never be fully understood, but it appears likely that officials in Victoria were afraid that Sproat's sympathetic Aboriginal attitudes would conflict with their long established development plans for that region.[71]

Rather than accepting Sproat's decision to set aside tracts of the railway belt as *Stó:lō* reserves, the province took action completely contrary to Sproat's intentions and passed the "Sumas Dyking Act of 1878." In this legislation they illegally granted land to a San Francisco business man named Ellis Luther Derby. Derby immediately commenced building dykes, and in the process took "possession of a considerable portion of the Matsqui Indian Reserve." He proposed extending his dyking activities "across the Sumas Indian Reserve" and then "diverting streams," thereby affecting the Chilliwack reserves. In Sproat's opinion, Derby unilaterally "used to the extent he wanted, two Indian reserves without asking permission of the Indians" or the federal government.[72] Derby's dyke cut across *Stó:lō* reserves without regard for *Stó:lō* people's rights or land use activities. The leader of the *Stó:lō* in Matsqui explained to Sproat that

> The crown long ago gave us land and by and by a white chief came and cut it down. We heard some years ago that our wishes would be listened to, and that a chief had been appointed who would come to look after the Indians, but ever since that time white men have continued to take land until now it is nearly all taken up. Mr. Derby, who may be a chief, has used our land up.[73]

Sproat clarified to both Derby and the provincial government that such dykes could only be made on such lands if the *Stó:lō* consented. In this instance, *Stó:lō* leaders were unanimously opposed to the project. With their endorsement, Sproat threatened legal action against the province, demanding that the Sumas Dyking Act be repealed and the lands returned to the *Stó:lō*. He even suggested that if the province failed to comply, he would recommend that the federal government invoke a little used clause in the

You Are Asked To Witness

constitution which gave the Dominion government to the right to "disallow" provincial legislation.[74]

Through Sproat's endeavours some *Stó:lō* reserves were ultimately enlarged, but overall the provincial government succeeded in out-manoeuvreing Sproat and further entrenching a small and marginal *Stó:lō* land base. Sproat recognized that dealing with Aboriginal land requirements on an ad hoc basis – reserve by reserve, pre-emption by pre-emption – doomed the process to failure. He realized that as long as the federal government failed to fulfill its fiduciary obligation toward B.C.'s Aboriginal people the Indian land question would forever haunt British Columbia. Short of negotiating treaties, Sproat maintained that it was incumbent upon the federal and provincial governments to ensure that the basic requirements of the Aboriginal population be met. Long before his resignation Sproat wrote to the Deputy Minister of the Interior expressing the opinion that

> I n all matters affecting Indians in this province there is one special consideration which I respectfully think extends in all directions. They have no treaties made with them, and we are trying to compromise all matters without treaty making... It is, with absence of treaties, all the more necessary to recognize the actual requirements of the people.[75]

Despite strong and repeated protests from *Stó:lō* leaders, and the establishment of yet another special Indian Commission in 1913, the Aboriginal land question has remained unresolved to the present day. Since the late 1860's *Stó:lō* people have been without a sufficient land base to pursue their traditional social, spiritual and economic activities. Simultaneously they have been denied the opportunity to meaningfully participate in the new European society. As the years went by and the *Stó:lō* population became even-smaller in relation to the *Xwelítem* community the dilemmas facing the *Stó:lō* communities likewise faded from mainstream public consciousness.

It is important to realize that Aboriginal demands for recognition of their title to the land did not disappear. To keep their claims alive and on the National political agenda Aboriginal leaders throughout B.C. began working together in more unified efforts in the early decades of the twentieth century. Ironically, this process of inter-tribal co-operation was in part facilitated by the residential school experience. Aboriginal children from different parts of the province were brought together at residential schools and compelled to speak only English. People who might otherwise never have met or who might not have spoken the same language forged lasting friendships which formed the foundations of subsequent political organizations. The Indian Rights Association of British

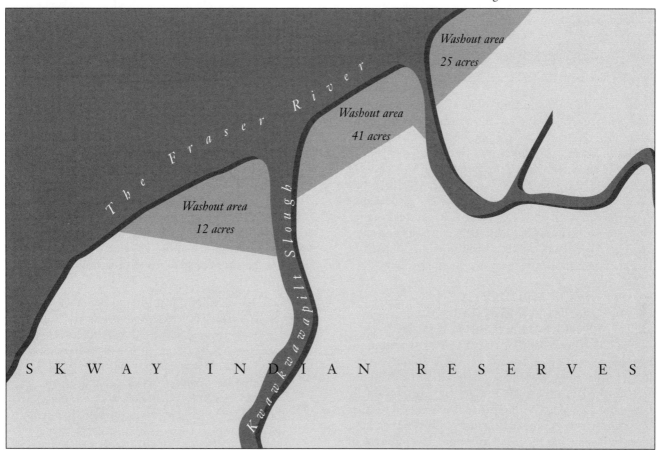

Erosion of *Stó:lō* reserves by the Fraser River has long been a problem. This map (created by Commissioner Sproat in 1879) shows where a 4.8 and a 16.4 hectare (12 and 41 acre) swath of land were washed away from the Skway Reserve over a few years.

The cultural and physical geography of the lower Fraser Valley has changed significantly in the past 200 years.

Columbia, the Allied Indian Tribes of British Columbia, The Native Brotherhood of British Columbia, the Aboriginal Native Rights Committee of the Interior Tribes of British Columbia, and the Aboriginal Native Rights Committee, were among the most well know of these broad based organizations. *Stó:lō* leaders like Chief Oscar Peters of Hope, and later *Stó:lō* leaders like Genevieve Mussell of Skwah, played pivotal roles in providing these organizations with focus and sustained energy. The Aboriginal people of the province refused to accept earlier government actions and inactions.

13 CONTEMPORARY LEGACY OF THE *XWELÍTEM* SETTLEMENT PROCESS ■

Today, the legacy of the *Xwelítem* settlement process is still strongly felt in *Stó:lō* communities. Reserves have never been restored to their original size as identified out by *Stó:lō* leaders and recognized by Governor Douglas. With railroad, highway, and utility line right-of-ways and easements, *Stó:lō* reserves have been reduced even further. Often, the development of such communication or utility routes cut communities in half, or destroyed delicate fish habitat and ecosystems along the edge of the Fraser River and its tributaries.

In the mid-1980's, the Canadian National Railway (CNR) planned to add a second track parallel to the existing railway through the Fraser Canyon. This threatened not only the environment, but also numerous *Stó:lō* sacred sites. In 1988, when discussing the potential impact on fisheries habitat and *Stó:lō* sacred sites, of the CNR's proposed "Twin Tracking" scheme, *Stó:lō* Elder Tilly Gutierrez of Chawathil commented on the seemingly insatiable appetite of the *Xwelítem* (hungry people) society. The frustration in her voice is representative of the way many *Stó:lō* people feel over the alienation of so much of their traditional land:

Okay, when *Xá:ls* [the youngest of the transformer siblings] went through [*Stó:lō* territory] making things right we had accepted him because he was nice to us. And pretty soon Christopher Columbus [came]; pretty soon Simon Fraser [came]; [then Governor James] Douglas, and you name them all – them big shots that came through. After [awhile] the *Xwelítem* started taking things away from us. Pretty soon the railroad and highways [took more *Stó:lō* land]. We got nothing.

You Are Asked To Witness

Here is where we lived on the edge of the road [Tilly points out the window towards Highway 7]. By the river there, that's where the railway and highway is going through. We still have our landmarks there; there is a few grave yards left here and there along the edge of the [proposed CN rail] route. Now why do... [the Canadian government and CNR] have to say "we can move this, and we're going to build another track?" No, not through our [reserve]. If we [accept] that, we're lost! I guess that's our survival right there. Sometimes people just have to say "no." Yeah! Well that [Stó:lō] guy who was brave laid in front of the [CN Rail Road] tracks [and said]: "Run me over if you want! If you want that land so bad, just go ahead and run over me." He laid there, [but] they couldn't do it. They just had to stop that... bulldozer. But he was willing to die for his piece of land there. That is "Indian" – God's man. [If you ever] wonder who's telling the truth, he is [the Indian] you know. And... [the Canadian government and the Courts] should be able to believe that. When you think of it – all the wars – why do they have to war anyway? Is that what "He"[76] wanted us to do? I don't think so. I think he wanted us to get along and be happy together – to get acquainted, like you and I. But here now the... Xwelítem are flying to the moon. They want the moon![77]

Stó:lō Sí:yá:m.

Beyond the alienation of *Stó:lō* land by government and corporations described by Tilly Gutierrez, *Stó:lō* land has been further reduced by the Canadian government's unwillingness to respond equitably to natural changes in the landscape. For example, only the upriver section of McMillian Island in Langley has been reserved for *Stó:lō* people, while the lower portion is private property owned by *Xwelítem* people. Each year the river erodes land from the Island's upper portion, depositing it on the down river section. This eroded land is lost to the *Stó:lō* forever. Interestingly, in areas where the erosion and deposits occur entirely on reserve land (such as Seabird Island near Agassiz, *Shxw'ow'hamel* near Hope, *Scowlitz* on the Harrison River, and *Skway* near Chilliwack), the land which washes away is officially lost; but deposits (called accretions) that occur on the down river side of the reserves become government crown land, and are not included within the official reserve boundaries.

Those reserves surrounded by dense urban development face different problems. For example, *Xwelítem* living on private property near reserves sometimes complain that drumming and singing associated with the *smílha*, or "Winter Dance," ceremonies disturb their sleep and infringe upon their right to peace and quiet. This places *Stó:lō* communities in an awkward position. They want to establish positive relationships with their neighbours, but do not want to compromise their right to practise their spiritual activities in accordance with tradition. Winter Dancing is integral to the spiritual lives of many *Stó:lō* people. It is estimated that there are nearly 900 *Stó:lō* winter dancers, and at least double that number attend Winter Dance ceremonies in other capacities.[78] Throughout the winter months, *smílha* ceremonies occur each night at various longhouses and community halls. The people gather during the afternoon and begin "the work" just as it gets dark. The ceremonies often continue until dawn the following day.

Logging activity, urban sprawl, and recreational activities (hiking, fishing, camping, kayaking, etc.) have curtailed the ability of the *Stó:lō* to practise traditional spiritual and food gathering activities in regions outside the official reserve boundaries. Areas like the Pitt and Alouette lakes, Sumas and Chilliwack mountains, and the Chilliwack and *Chehalis* River Valleys to name but a few, have been heavily utilized by *Stó:lō* hunters and spirit dancers. *Stó:lō* people who continue such activities in these and other areas are increasingly disturbed by outsiders. In the most extreme cases, the destruction and transformation of the environment prevents the *Stó:lō* from practising their culturally important traditional activities.

14 CONSIDERING SOLUTIONS AND RESOLUTION ■

The Canadian Constitution guarantees Aboriginal people certain rights, based upon their occupation of the land prior to European contact. Among these are the right to self-government. Currently, this right remains legally undefined. Many *Stó:lō* leaders have, however, expressed what self-government means to them. *Stó:lō* Nation Chief's Representative Steven Point has defined *Stó:lō* self-government as a process whereby the *Stó:lō* regain control of their lives – become self-supporting, and self-determining. This implies breaking free of the demoralizing cycle of dependency on government grants and subsidies. To accomplish this, the *Stó:lō* require a sufficient land base to meet their cultural, residential, and economic needs. They maintain that they require at least the land base originally surveyed under the direction of Governor Douglas. Of course, with the extent of private land now alienated in the Fraser Valley, it would be difficult to re-establish the original reserves. But, the *Stó:lō* are willing to consider options.

Along with increased reserve size, the *Stó:lō* require an economic base. In 1990, federal, provincial and Aboriginal government's committed themselves to negotiating treaties through the newly established B.C. Treaty Commission. In 1995 the *Stó:lō* Nation filed a statement of intent to participate in these negotiations. The *Stó:lō* are acutely aware that the rivers, lakes, forests, and minerals within traditional *Stó:lō* territory all provide regular revenue to the federal and provincial governments. These resources still belong to the *Stó:lō*. Fair and equitable treaty agreements will provide the *Stó:lō* with the financial and economic resource base to once again become self-supporting and self-sufficient. However, until the legacy of the B.C. government's past unwillingness to recognize Aboriginal title and legitimate land and resource requirements is addressed in a meaningful manner, the physical, social and political dilemmas confronting Aboriginal communities will continue to haunt both mainstream and *Stó:lō* society.

Recommended Further Readings

British Columbia, *Indian Land Question:* 1859-1875, 1877, Victoria: Government Printers, 1987 (reprint).

Fisher, Robin, *Contact and Conflict: Indian European Relations in British Columbia,* 1774-1890, Vancouver, University of British Columbia Press, 1992 (second edition)

Tennant, Paul, *Aboriginal People and Politics: The Indian Land Question in British Columbia,* Vancouver: University of British Columbia Press, 1990.

Wells, Oliver, *The Chilliwack and Their Neighbours,* Vancouver: Talonbooks, 1987.

Footnotes

1 Joe Louis, in conversation with Imbert Orchard, in *Forest and Floodland: Memories of the Chilliwack Valley* Sound Heritage Series Number 37 (Victoria:Sound and Moving Image Division, Province of British Columbia), p.5.

2 *Yewal Sí:yà:m* is a *Halq'eméylem* expression which translates roughly as community leader. A *Yewal Sí:yà:m* is a highly respected member of a *Stó:lō* community or extended family. The term is experiencing a revival of formal use among *Stó:lō* people as the *Stó:lō* Nation seeks to reinvest Chiefs and other contemporary leaders with more traditional roles and responsibilities.

3 Albert "Sonny" McHalsie in conversation with Keith Thor Carlson, April 1995. Tape on file at *Stó:lō* Nation Archives (SNA).

4 Gordon Mohs, "*Stó:lō Sacred Grounds*," *Sacred Sites, Sacred Places,* edited by David L. Carmichael, Jane Hubert, et al. (New York, New York: Routledge, 1994) p.189 and 190.

5 Old Pierre, as quoted in Diamond Jenness, *The Faith of a Coast Salish Indian,* edited by Wilson Duff (Victoria: British Columbia Provincial Museum, 1955), p.35. In this manuscript Old Pierre provides a fascinating discussion of *XeXà:ls* (the transformers) and the role they played in arranging the world into its present state.

6 Tilly Gutierrez in conversation with Keith Thor Carlson, July 10, 1996. Tape on file at SNA

7 To read more *Stó:lō swoxwiyà:m* (legends) consult Norman Lerman, *Legends of the River People;* Oliver Wells, *The Chilliwack and their Neighbours;* Ralph Maud, *A Guide To B.C. Indian Myth and Legend.* To better appreciate *Stó:lō swoxwiyà:m,* consult Chapter 11 this volume.

8 Paul Tennant, *Aboriginal Peoples and Politics: The Indian Land Question in British Columbia,* 1849-1989 (Vancouver, B.C.:University of British Columbia Press, 1990), p.10.

9 Ibid., p.10.

10 Ibid., p.11.

11 Brain Slattery "The Hidden Constitution," in

Menno Boldt and J. Anthony Longs, ed., **_The Quest for Justice: Aboriginal Peoples and Aboriginal Rights_** (Toronto: University of Toronto Press, 1985), p.121.

12 For a more detailed explanation of the relationship between the _Stó:lō_ and the furtraders, refer to Chapter 2 this volume.

13 Margaret Ormsby. **_British Columbia: a History,_** (Vancouver: The MacMillan Company, 1958.) p.138.

14 G.P.V. Akrigg. "The Fraser River Gold Rush," in **_The Fraser's History from Glaciers to Early Settlements._** Papers from a seminar presented at the Annual Meeting of the British Columbia Historical Association on May 27, 1977. (Burnaby, BC.), p. 32

15 Evans, Elwood "The Fraser River Excitement, 1858." (Unpublished manuscript,) BCARS.

16 Ormsby, Pp. 138-140.

17 James Douglas, to Home Government, April 6, 1858, Colonial Correspondence. BCARS.

18 James Douglas, "Correspondence relative to the Discovery of Gold in the Fraser's River District," London, 1858, p.5. in T.A. Rickard, "Indian Participation in the Gold Discoveries." **_British Columbia Historical Quarterly_** (BCHQ). January 1938.

19 Angus MacLeod Gunn, "Gold and the Early Settlement of British Columbia," 1858-1885. Unpublished M.A. Thesis, UBC Department of Geography. 1965. Table II, p.28.

20 Rickard, "Papers relative to the Affairs of British Columbia", Part I., London, 1859, p.16.

21 Sonny McHalsie in conversation with Keith Thor Carlson, March 1995.

22 Douglas, "Papers Relative to the Affairs of British Columbia", Part, II., London, 1959, p.5. BCARS.

23 Sonny McHalsie in conversation with Keith Thor Carlson, March 9, 1995. Transcript on file SNA.

24 Harold Wells in conversation with Keith Thor Carlson and Brian Thom at Mr. Wells' home, near Hope, Feb 21, 1995. Transcript on file at SNA.

25 Ware, p. 83.

26 "Articles of British Columbia" printed in the **_London Times._** Aug. 4 - 15, 1858; September 12, 1858, (E,B,F86, BCARS).

27 John Hayman (editor). **_Robert Brown and the Vancouver Island Exploration Expedition._** (Vancouver: UBC Press, 1989). p. 44.

28 "Articles on British Columbia" printed in the **_London Times,_** Various issues, Summer and Autumn 1858. BCARS. Also, Edward McGowan, "Reminiscences of Edward McGowan", _Argonaut,_ 1878, copy at BCARS.

29 McGowan, BCARS.

30 McGowan; see also op. cit. Howay; Akrigg.

31 "Articles of British Columbia" printed in the London Times, Aug. 4, 1858 - Aug 15, 1862. E,B,F86, BCARS. September 12, 1858. Moreover, Aboriginal oral traditions surrounding the confrontation explain that the company of American militia/miners stopped at the Nlakapamexw village of Spuzzum on their way up the Canyon to make war and burned the local grave houses in an attempt to affront and provoke the Aboriginal community. (Personal communication with Sonny McHalsie who recalls Annie York telling him this story in 1988).

32 Otis Parsons, **_Unpublished Diary,_** June 29-September 19, 1858, BCARS

33 "Articles on British Columbia" printed in the **_London Times._** Thursday Feb 17, 1859. BCARS.

34 Interview with Dan Milo and Imbert Orchard. "Imbert Orchard Collection," 1963, BCARS.

35 Tilly Guiterrez in conversation with Keith Thor Carlson, March 1995. Transcript on file SNA

36 F.W. Howay, "The Introduction of Intoxicating Liquors Amongst the Indians of the Northwest Coast", BCHQ, VI, 3, 1942.

37 It is interesting to note that as more women of European descent settled in the new colony of British Columbia, the respected position held by women of mixed Aboriginal and European ancestry, like Lady Douglas, declined. The early colonial elite were primarily people from the fur trade era. These people generally accepted and respected Lady Douglas. This was increasingly less the case as time went on and as prominent figures from the fur trade became a minority.

38 Dispatch from Governor Douglas to the Right Hon.

Sir E.B. Lytton, March 14, 1859, **British Columbia, Papers Connected with the Indian Land Question,** 1850-1875, (Victoria: Government Printer, 1875), p.16-17. (Cited hereafter as BC, **Papers**.)

39   Ibid.

40   The question of whether B.C. colonial officials were aware of their obligations under British Common law remains unanswered. For the most recent discussion on this topic, and a very balanced perspective, see Hamar Foster, "Letting Go the Bone: The Idea of Indian Title in British Columbia, 1849-1927," in Hamar Foster and John McLaren, eds., **Essays in the History of Canadian Law,** Vol. VI, B.C. and the Yukon, (Toronto: Osgoode Society, 1995). Pp. 28-86.

41   Chief James of Yale, testifying before the Royal Commission. Copy on file at SNA.

42   Chief William Sepass, Testimony before the Royal Commission, January 14, 1915, p.196 SNA.

43   Chief Charlie of Matsqui, testifying before the Royal Commission, January 11, 1915., p, 196 SNA.

44   Chief Harry Edwards, Testimony before the Royal Commission, January 13, 1915, p.171 SNA.

45   Conversation between P.D. Peters and Larry Commodore, July 21, 1985. Tape on file at SNC.

46   Moody to E.H. Saunders, Land and Works Correspondence Outward, BCARS C/AB/30.7j3.

47   Parsons to Sapper Turnbull June 1, 1861, BCARS C/AB/30.7j2.

48   Instructions to McColl From Chartres Brew, April 6, 1864, **Papers Connected with the Indian Land Question.**, p.43.

49   Moody to W. McColl, June 2, 1862, Land and Works Correspondence Outward, BCARS   C/AB/30.7j1.

50   Evangeline Pete in a conversation with Gordon Mohs, 1985, quoted in Gordon Mohs, "Stó:lō Sacred Ground," in David L. Carmichael et al, **Sacred Sites, Sacred Places,** (New York, New York: Routledge Press, 1994), p.185.

51   Jimmie Peters in a conversation with Gordon Mohs, 1985, quoted in Gordon Mohs, "Stó:lō Sacred Ground," in David L. Carmichael et al, **Sacred Sites, Sacred Places,** (New York, New York: Routledge Press, 1994), p.200.

52   Albert Phillips in a conversation with Gordon Mohs, 1984.

53   Robin Fisher, **Contact and Conflict,** (Vancouver, University of British Columbia Press, 1992) p.159.

54   Fisher, p.160 - 161.

55   For further discussion on this subject see Chapter 2 this volume.

56   Truch to Acting Colonial Secretary, August 28, 1867, in **Indian Land Question,** p.42.

57   Ibid.

58   **The British Columbian,** December 2, 1865.

59   Ibid., August 4, 1866.

60   Ibid., December 2, 1865.

61   Letter from C. Brew to J. Truch, November 21, 1865. Copy on file at SNA.

62   Chief of Police, Chartres Brew, to Chief Commissioner of Lands and Works, Joseph Truch – See margin notes by Truch – December 1,1865. Copy on file at SNA.

63   The amended law made it impossible for Aboriginal people to pre-empt land without the written permission of the colonial governor. Prior to this amendment Col. Moody of the Royal Engineers had written Gov. Douglas to report that Stó:lō "Indians are pre-empting land as freely as the white man." There is no evidence that any Stó:lō person pre-empted land after the amendment was passed.

64   Chief Peter Ayessick of Hope and Chief Alexis of Cheam, 14 July 1874, "Petition of Chiefs of Lower Fraser... to I.W. Powell." BCARS.

65   Ibid.

66   Memorandum from David Laird, Minister of the Interior to I.W. Powell, Superintendent of Indian Affairs, November 2, 1874. in **Indian Land Question,** p.151.

67   Minister of the Interior (Mills) to I.W. Powell.

68   Sproat to Chief Commissioner of Lands and Works, May 18, 1878.

69   Ibid.

70   Sproat to E. Dickson, Government Agent at New Westminster, May 21, 1878.

71   Sproat to Chief Commissioner of Lands and Works, June 3, 1878; Sproat to Superintendent General, July 1, 1878.

72   G.M. Sproat to Superintendent General, November 25, 1878. Copy on file in SNA.

73   Ibid. (Aboriginal voice presented in first person by author).

74   Sproat, January 25, 1879; Sproat to Superintendent General, March 17, 1879. Copy on file at Stó:lō Nation Archives.

75   Sproat to the Deputy Minister of the Interior November 6, 1878. Copy on file at Stó:lō Nation Archives.

76   By "He" Tilly is referring to God or Xá:ls. She frequently refers to Xá:ls as "the little Christ" who came to visit the Stó:lō "after he had been in the Middle East as recorded in the Bible." This blending of Christian and traditional Stó:lō belief systems is common among many Stó:lō Elders.

77   Conversation between Tilly Gutierrez, Sonny McHalsie, Randall Paul and Richard Dally, September 20th, 1988. Tape at SNA.

78   Personal communication with Tracey Joe, July, 1996.

CHAPTER 5

EARLY NINETEENTH CENTURY
Stó:lō Social
Structures
and Government
Assimilation
P O L I C Y

Keith Thor Carlson

INTRODUCTION:

Two aspects of *Stó:lō* society – the specific status based social structures and unique relationships with the Spirit world – clearly distinguish and set it apart from many other Aboriginal communities. Recognizing this cultural distinctiveness is extremely important if one wishes to truly appreciate *Stó:lō* people and *Stó:lō* history. *Stó:lō* society is as distinct from other North American Aboriginal societies as Spanish culture is from different European cultures. Just as you would never try to learn about Spain by studying Swedish or Ukrainian society you would not try to learn about the *Stó:lō* by studying the Iroquois or Cree. And yet, government policy towards Aboriginal people in Canada has never appreciated these cultural and geographic differences. Indeed, one of the few things shared by all Canadian Aboriginal peoples is the experience of colonization.

Interior of a winter longhouse. Temporary mat partitions divided the interior of the building, and individual families had their own fire-pits.

This chapter seeks to shed light upon the attempts by the British/Canadian government and its agents to eradicate and assimilate *Stó:lō* cultural identity. To accomplish this, the paper first describes in some detail the way in which *Stó:lō* society was originally structured in the immediate pre-contact, and early contact era. It then discusses the official government policy towards Aboriginal people and documents the local *Stó:lō* experience with these policies. The *Stó:lō* response to these external threats is indicative of the adaptive and flexible nature of their culture, and in particular, their leadership.

1 EARLY NINETEENTH CENTURY STÓ:LŌ SOCIAL STRUCTURES AND POLITICAL CULTURE: STATUS AND LEADERSHIP ■

Extended family ties remain the most important social bonds within *Stó:lō* society. Such connections continue to be far more meaningful than any ties joining unrelated people who lived within the same village. This is reflected even in the architecture and occupancy patterns of traditional *Stó:lō lálém* or longhouses. Typically, members of one extended family lived together in large shed roofed longhouses. They averaged 6-18 m in width, and 12-36 m in length, but were also known to be much larger. For example, when Simon Fraser visited *Stó:lō* territory in 1808, he observed a single longhouse at Matsqui (near Abbotsford) that was 192 m long and 18 m wide (640 x 60 feet), or larger than two football fields. Inside, the giant house was divided by hanging woven mats into "square apartments." *Stó:lō* Elders explain that these rooms were the separate living quarters of individual nuclear families. The mat walls could be easily removed when larger areas were required for ceremonies and celebrations. The only room in the longhouse significantly different from the others belonged to the leader of the extended family. Within the large longhouse Simon Fraser observed in 1808, the extended family's leaders room was 27 m (90 ft.) long. Unlike the other smaller compartments, it was elaborately decorated with carved figures and other signs of wealth.

Cranial deformation.

Stó:lō social status was reflected both in the physical space people occupied within their longhouses, as well as the positioning of their longhouses within the village. *Stó:lō* society was divided into three distinct social groupings. The majority of people were considered high status, a somewhat smaller number were low status, while the smallest group consisted of slaves. Slaves lived with their masters, but were confined to sleeping near the drafty doors of the longhouse, where they would be the first to encounter any raiders who attacked during the night. Members of an extended family who lived in the same village often shared a longhouse, with high ranking family members occupying the most comfortable and protected spaces. Longhouses of low status people were typically constructed along the village edges, in less desirable and more vulnerable locations. In a few instances, entire villages were comprised of low status people. Low status longhouses were also distinguishable because they were typically clad with cedar bark slabs rather than the more valuable split cedar planks used by high status families.

High Status: *smelá:lh*

Stó:lō people's status was derived not only from their personal achievements, but also from their family's position. High status people usually came from high status families. *Smelá:lh*, which translates as "worthy people," is the *Halq'eméylem* term for high status families. To be *smelá:lh* – that is "worthy" – a person had to be from a family that "knew its history." Knowing your history meant, among other things, knowing which productive fishing or berry picking sites your family owned, legends about the mythological past, special information about plants and other resources, and having a relationship with the spirits of prominent family ancestors. Children of worthy parents had certain advantages over other children. Special inherited high status family names guaranteed access to and ownership of family assets.

According to the *Stó:lō* Elders who shared information with the anthropologist Wilson Duff in the 1940's, *smelá:lh* parents from *Stó:lō* communities between present day Langley and the ocean flattened the foreheads of their infants to distinguish them from children of lower status families.[1] This process, called "cranial deformation," was permanent and irreversible. Moreover, it could not be performed after an infant was more than a few months old, by which time the skull becomes hard and impossible to manipulate. In this way,

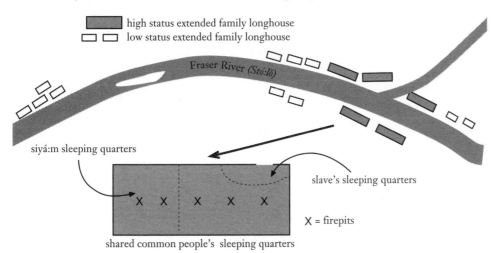

high status extended family longhouse
low status extended family longhouse

Fraser River *(Stó:lō)*

siyá:m sleeping quarters

slave's sleeping quarters

X = firepits

shared common people's sleeping quarters

Status was reflected in the physical space *Stó:lō* people occupied within villages and longhouses.

Left: Canoes, situated at an encampment on the shores of the Fraser River, were a symbol of wealth.

siyá:m

smelá:lh high status "worthy people" who know their history

s'téxem low status "worthless people" who "have forgotten their history"

skw'iyéth slaves

Chart illustrating aspects of *Stó:lō* social structures.

certain outward signs of status were ascribed by birthright. Likewise, some high status people pierced their nose and spoke a special dialect which further distinguished them from low status people.

Low Status: *s'téxem*

People from low status families were typically referred to as *s'téxem*, which translates as "worthless people." Other English terms used by *Stó:lō* Elders to describe people of this lower status are "poor people," "nothing people," or "younger children."[2] Elders explain that *s'téxem* implies "people who have lost or forgotten their history." People without a history could not access the hereditary privileges of high status families. As a result, upward social mobility was a rare occurrence. The stigma of having *s'téxem* ancestry always haunted low status people regardless of their personal achievements. Someone from a worthless family had no opportunity to learn good manners or access the private knowledge of high status people, let alone have rights to the best fishing sites and berry patches.

Slaves: skw'iyéth

Skw'iyéth, or slaves, were the one segment of *Stó:lō* society whose status was entirely determined by birth. Children of slaves were destined to be the property of their parents' masters as well. To distinguish them, slaves were compelled to keep their hair cut short.[3] Long hair was associated with aspects of spirit power. High status slave owners may have prohibited their slaves from growing long hair to ensure they did not become spiritually powerful and thereby potentially more rebellious or inde-

pendent. Whatever the cause, short-haired slaves were easily and immediately distinguishable from other community members.

Not all slaves, however, were born into servitude. Some (typically women) were captives taken from other communities during raids. Others were purchased from neighbouring villages, acquired at potlatches, or accompanied high class women as wedding dowry. *Stó:lō* Elders explained that slaves lived with their owners and carried out their menial tasks. But, as anthropologist Wayne Suttles explains, they were socially "non-persons" in that they could not receive a special name or inherited privileges and, as such, slaves "mainly lived lives of drudgery."[4]

Swōqw'elh, a goat wool blanket, which represented of wealth.

Leadership: *sí:yá:m*

Some high status *smelá:lh* people became especially respected and developed a reputation for leadership. Such people were referred to as "*siyá:m*," (*sí:yá:m* when referring to more than one). *Siyá:m* implies "unblemished ancestry,"

You Are Asked To Witness

"political" *siyá:m*	*shxwlá:m*	*stómex*	*tewit*
provided leadership in	*provided leadership in*	*provided leadership in*	*provided leadership in*
dispute resolution and regulating access to family owned resources.	important areas of health care (often women).	organizing and executing raids and counter raids.	in aspects of resource procurement relating to hunting.

Different people had leadership responsibilities over various aspects of early nineteenth century *Stó:lō* society.

"good manners," "extrahuman support," and "wealth."[5]

The requirement for unblemished ancestry illustrates how important hereditary status, or "pure blood" was to the *Stó:lō*. Good manners were an outward expression of a quality education and healthy home life. Extrahuman support refers to spirit power. The *Stó:lō* believe the spirits of their ancestors and spirits of certain animals play important interactive roles in people's day to day lives. Expert hunters or fishermen attributed much of their success to their special spirit power, as did spiritual leaders (many of whom were women) and warriors. Likewise, *sí:yá:m* were careful to credit aspects of their historical knowledge and oratory skills to the assistance of prominent ancestral spirits who guided them in their activities. *Stó:lō* spiritual leaders explain that spirits often interacted with people in a manner similar to a memory, but other times they were specially acquired during "spirit quests." They involved a person going into seclusion for a number of days, in which they fasted, did strenuous exercise, and meditated.

Sí:yá:m also needed to be wealthy. In fact, when used as a verb, the word *siyá:m* literally translates as wealthy.[6] In *Stó:lō* society, high status people demonstrated and reinforced their social position by throwing elaborate ceremonial potlatches (known in *Halq'eméylem* as "*stl'éleq*"), wherein they redistributed vast amounts of wealth within their communities. *Sí:yá:m* accumulated wealth in a number of ways. This was commonly done through the ownership, regulation, and control of productive resource sites such as fishing rocks and berry patches. Wealth also came in the form of gifts, received in recognition for assisting people to resolve a dispute. It was also acquired by recognition for acting as a speaker or master of ceremonies at large public gatherings. The more respected a leader became, the more gifts they would receive. Each gift was wealth, and the greater a leader's wealth, the higher their status.

The expression *siyá:m* can also be understood as meaning "respected extended family leader." As mentioned, extended families ties were the most important social bonds within traditional *Stó:lō* society. These connections were far more meaningful than any ties joining unrelated people who lived within the same village. A *siyá:m* controlled the most important extended family ceremonial rights and names, and regulated access to productive family owned resources sites. It is important to note, however, that the word "*siyá:m*" was not an official title, nor was being *siyá:m* a specific political or economic office with prescribed rights and responsibilities. *Sí:yá:m* were neither appointed nor elected officials, and they had no means of enforcing their will or decisions upon others. People simply respected their opinion, and tended to accept their advice and follow their lead.

Drawing on information acquired in the 1940's during interviews with prominent *Stó:lō* Elders, Wilson Duff explained that,

Within each extended family there was no doubt one man who made everyday decisions on matters involving the family. In multi-family villages, heads of families were no doubt loosely ranked by prestige, with one man standing above the others and holding the most sway over the village as a whole. This man... spoke and others listened, he suggested and exhorted and the others took action. His power over his own kinsmen was considerable, since he had the greatest voice in controlling the family's property, names, and actions as a group. His power over unrelated families was less, depending upon his personal reputation for wisdom in leadership. Yet, apparently he did tend to develop a habit of leadership' over the whole village and undertook certain duties as a village official.[7]

Duff further observed that all *Stó:lō sí:yá:m* were "ranked in ascending scale regardless of place of residence, but this was a social ranking and only incidentally and to a limited degree a political one."[8] People living in one village often accepted that their local extended family *siyá:m* might not be as highly respected as another *siyá:m* from the same extended family in a different village.

Being recognized as an extended family *siyá:m* did not mean a person was the leader over all aspects of family or community life. While the term *sí:yá:m* is generally used to describe people who are recognized as political or social leaders, other people had expertise, responsibilities, rights, and privileges in other fields. For example, in the early nineteenth century there remain at least three types of healers or "doctors" (*shxwlá:m*, *syuwí:l*, and *syéwe*), each of

Family owned dip netting site located along the Fraser River.

ticular leaders. This sometimes confuses *Xwelítem* people, because it does not easily coincide with the structures they are accustomed to. However, by becoming more aware of *Stó:lō* social structures we can hopefully better appreciate how difficult it has been for the *Stó:lō* to adapt to mainstream Canadian political society. For the purposes of this chapter, focus will be given to the family *siyá:m* who assumed leadership roles which most closely correspond to what mainstream society defines as political leadership.

The Political Process: Checks on the Influence of *Siyá:m*

which are responsible for various aspects of their extended family's health. Many *Stó:lō* spiritual leaders are women. Women also exercised special leadership roles concerning the passing down of hereditary privileges such as the right to wear a *sxwó:yxwey* mask. Likewise, there were people called, *stómex*, who assumed responsibility for organizing and conducting raids and counter-raids on members of unfriendly extended families in other villages. Expert hunters who led their extended families in catching winter supplies of game were called *tewít*. Thus, even today leadership and *siyá:m* are distributed within *Stó:lō* society. People with special skills, knowledge, and spirit power become acknowledged as leaders within certain fields.

Commenting on the flexible and informal nature of traditional *Stó:lō* leadership, anthropologist Michael Kew observes that "there was a lack of uneasiness among the *Stó:lō* over the imprecision of social roles."[9] In other words, the *Stó:lō* were not overly preoccupied with assigning prescribed political authority to par-

In the early nineteenth century, when an extended family had to make a major decision, the various family leaders met to discuss the matter. In such instances, *siyá:m* sought to harmonize extended family interests, and achieve a consensus of opinion. If agreement could not be reached easily, discussions might continue for days. If consensus ultimately proved unattainable, the matter was typically set aside and left unresolved. It was not uncommon, however, on occasions when only a few people refused to follow the advice of their local *siyá:m*, that the dissenters relocated to anoth-

At St. Mary's Mission on the Fraser River in May, 1867.

You Are Asked To Witness

Coast Salish raiding party, painted by Paul Kane, 1863.

er village and lived under a different family *siyá:m*.

As described, traditional *Stó:lō* leaders exercised their authority very differently than contemporary Canadian political leaders, and were not elected for prescribed terms of office. *Sí:yá:m* did not need to pass laws and record them in books for others to obey. They had no need for a police force or army to enforce their will, and did not require a separate judicial system to interpret laws. The actions of both the leaders and the extended family were regulated by customs, not laws. People listened to *sí:yá:m* and typically followed their leadership because they respected their wise opinions, conflict resolution skills, and proven good judgement.

Sí:yá:m were responsible not only for their extended family's general welfare, but also for their actual comfort.[10] Extended families had a number of

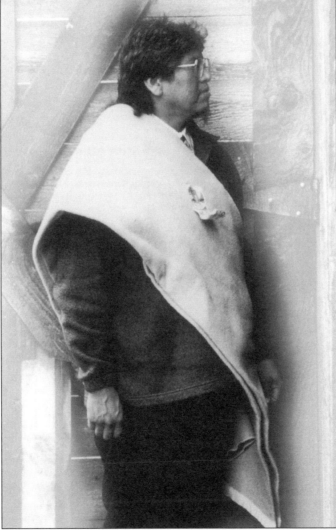

Contemporary *Stó:lō siyá:m* Sonny McHalsie.

options if their local *siyá:m* failed to provide for them or did something offensive. Typically, when *sí:yá:m* became discredited, their extended family stopped deferring to their opinion or following their leadership. If this happened, a *siyá:m* quickly dropped in influence and status.

Gossip, an important tool of social leverage, was employed to ensure that all people knew of a tarnished leader's failings. *Sí:yá:m* who lost their family's support could attempt to regain it, but loss of status was a difficult thing to overcome. Yet, it is important to note that *sí:yá:m* worked very hard to retain their family's respect. For instance, within the recorded oral history of the Chilliwack people there is only one instance of a top ranking *siyá:m* ever being rejected and deposed.

In rare cases when members of an extended family determined that a prominent person's behaviour threatened the community, various extended family leaders occasionally arranged to depose of the person. In 1952, anthropologist Wilson Duff was told a story by *Stó:lō* Elder Edmond Lorenzetto which illustrated the lengths *sí:yá:m* would go to restore inner-family tranquility and inter-family peace. Mr. Lorenzetto told of a great *siyá:m* named *"Likwetem"* from a village near the present town of Yale in the Fraser Canyon. *Likwetem* had three brothers "who did a lot of killing for little things." When a *siyá:m* from a village near the present town of Hope passed Yale on his way to obtain dried salmon from his storage area in the canyon, one of *Likwetem's* brothers shot at him. The Hope *siyá:m* landed his canoe and shot *Likwetem's* brother dead. This did not upset *Likwetem*, who appeared glad that the "trouble maker" had been killed. However, *Likwetim's* other two aggressive brothers organized a raiding party and attacked the village near Hope in retaliation. The raid ended with a second of *Likwetem's* aggressive brothers' death. Later, *Likwetem* "gave some Hope people permission to do what they wanted with his third brother." Two men from Hope secretly travelled to Yale and set up an ambush. As *Likwetem's* canoe passed by, the people from Hope shot dead the last of *Likwetim's* brothers. *Likwetem* did not stop his canoe, but rather "just told his pullers to keep on paddling." As Lorenzetto explained, *Likwetem* "knew that the business was done."[11]

The drastic action of killing a bad leader was rare, even in the nineteenth century. Such practises certainly do not occur today. However, the traditional *Stó:lō* technique

Contemporary *Stó:lō siyá:m* Michelle Douglas receiving traditional recognition when appointed to the *Stó:lō* Nation Special Chiefs' Council.

of quietly casting aspersions upon a discredited leader while publicly ignoring them does remain a powerful instrument of social control in contemporary *Stó:lō* society. For example, in the 1980's the *Stó:lō* Nation publically recognized certain *Stó:lō* leaders for having consistently given of themselves over their lifetime to better the entire *Stó:lō* population. These people were given the honourary title of "Grand Chief." A few years later, one of these men was accused, and ultimately convicted in the BC provincial court, of sexually abusing children. News of his guilt spread quickly throughout *Stó:lō* extended families. While no official action was ever taken by the *Stó:lō* Nation to strip away this man's honourary title, people

everywhere stopped referring to him as a "Grand Chief" – he had ceased to be *siyá:m*. No longer was he "called as a speaker" at important public gatherings. When other chiefs and respected Elders were introduced or "called as witnesses" his name was conspicuous by its absence. The dishonoured "Grand Chief" became a social and political outcast, ostracised from respectable high status *Stó:lō* society. By dealing with the issue in a traditional and culturally appropriate manner, the *Stó:lō* quietly exercised their own form of justice and a version of self-government.

2 GOVERNMENT ASSIMILATION POLICY ■

In order to appreciate the ways government legislation has impacted traditional *Stó:lō* social structures and leadership styles, it is necessary first to review the earlier British laws which dealt with Aboriginal people in what is now central Canada. Early in the nineteenth century, the British government adopted policies to "protect and civilize" British North America's Aboriginal people. They wanted to "protect" Aboriginal people from the fast encroaching settlers and whiskey pedlars, and then "civilize" them so they could be integrated into mainstream society.

British Attitudes Towards Aboriginal People

Most Europeans of this era accepted the Biblical teaching that God had given humankind a divine right to "subdue the earth and have dominion over the animals." Europeans had traditionally interpreted this to mean that most of the earth's natural resources were predestined to eventual exploitation. However, a growing number of people living in Britain and along the eastern Canadian seaboard, where nature had already been transformed, began pressuring the government to protect Aboriginal people in their natural environment. This protection required that unspoiled land be "reserved" for Aboriginal people's exclusive use, at least for the short term, until they could be assimilated into the broader European culture.

Responding to these pressures, in the 1830's British Parliament passed several laws designed to "protect" and "civilize" (or assimilate) Canada's Aboriginal population. These laws were viewed as an experiment in civilization, and formed the basis of Canada's future Indian reserve policy and the "Indian Act." Accordingly, in what is now central Canada, relatively large centralized Indian reserves were created. They became social laboratories, where well-intentioned, but ethnocentric *Xwelítem* sought to remake Aboriginal people in a European mould. They were intended to strip away the fabric of Aboriginal society and replace it with that of European "civilization." In accordance with the scientific method, the experiment placed Aboriginal people into a controlled environment called an "Indian reserve." According to the theory, once in this controlled environment, Aboriginal people's interaction with undesirable stimuli – in particular whiskey pedlars – could be

RED JACKET
STOMACH BITTERS

Nineteenth century patent medicine labels portraying the stereotypical image of the "noble savage" suggested that life in the "natural state" was more healthy than living in urban industrialized cities.

The Biblical verse in which God said to Adam and Eve "subdue the earth" was interpreted quite literally by many people and businesses in the nineteenth century. Here we see the effects of nineteenth century logging techniques in *Stó:lō* territory.

regulated, while positive stimuli – Christian missionaries, respectable farmers, and the like – could be introduced to act as catalysts for "positive" change.

By the 1850's the British government determined that their early experiments were not working as well as originally anticipated. They decided part of the reason for their failure was that Aboriginal people's exposure to the best elements of Euroamerican society had not been intense enough. A two-pronged approach was then adopted to accelerate the assimilation process; the first focussed on either replacing or assimilating extended family leaders – *sí:yá:m*, and the second targeted Aboriginal children. The government realized that *sí:yá:m* people carried great influence. It was felt that by winning them over or replacing them, the assimilation process would be more effective with the rest of the community. With regard to children, the government assumed that by assimilating young children their efforts would be essentially completed after one or two generations, as soon as the "old people" had died off and been replaced by the new assimilated generation.

ASSIMILATION TECHNIQUE #1: UNDERMINING ABORIGINAL LEADERS

Missionary Activity

Some of the initial foot soldiers in the government's assimilation policy were Christian missionaries. Prior to the 1858 gold rush few missionaries had visited *Stó:lō* territory, and what visits did occur were brief.[12] It was only after the arrival of over 30,000 *Xwelítem* miners into *Stó:lō* territory that serious and concerted missionary activity occurred among the *Stó:lō* people. These were initiated at the request of the colonial government who was primarily interested in having the missionaries counteract the affects of unscrupulous whiskey pedlars who followed the miners to the gold fields. Father Chirouse, the first missionary to arrive in *Stó:lō* territory in the wake of the gold rush, recorded that the concoction being passed off to the *Stó:lō* as alcohol was in reality a toxic "mixture of camphor and tobacco juice." Chirouse estimated that alcoholism was effecting well

over half of all *Stó:lō* families.[13] While the missionaries, no doubt, had reasons to paint as bleak a picture of the situation as possible in order to encourage their supporters to make financial contributions, there is no reason to dispute the general assumption that alcohol had become a significant problem for *Stó:lō* communities during the gold rush.

The first missionary to settle permanently among the *Stó:lō* was the Catholic Oblate priest Father Leon Fouquet. The current name for the site where he first began his work continues to bear testimony of his activities to this day. Founding his "Mission" in 1861, Father Fouquet immediately set about learning the *Halq'eméylem* language and studying *Stó:lō* culture to learn the best way to gain their acceptance and win them over to his cause. Once he understood aspects of *Stó:lō* society he designed his missionary activities to take advantage of *Stó:lō* concepts of *sí:yà:m*. To accomplish this the Oblate priest identified sympathetic traditional *Stó:lō siyá:m*, and with their assistance established "Temperance" or "Sobriety" Societies. To assist the *siyá:m*, Fouquet and the other Oblates identified *Stó:lō* community members who were supportive of the missionaries' work and appointed them "captains" or "watchmen."

The missionaries were initially viewed with some suspicion by the *Stó:lō* leadership. Their experience during the gold rush had taught them to be cautious of *Xwelítem*. However, according to the Oblates, the majority of the *Stó:lō* quickly came to appreciate the missionaries' assistance. Whereas "during the first five or six months the Indians would not even approach the missionaries" by 1861 "everywhere, the Indians, en masse, (had) enrolled under the Banner of Temperance... With the Chiefs at the head, captains and watchmen were organized in every camp."

The first concerted Oblate effort to counteract the whiskey pedlars occurred at the *Stó:lō* village of Cheam, near Chilliwack. The main local *siyá:m*, a man named Alexis, was instrumental in assisting Father Chirouse. In describing the event, Chirouse said that after he had addressed the community he found that nearly 200 *Stó:lō* had gathered around him and Alexis, while only 15 remained at the whiskey pedlars shack which had been built right among the *Stó:lō* homes. Alexis then recommended that they burn the shack down. Following this incident Chirouse claims the Oblates "received many requests to visit other camps and establish 'sobriety societies.'"[14]

The story of the battle against the gold rush era whiskey pedlars has great contemporary meaning for *Stó:lō* people. In the summer of 1996 Ohamil Elder Ralph George invited the RCMP and a TV news team to visit his community so he could show them the devastating impact drug pushers were having on *Stó:lō* society. With Mr. George's assistance the RCMP were able to destroy a marijuana crop with an estimated street value of $150,000. When a CBC radio reporter asked Mr. George if he was concerned for his safety he replied that he was more afraid for the safety of the children:

I'm an old man. If the Vancouver motor bike gang who grows these drugs and pushes them on our kids wants to get me I don't care. I've lived a full life and I've seen the damage drugs and alcohol have on our communities. If I try to stop the drugs I might get hurt, but if I don't, a lot of children are going to get hurt for sure. Its just like the whiskey pedlars from the old days. The Elders and *sí:yá:m* have to stand up and say we won't stand this sort of abuse of our communities."[15]

Elder Ralph George is a legacy of the *sí:yá:m* of the last century.

Recognizing that they could not achieve their goals if the *Stó:lō* leadership was hostile towards them, and encouraged by their close and apparently successful relationship with Chief Alexis of Cheam, the Oblates, and later the Methodists, moved to promote the conversion and assimilation of *Stó:lō* community leaders. The assumption was that if they could convert the elite, the rest of the community would follow. Not surprisingly, then, when the missionaries could not convert an existing leader they often attempted to undermine that person's position by promoting a new leader who was more receptive to their objectives.

All too often, communities were pulled apart by interdenominational feuding between the different missionaries.[16] Reporting on the activities of the Methodist Missionary Thomas Crosby at Chilliwack, the Oblate Priest Father Marshal proudly commented that Crosby was "set up in the centre of these (Catholic) villages, unable to spread his work." However, Marshal noted that according to his *Stó:lō* supporters, the Methodist was intimidating *Stó:lō* people into becoming Protestants by threatening them that those who rejected the Protestant faith in favour of Catholic doctrine "would be chased from this land and transported along with the Catholic priest to an island of the ocean, where there is no sweet water, no drink and no food of any kind; where he would soon die of misery."[17] On the other hand, in his autobiography *Among the An-ko-me-nums*, Reverend Crosby paints the picture in reverse, stating that the Catholics subjected those *Stó:lō* who had shown interest in the Methodist faith to "the most bitter persecution;" circulating illustrations of Catholic Indians going to Heaven, while "Crosby and his friends went head first into the lurid flames of hell-fire."[18]

Competition, for the loyalty and allegiance of *Stó:lō* leaders remained a characterizing feature of Catholic-Protestant and interdenominational Protestant relations in the Fraser Valley throughout the nineteenth century. In 1886, the Oblate priest Father Edward Peytavin described the competition between the Catholic Church, the Methodists and the Anglicans for the souls of the Skw'átets community (now called Peter's Reserve). He claimed that of a total population of fifty-one, thirty six were Catholic; the remainder Protestant. The traditional community leader was reportedly an Episcopalian Anglican and the Methodist families allegedly "refused to recognize an Anglican Chief." In response, the Methodist Minister had appointed a "Methodist Chief." This action, according to the Oblate, was unacceptable to the remaining Catholic population. Thus, in order to "maintain peace and discipline among the Catholics," Peytavin reported that he "had to choose a Catechist or Zealator," for the Catholic majority. Once appointed, the Catechist was allegedly given by his "co-religionaries" the "title of Chief:" "There are now three (chiefs) in this little village, it is the Catholic Chief who has the most subjects, the Methodist Chief is in Control of thirteen, and the Episcopalian has only his wife to govern. This situation causes much laughter among whites and Indians." Father Peyatvin's report described a similar situation existing at *Shxw'ōwhamel* (just down river from Hope), only in that community, the priest lamented, the Catholics were "losing ground."[19]

In all probability, there was much more going on at *Skw'átets* and *Shxw'ōwhamel* than the Oblate Father's simple description might imply. Interdenominational Christian disputes were often more a vehicle for Indigenous politics than the causal factors Peyatvin's description suggests. Archaeological research suggest that intense rivalries between families for community leadership had been a feature of *Stó:lō* society for at least the past 1400 years.[20] Today, as has been shown, families continue to compete for position within the social and political hierarchy of *Stó:lō* society. Yet, regardless of the true cause of such conflicts, it remains that the Christian Missionaries were accentuating, if not provoking, inter-community disputes in their efforts to control *Stó:lō* leadership.

Xá:ytem, a "transformer rock" located in Mission.

Government Activities: The "Civilization Act"

The colonial, and later provincial and federal governments did not leave the matter of assimilation to the missionaries alone. Specific legislation was also drafted to expedite the assimilation of Aboriginal leaders. This law was called the "Civilization Act."[21] It defined "Indians" or Aboriginal people as wards of the government. They were not citizens, and therefore did not possess all the rights of Canadian citizenship. The government decided that full citizenship and integration into mainstream *Xwelítem* society was the goal all Aboriginal people should aspire to.

The "Civilization Act" established a rigid criteria for Aboriginal people to fulfill before they could be "promoted" to full and equal citizenship and be recognized as "civilized." They had to be able to read and write, be free of debt, and of good moral character. As long as they failed to meet any of these criteria, they were regarded as inferior to people of British descent – they were legally and socially "Indian."

It is useful to consider the standards the government established for citizenship. In the nineteenth century most full Canadian citizens of British or European descent could not even meet all the citizenship requirements established for "Indians," yet they were considered "civilized" from birth. Thus, to become a citizen and be considered equal, Aboriginal people were expected to become more "civilized" than Europeans.

Able to Read and Write

For the *Stó:lō*, it was almost impossible to fulfill the government's literacy requirements and still live within the framework of their traditional oral culture. In pre-contact times, the *Stó:lō* had not found it necessary to develop a written language to preserve their history. Instead, they recorded important information in elaborate oral narratives (and sometimes in images they painted and carved into rocks and cedar houseposts). Such stories were passed from generation to generation in a carefully prescribed manner. One particularly well known *Stó:lō* oral narrative surrounds the transformer stone "*Xá:ytem*," located in Mission. It relates how the transformers *XéXa:ls* punished three *sí:yá:m* for not adopting new ways to preserve and protect *Stó:lō* traditions and knowledge. For *Stó:lō* culture to survive the government's assimilation policy, leaders needed to heed the lessons of *Xá:ytem* and be innovative and adaptive. However, people who had been raised in an oral environment could not be expected to adapt to a written culture overnight. It took time.

Free From Debt

The second criteria for citizenship under the "Civilization Act" was freedom from debt. Interestingly, many British-born Canadian citizens accumulated significant debts throughout their lives as they purchased land and built homes or businesses, yet they were not denied citizenship. For the *Stó:lō*, debt was a central facet of life. As explained, the *Stó:lō* accumulated wealth primarily to

A nineteenth century potlatch ceremony in which a blanket is being thrown off a platform to the people below.

redistribute it at special feasts and potlatches. Whenever a major feast or potlatch was held the *siyá:m* hosting the event always borrowed from their relatives to ensure enough food was available. The hosts were expected to repay this favour with interest at a future potlatch. In other words, the hosts became indebted. In this way all who participated in *Stó:lō* potlatches (and everyone did) was by definition "in debt" and ineligible for Canadian citizenship.

"Good Morals"

Morality, the third criteria of the "Civilization Act," also impacted the *Stó:lō*. Morality is something that society is constantly redefining. It is also interpreted differently by various groups within society. People of different economic classes, ethnic backgrounds, religions, ages, and genders, often do not agree on a single definition of what is moral and immoral. For example, in the late-nineteenth century, upper class Americans felt it was immoral for a woman to reveal any portion of her leg in public. Observance of this definition of morality resulted in some people covering the legs of their pianos because they thought the graceful curved carvings too closely approximated the female figure. Currently, many young people enjoy watching music videos. They find them entertaining and harmless. Yet, other members of contemporary society (primarily conservative older people) view the content of many such videos as offensive and immoral.

Through the "Civilization Act" immorality was carefully interpreted using the value judgements of upper-class British Society. The Act defined slavery and polygamy (having more than one wife), as immoral.

Therefore, any Aboriginal person who owned slaves or had more than one wife was considered "uncivilized" and ineligible for "citizenship." For nineteenth century *Stó:lō* people conforming to such definitions required fundamental readjustments of their social structures. As explained, *sí:yá:m* were required to demonstrate their wealth. Slaves were not only symbols of wealth, they were wealth in themselves, for their labour contributed to their owner's possessions and made his family's life easier. A census taken by the Hudson's Bay Company in 1839 indicates that 15% of the *Stó:lō* population were slaves.

It was also common for *Stó:lō sí:yá:m* to have more than one wife. The main reason for this practice was to access new resources by forging new family alliances. Having more than one wife also indicated that a *siyá:m* was wealthy enough to support a large family. Often times, *sí:yá:m* acquired slaves so their high status wives would not have to work too hard. Thus, for *sí:yá:m* to meet the "citizenship" requirements of the Civilization Act meant abandoning certain important traditional activities and practises.

Gradual Enfranchisement Act

In 1869 the Canadian government passed another act which impacted upon Aboriginal people – the "Gradual Enfranchisement Act." Like the "Civilization Act," the "Gradual Enfranchisement Act" applied in British Columbia after Confederation in 1871. "Enfranchisement" refers to the ability to vote in an election. The Gradual Enfranchisement Act was part of the government's "civilization" policy. It was intended to encourage Aboriginal communities to adopt British style elections. The Act also enabled government agents to remove traditional leaders and replace them with elected councils. As a result, traditional *sí:yá:m* were replaced with "municipal style" councils, where "chiefs" were elected like "mayors" and "councillors" like "aldermen." If elections were not held, the legislation gave the Indian Agent the authority to "appoint" Chiefs. Typically, the Indian Agent appointed people who had already been selected by the missionaries as "Church Chiefs" and "Watchmen."

Not surprisingly many Aboriginal leaders opposed such changes. The government assured Aboriginal communities they would only use this law to remove

You Are Asked To Witness

Aboriginal leaders who were unfit or unqualified to hold office. However, as we have seen, *Xwelítem* and Aboriginal definitions did not always correspond. A *siyá:m* who could not read or write was deemed incompetent and unfit by the government's standards. And a *siyá:m* who had more than one wife or owned slaves was considered by the government to be immoral and equally unfit for a position of authority.

More "Indian Laws"

In 1880 and 1895, the Canadian government amended their "Indian Laws" once again. As with previous government initiatives, these changes were designed to intensify the assimilation process. Traditional leaders were now "prohibited from exercising any power unless they had been elected." Those communities that retained their traditional leadership structures discovered their *sí:yá:m* had less legal authority than those chiefs who had been "elected" or "appointed" under the new legislation. In fact, all Chiefs were now regarded as "appointees of the government," and therefore subject to removal by Indian agents.

Anti-Potlatching Law

In 1884, the Indian Act was amended to include the infamous "anti-potlatch law." The Act now made it illegal for Aboriginal people to gather together in a ceremonial dance, funeral, marriage, naming ceremony, or any other kind of traditional event where gifts were given out. People who violated this law were "liable to imprisonment for a term of not more than six nor less than two months in any gaol [jail] or other place of confinement."[22]

The main objective of this new law was to promote the assimilation of Aboriginal people by subverting one of their main economic and social institutions. Many missionaries and Indian agents who had observed these gatherings viewed them as "heathen," "immoral," and "communistic," because they allegedly appeared un-Christian and discouraged savings thereby making paupers out of rich people.

The first person to be arrested and convicted for violating the anti-potlatching law was a *Stó:lō* man from Chilliwack named Bill Uslick. In January 1896 Indian Agent Frank Delvin reported to the police that he had witnessed a potlatch ceremony where Mr. Uslick gave away almost all his wealth. In his report Delvin stated that he was convinced that:

The Indian mentioned ... Bill Uslick ... is one of those Indians that is very hard to manage. He still wishes to keep up the old habits and customs, and would like to be a leader among the Indians of the neighbourhood. The Potlatch given by Bill Uslick was simply a Potlatch. I am not aware that any human, or animal bodies, were mutilated, or anything of that kind occurred. There certainly was a great waste. He practically left himself destitute, having given everything away that he had in the world. I am of the opinion if he was brought before the Court and got a couple of months in prison, that it would have a good effect, and would deter others from following his example...[23]

Uslick was arrested on February 1, 1896, and sentenced to two months in prison.

In the following years several other convictions occurred up and down the coast. To even more effectively undermine Aboriginal society, the anti-potlatching law was amended to prohibit "any Indian festival, dance or other ceremony of which the giving away or paying or giving back of money, goods or articles of any sort forms a part."[24] This amendment was made to prohibit virtually any gathering of Aboriginal people, effectively eliminating their ability to legally practise their traditional spiritual or economic activities.

While some *Stó:lō* people complied with the anti-potlatching law, others moved the potlatch along with the winter ceremonials and other public gatherings underground. Public occasions such as weddings and funerals were held in various churches, although with a distinctly *Stó:lō* flavour. The clandestine efforts of *Stó:lō sí:yá:m* like Richard Malloway of Yakweakwioose in Sardis enabled the potlatch and the winter ceremonial to survive through the prohibition period and into the present.

No Lawyers

In the early twentieth century the "Civilization Act," "Gradual Enfranchisement Act," and "Advancement Act" were unified into a single piece of legislation known as the "Indian Act." It retained all the essential elements of its predecessors and continued the policy of assimilation. In 1929, in order to stop Aboriginal people from taking legal action against the government, the Indian Act was again amended, making it illegal for any lawyer to work for an Aboriginal person or organization in a suit against the federal government. This ban remained in effect until 1951 when certain amendments were made to the Indian Act to remove the most offensive aspects of the legislation. While the Indian Act no longer prohibited the potlatch or prevented Aboriginal people from hiring lawyers, the changes did not affect the central assimilationist policy of the government's Indian policy. Rather, the changes simply provided greater administrative independence for those Aboriginal communities which had proven to be the most assimilated. Throughout the 1950's and 60's, most *Stó:lō* communities attempted to work within the parameters of the Indian Act. These communities functioned essentially as federal municipalities with elected mayors (chiefs) and councils.

The preceding discussion outlines the major government efforts to undermine the positions of Aboriginal leaders. To fully appreciate the government's assimilationist intentions it is also necessary to look at those policies which focussed on pediatric societal manipulation, or the transformation of Aboriginal society through the acculturation of children.

Residential Schools

Recently many of the more sinister aspects of residential school life have been documented and published. Numerous accounts of physical, psychological and sexual abuse by people who were responsible for children's care vividly illustrate the most personally tragic aspects of many Aboriginal student's residential schools experience. The role of residential schools in contributing to the haunting legacy of poverty, suicide, alcoholism, and loss of parenting skills among Aboriginal people may never be fully appreciated. The history of residential schools is more than the sum total of stories of personal tragedy, it also an aspect of the broader process of assimilation. It was part of a system that was designed to strip Aboriginal children of their traditional culture by removing them from the supposedly "harmful" influences of their parents and extended families.[25] As the educational historian Jean Barman has written, "while teachers and administrators of good will were able to ameliorate the worst aspects of the system for their pupils, all the individual good will in the world could not

Nineteenth century *Stó:lō* people participating in the Easter Passion Play at St. Mary's, Mission, organized by Catholic Missionaries.

have rescued a system that was fundamentally flawed."[26]

Indian residential schools were operated by both Catholic and Protestant Churches. Children were placed in residential schools because the *Xwelítem* believed it was in Aboriginal people's best interest to have their "character" redesigned after a European model. In *Stó:lō* territory there were two residential schools. The first, St. Mary's, was operated by the Catholic Church. Later the Methodists (now called the United Church of Canada)

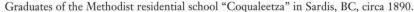

Graduates of the Methodist residential school "Coqualeetza" in Sardis, BC, circa 1890.

opened Coqualeetza residential school. Many *Stó:lō* children were also sent to other residential schools operating in places like Alberni, Kamloops, Kuper Island, Lytton and Sechelt.[27]

B.C.'s modern residential school history begins in 1863 when Father Florimond Gendre, a Roman Catholic Oblate priest, established St. Mary's residential school at Mission in the Fraser Valley. For the first years of its operations, St. Mary's only accepted male students but it did not take long for a second building to be constructed for girls. The girl's school was operated by the Sisters of St. Ann.[28] As previously mentioned, St. Mary's residential school was an extension of the earlier missionary activities of Father Leon Fouquet who had begun working among the *Stó:lō* in 1861. The Oblate priests modeled their activities after the efforts of seventeenth century Catholic Jesuit missionaries in Paraguay who had sought to establish "model Christian village communities." Graduates of the Jesuit's schools were encouraged to settle near the Catholic missions where, it was hoped, they would adopt a European lifestyle.

St. Mary's residential school was named after the biblical prostitute "Mary," who had been "saved" from a life of sin by Christ. The selection of this name provides insight into the way the *Xwelítem* viewed the *Stó:lō*. The Catholics had been invited to establish their residential school by the colonial government. The government hoped missionaries would be able to save the *Stó:lō* from "whiskey pedlars" and other unscrupulous *Xwelítem* who had followed the gold miners into *Stó:lō* territory during the 1858 gold rush. The *Stó:lō* were viewed as contemporary reflections of the Biblical St. Mary – an innocent woman who had been corrupted by immoral men. Provided with the opportunity to follow Christ and redeem herself, St. Mary had immediately reformed and became a model Christian citizen. Likewise, the *Stó:lō* were viewed as innocent children of the forest who had been debauched by the most despicable representatives of *Xwelítem* society. Missionaries anticipated that by removing *Stó:lō* children from their traditional "heathen" environment and the influence of the whiskey traders, they could "be saved" in Christ's faith. Once they had been saved from the *Xwelítem* whiskey pedlars the Catholic priests could direct their efforts toward replacing traditional *Stó:lō* spirituality and culture with Catholic religion and European society. Placing them in

residential schools appeared to provide the best means of accomplishing this.

The idea of having children raised by foreigners in an isolated residential school was distressing for the *Stó:lō*. Traditionally, child rearing had been the prerogative and

The Coqualeetza Residential School boys' dormitory in the 1920's, Sardis, B.C.

responsibility of grandparents, great aunts, and uncles. Initially, some *Stó:lō* parents (primarily ones from high status families) did not allow their children to attend. For this reason, in the early years (before the government made residential school attendance compulsory) a large proportion of *Stó:lō* children who were taken by missionaries to either St. Mary's or Coqualeetza were from low status families, orphans, or sick children.[29] By the time the government legislated mandatory school attendance in 1884, and began to strictly enforce it after 1920,[30] several *Stó:lō* children had already been admitted to public day schools where they could return home each night. Yet, many *Stó:lō* children were still taken from their communities and raised in institutions where they were deprived of their family's love and frequently subjected to physical and sexual abuse.

Isolation from family was central to the residential school philosophy, to prevent children from adopting the culture of their parents. However, the policy was severely misguided. Children raised in institutions were not provided with the opportunity to develop healthy family relationships. Even the kindest and best intentioned priest or nun could never replace the love and emotional connection provided by a parent. Because *Stó:lō* children in residential schools were never parented they never learned to become parents themselves:

I didn't even know my brothers and sisters were there. I didn't really have a close relationship with them. I never had a close relationship with my mother and I never developed a close relationships with any of my cousins either, whether they were at home or school or wherever, just because of the way we were raised. The residential school experience resulted in the total destruction of family structure... They basically took away the family experiences that I should have enjoyed and should have been able to pass on to my kids. I know that because of my experiences at residential school I didn't treat one of my older kids very well at all...

At residential school I was taught that punishment is supposed to make you do something and make you change. Because of learning these things I lost my traditional family values. Parents should be able to deal with their children in a better manner than how I was treated... When I became a parent I probably realized to a certain extent that I wasn't doing the right thing all the time. But it wasn't until after my older son moved out, and eventually died, that I thought about things, about how I was treated. It was then that I realized that you can't change what's done. My son was killed by a couple of people after he moved out of our house. To a certain extent, the way I treated him probably helped him to move away.[31] 😊

It was this "destruction of family" which many *Stó:lō* people refer to as the most devastating legacy of Indian residential schools.

Part of the residential school assimilation process involved training *Stó:lō* children to become good agricultural farm hands and industrial labourers for the growing *Xwelítem* economy. This became especially true after the federal government assumed administrative responsibility for residential schools in 1884. With federal administration came federal funding. However, Ottawa supported Aboriginal students at a much lower rate than the province supported *Xwelítem* students.[32] For this reason Indian residential school had to generate much of their own operating costs. To do this they used their students as labourers (typically farming or taking in laundry) with the proceeds going to the school.

In addition to lower funding, residential schools also emphasized industrial training over academics because it was commonly thought that Aboriginal students were unsuited to intellectual life. Racist public attitudes prevented Aboriginal people from being seen as equals. They were regarded as members of an inferior race and as such the federal government was not prepared to waste money on educating Aboriginal children for

careers they would never be socially accepted into.

Finally, it was assumed that traditional Aboriginal work habits – centering on seasonal changes in the environment – made Aboriginal students unsuited to regulated industrial labour. As such, it was thought Aboriginal children needed to be indoctrinated into the European institutionalized and industrialized mind set. Deviation from the prescribed model was not tolerated. Lives were regimented around the clock to inculcate a healthy work ethic. To ingrain the European work ethic it was considered a better use of time to have Aboriginal children spend more of their day working in the fields or in the laundry room than to have them sitting behind a desk learning less practical skills that they would never be able to use in a prejudice filled society. Personnel files were kept for each pupil and "offenses" were greeted with strict "punishments." The fragmentary records of one turn-of-the-century British Columbia Oblate residential school paint a vivid picture of the disciplinary techniques of the supposed "civilizers":[33]

Offence	Punishment
Insolence	Writing 400 lines
Communicating with girls	Half hour of kneeling
Playing in school	Kneeling down
Stubbornness	Kneeling during breakfast
Pulling carrots	Kneeling during supper
Chewing tobacco	Kneeling during supper
Breaking bounds	Public Reprimands
Using tobacco	Public Reprimand
Late	Confinement
Talking Indian	Work during recess
Laziness	Work during recess
Fighting	Extra Work
Talking in Bed	Extra Work
Indian Dancing	Extra Work
Playing forbidden games	Extra Work
Stealing apples	One day's confinement
Truancy	Confinement and humiliation
Breaking plaster	Three lashes
Disturbance in dormitory	A few slaps
Runaway	Five strokes of the lash
Breaking into girl's dorm	Expulsion
Setting fire to boy's dorm	Expulsion

It is interesting to note how closely the government policies which sought to undermine the positions of traditional Aboriginal leaders fit with the policies directed toward assimilating children. The provisions of the "Civilization Act" which enabled Indian Agents to remove from power any *síyá:m* who had more than one wife, owned slaves or participated in potlatches, meant that the only people who were legally qualified to become Chiefs were residential school graduates. They could read and write English, and had not incurred a debt by potlatching, therefore were not considered incompetent. Because they had been educated as Christians and did not

You Are Asked To Witness

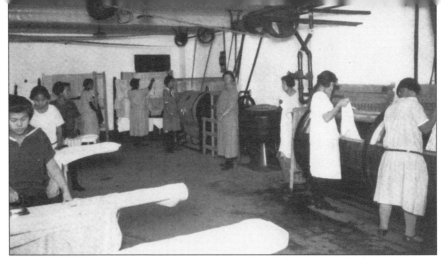

own slaves or have more than one wife they were not considered immoral. In this way the Indian Agents replaced many traditional *siyá:m* with people who had been raised and trained in a completely non-traditional environment.

By the 1950's, after the Indian Act had been revised to allow Aboriginal people to hire lawyers and practise their traditional ceremonial and spiritual activities, Aboriginal people began to articulate their dissatisfaction with residential school education. While the *Xwelítem* government was not ready to abandon its policy of assimilating

Aboriginal girls working in the laundry of the Coqualeetza Residential School, Sardis, B.C.

Aboriginal children, the general public was becoming more sensitive to the injustice of providing Aboriginal children with a second rate education. Studies showed that many residential school teachers had been rejected by the public school system. The obvious injustice of a system which claimed to prepare students for integration into mainstream society, but which had inferior academic training standards made it difficult for even the most dedicated supporter of the residential school system to defend its existence. As a result, the federal government began closing down Indian residential schools and integrating Aboriginal children into the public school system. In an odd way, the motivation for closing the residential schools stemmed not from an abandonment of the assimilation policy, but from a distorted perception that the assimilation process had been successfully completed.

By the late 1960's the illusion that the assimilation process had been successful was generally accepted by federal politicians and bureaucrats. In 1969, under the leadership of Prime Minister Pierre Trudeau and Minister of Indian Affairs, Jean Chretien, the government unveiled a major policy proposal – the infamous "White Paper." This document proposed that within five years the entire Department of Indian Affairs would be dissolved and all Aboriginal rights abolished. Assimilation would be complete – Aboriginal culture was believed to be extinct.

The government genuinely appeared to have expected Aboriginal people to celebrate the supposed success of the assimilation policy, and the eradication of Aboriginal society and culture. Instead, Aboriginal people throughout Canada rejected the "White Paper" and what it stood for. The "White Paper" acted as a lightning rod, focus-

Class photo of the Coqualeetza Residential School Brass Band, which performed throughout the Fraser Valley.

ing Aboriginal resentment and providing an avenue and opportunity for the reassertion of Aboriginal distinctiveness and identity. Until this time, many Aboriginal people had felt overwhelmed by the assimilationist society around them. To succeed, even to get along, they tried to hide their Aboriginal ancestry and cultural identity. As Soowahlie Elder Wesley Sam explained, for the generation growing up in the pre-White Paper era "no one wanted to be a chief. It was bad enough having whites treat you differently because you were Indian. You didn't want to make matters worse by being really Indian; by being Chief."[34]

The "White Paper" made it clear to Aboriginal leaders that unless they vigorously asserted their Aboriginal rights and openly expressed their unique cultural identity, they could soon cease to be an identifiable people. The feelings of cultural inadequacy and personal shame experienced by many Aboriginal people as a result of residential school and government assimilation policy needed to be challenged and overturned. To accomplish this, a number of regional and national Aboriginal organizations were formed to advocate Aboriginal rights before provincial and federal authorities. One of these was the Union of British Columbia Indian Chiefs. More locally, the Chilliwack Area Indian Council and the Vancouver Alliance Council were formed. Later, the Chilliwack Area Indian Council evolved into the *Stó:lō* Nation.

In the face of united Aboriginal opposition, the government reversed its "White Paper" policy proposals. They acknowledged that no one group of people have the right to impose their culture, values, and belief system onto another. The government publicly apologized for insulting and patronizing Aboriginal people, and took the first hesitant steps towards dismantling over a century of assimilation initiatives. Over the next three decades the federal and provincial governments recognized that Aboriginal people have the right to exist as self-governing, culturally unique entities within the Canadian fed-

eration. In British Columbia, where few treaties have been signed, formal negotiations are occurring between federal and provincial representatives and Aboriginal communities. This will allow BC Aboriginal people to receive compensation, as happened in all other parts of Canada, for the loss of their exclusive use of their traditional land and resources. It will also allow Aboriginal people to play a meaningful role in the management of the remaining natural resources within their territories, thereby ensuring that resources will be preserved for future generations, and Aboriginal communities will become economically self-sufficient.

Clearly, the government's assimilation policies had a significant and devastating impact upon *Stó:lō* society. In many ways the position of the *sí:yá:m* were greatly undermined as non-Aboriginal Indian agents and missionaries assumed ever increasing responsibility for regulating the lives of Aboriginal people. Ironically, however, at the same time that the government was seeking to undermine and subjugate Aboriginal leadership, other factors were acting to enhance and institutionalize the position of the *sí:yá:m* vis a vis those people who had held positions of respect and leadership over other aspects of *Stó:lō* life. For example, by the end of the nineteenth century, the imposition of British/Canadian law had effectively ended Aboriginal inter-community wars and raids. *Stomex*, the traditional leaders of raiding parties then ceased to have a purpose. Likewise, traditional *Stó:lō* doctors became somewhat discredited when they were unable to effectively treat introduced bacterial and viral infections. This loss of status was compounded by the growing influence of *Xwelítem* physicians.

Despite the assimilationist policies, in many ways *sí:yá:m* were among the only traditional leaders to find a place in the new *Xwelítem* dominated society. And so while many *sí:yá:m* were pushed aside by government legislation, others, by converting to Christianity and becoming priest appointed "Church Chiefs" or attending residential school

The Union Of British Columbia Indian Chiefs formed after the release of federal government's "White Paper".

You Are Asked To Witness

and then being elected or appointed "chiefs" by the Indian agent, were able to accentuate the traditional responsibilities of the *sí:yá:m* under the new and more institutionalized title of "Chief."

3 THE CONTEMPORARY *STÓ:LŌ* NATION – CREATING SELF-GOVERNMENT ■

Understanding some of the processes and historical events which shaped the way the *Stó:lō* have governed themselves, and been governed by others over the past 150 years, provides a context for appreciating the contemporary structure of the *Stó:lō* Nation. The Canadian Constitution recognizes that Aboriginal people have the right to be self-governing. This right is not based upon their "race," but, like all other Aboriginal rights, upon Aboriginal people's prior occupation of Canada. However, the Constitution does not define self-government. For the *Stó:lō*, self-government is something being achieved and implemented incrementally. As *Stó:lō* Elder, and Chief of the Yeqwyeqwi:ws community, Frank Malloway explains that

Self-government is controlling your own resources and being able to take control of your lives. It means being able to develop land the way you want, and to use money as you see fit. To be able to decide things without Ottawa having to check and then rubber stamp everything. 🔲

Frank Malloway's sentiments are echoed in the words of *Stó:lō* Grand Chief Clarence Pennier, who is also the Executive Director of Aboriginal Rights and Title Department of the *Stó:lō* Nation. He explains that

We have to look at the past to see how things were organized and then look at today and ask how we want to change. We have to have more control over how land is developed and over how resources are extracted. We have to look after the environment for our children's children. Elders have to become more involved and have a larger role in the community.[35] 🔲

Steven Point, Chief of the Skowkale Community and *Yewal Siyá:m* (Chief's Representative) for the entire *Stó:lō* Nation, discusses self-government in these terms:

We want to be self-governing. We believe that our rights to self-government, our sovereignty as a nation, has never been affected. Our rights have never been extinguished even though foreign countries have come here and established governments and taken our lands.

...re-asserting the right to hunt and fish and trap does not go far enough... If it is to become a reality, self-government must be a process, not a destination. There must be an internal change which transcends where we were as wards of the government, to political organizations pressuring government, to actually becoming self-governing.

Self-government is becoming a reality. We are taking on more jurisdiction, more responsibilities. We are becoming self-governing.[36] 🔲

Stó:lō Chiefs at the *Stó:lō* Nation unity ceremony of 1994.

Appendix:
The Contemporary *Stó:lō* Nation

The following is a brief description of the *Stó:lō* Nation organization as it exists in 1996. If you require more detailed information, contact the *Stó:lō* Nation directly and request to speak with a representative for one of the departments.

Political Arm

To facilitate the "process" of self-government, *Stó:lō* communities have organized themselves into the *Stó:lō* Nation, an umbrella organization which provides services to its 21 member communities. It is composed of a political arm and a bureaucratic arm, much the same way the federal provincial or municipal government is. The political arm, like the Canadian federal government, consists of three branches.

i) *Lálém Te Stó:lō Sí:yá:m*
   ("House of Respected *Stó:lō* Leaders")

The first branch of the political arm of the *Stó:lō* Nation is the *Lálém Te Stó:lō Sí:yá:m*. It is based upon proportional representation. Each *Stó:lō* community has at least one representative and larger communities have up to three votes. It is in the *Lálém Te Stó:lō Sí:yá:m* that *Stó:lō* legislation and laws originate. This is the main political body of the *Stó:lō* Nation. The chiefs in the *Lálém Te Stó:lō Sí:yá:m* elect a five person cabinet called the "Special

Chiefs' Council" (SCC). It consists of one representative for each bureaucratic department of the *Stó:lō* Nation. These representatives are "Portfolio Chiefs," who oversee the bureaucratic or business operations of the *Stó:lō* Nation and report back to the *Lálém Te Stó:lō Sí:yá:m*. The SCC is chaired by the *Stó:lō* Nation Chief's Representative. This person is the primary political spokesperson for the *Stó:lō* Nation, and directly accountable to the *Stó:lō* chiefs.

ii) *Lálém Te Sí:yelyó:lexwa* ("House of Elders")

The second branch of the political arm of the *Stó:lō* Nation is the *Lálém Te Sí:yelyó:lexwa* At least one Elder from every *Stó:lō* community sits on this council. It functions in a manner similar to the way the Canadian Senate was designed to operate. The *Lálém Te Stó:lō Sí:yá:m* is also responsible for overseeing all matters pertaining to culture and tradition.

iii) House of Justice

The final branch of *Stó:lō* Nation's political arm is the "House of Justice." This body is not yet fully functional, but will deal with justice issues of particular concern to *Stó:lō* people. *Stó:lō* concepts of justice emphasize "rehabilitation." Many non-Aboriginal people find the thought of a separate justice system for the *Stó:lō* disconcerting. *Stó:lō* leaders assure people that they have nothing to fear from a parallel *Stó:lō* justice system. One important function of the "House of Justice" will be to deal with justice issues that are Aboriginal in nature. For the *Stó:lō*, certain songs and stories are "owned" by particular individuals or

MAP KEY	
BLDG #	**BLDG NAME**
1	Siya:m Lalem 3 storey brick
2	Stó:lō Nation Fisheries
3	Coqualeetza Shop
4	Offices (rented)
5	Stó:lō Centre 3 storey brick
6	Living Quarters
7	Church 1 storey brick
8a	Workshop Stucco w/chimney
8b	Meeting Hall Stucco w/chimney
9	Storage
10	Storage
11	Maintenance
12	Stó:lō Shxweli
13	Counselling Centre
14	Storage
15	Stolo Employments Service/PREP
16	Alternate School Classroom
17	Offices (rented) Dark Brown
18	A.B.E. Classroom Lt. tan w/green trim
19	Shxwt'a:selhawtxw
20	Coqualeetza
21	Coqualeetza
22	Coqualeetza Longhouse
23	Alternate School Classroom
24	Alternate School Classroom
25	
26	Kitchen/bathroom

Partial map of the Coqualeetza grounds showing the *Stó:lō* Nation.

families. If a *Stó:lō* person were to go to a provincial court house and ask a judge to adjudicate who had a right to sing a song or tell a story, the judge would be at a loss as how to proceed. Similarly, *Stó:lō* families "own" specific fishing sites along the Fraser River. These rights are based upon complex family laws and customs which the mainstream legal system is unfamiliar with. Such matters are very serious to *Stó:lō* people. Through the *Stó:lō* "House of Justice," these and other culturally specific justice matters could be dealt with by *Stó:lō* people within a *Stó:lō* justice setting.

Similarly, other justice and legal matters may one day also be dealt with by the *Stó:lō* "House of Justice." Property crimes and violent crimes between *Stó:lō* people may be handled more effectively within the context of *Stó:lō* justice system.

Administrative/Business Arm

The administrative arm of the *Stó:lō* Nation is divided into five departments:

Stó:lō Nation Special Chiefs' Council, 1995.

1) Health and Social Services;
2) Community Development and Education;
3) Aboriginal Rights and Title;
4) *Xolhmi:lh* (Child Welfare); and
5) Finance.

Each department is headed by an executive director. Together the directors are in charge of the "business" of the *Stó:lō* Nation.

i) Health and Social Development

The Health and Social Development Department is the largest of the *Stó:lō* bureaucracies in terms of staff. Their full time employees include nurses, psychologists, addictions counsellors, social workers, community support workers, and cultural support workers.

ii) Community Development and Education

The Community Development and Education Department is the largest department, with regards to the programs they run. Their staff deal with job training, life skill training, economic and human development, adult education, school based education initiatives, community planning, and housing development.

iii) Aboriginal Rights & Title

The Aboriginal Rights & Title department is concerned with issues of heritage management, treaty negotiations, archaeology, history, justice, language revival, fisheries, and some education and cross-cultural awareness matters. Much of their time is spent dealing with issues such as urban expansion, and heritage overviews for proposed development sites.

iv) *Xolhmi:lh* (Child Welfare)

Until recently Aboriginal children were the victims of federal and provincial jurisdictional disputes. The Canadian Constitution defines child welfare as a provincial responsibility. However, all matters dealing with Aboriginal people fall under federal jurisdiction. Aboriginal children therefore "fell between the cracks." As part of the self-government process, responsibility for child welfare has been transferred directly to the *Stó:lō* Nation. The *Xolhmi:lh* program combines traditional *Stó:lō* child care techniques with social work to help recreate healthy families.

v) Finance

The *Stó:lō* Nation Finance Department provides financial support to all other departments.

Indian Bands

There are currently of 24 *Stó:lō* villages. These village communities are referred to as "Indian bands," a legal description created by the Canadian government. Villages were arranged into administrative units by the federal government to better regulate finances and services. Indian bands within *Stó:lō* territory have the option of formally joining the *Stó:lō* Nation or remaining "independent." There are 24 *Stó:lō* bands between the Fraser Canyon and Langley, three of these were "independent" at the time this chapter was written in 1996. All *Stó:lō* communities communicate and share resources regardless of their affiliation with *Stó:lō* Nation.

Recommended Further Readings:

Wilson Duff, *The Upper Stó:lō Indians,* 1952.
Wayne Suttles, *Coast Salish Essays,* 1990.
Paul Tennant, *Aboriginal People and Politics,* 1990.
Cecilia Haig Brown, *Resistance and Renewal,* 1988.

Footnotes

1   Wilson Duff, *The Upper Stalo Indians of the Fraser Valley, British Columbia,* (Victoria: British Columbia Provincial Museum, 1952), pp. 90-91.
2   Wayne Suttles, "Private knowledge, Morality, and Social Classes among the Coast Salish," in Wayne Suttles, ed., *Coast Salish Essays,* (Vancouver: Talonbooks, 1987), p.6.
3   Duff, p.82.

4   Wayne Suttles, "The Central Coast Salish," in Wayne Suttles, ed., *Handbook of North American Indians, Vol. 7, The Northwest Coast,* (Washington DC: Smithsonian Institute, 1990), p. 465.

5   Ibid, p.465.

6   Dr. Brent Galloway, personal communication. November 27, 1995.

7   Duff, p.81.

8   Duff, p.81.

9   Dr. Michael Kew, personal communication, November 27, 1995.

10 Charles Hill-Tout, *The Salish People* (Vancouver: Talonbooks, 1978), p.358. Moreover, as previously explained, special doctors, or "spiritual leaders" assumed principal responsibility for the emotional and spiritual well being of *Stó:lõ* communities, and other men were responsible for raiding and counter raiding enemies in other villages.

11 Duff, p.89.

12 See Wayne Suttles, "The Plateau Prophet Dance Among the Coast Salish," in Wayne Suttles, *Coast Salish Essays,* (Vancouver: Talonbooks, 1987), pp.152-198. The lack of missionary activity should not be taken as an indication that Christian influences did not reach the Fraser Valley.

13 "Records of the Oblates of Mary Immaculate," Letter of July, 16, 1862, (copy atSNA).

14 ibid.

15 *Shxw'õwhamel* Elder Ralph George, personal communication. Discussing the news media coverage of his fight against drugs. September 27, 1996.

16 James W. Redford, *Attendance at Indian Residential Schools in British Columbia, 1890-1920,* (M.A. Dept. of History, U.B.C., 1978), p.32.

17 "Records of the Oblates of Mary Immaculate," Letter from R.P. Marshal to R.P. Durieu, February 12, 1871, Photocopy in SNA.

18 Thomas Crosby, *Among the An-ko-me-nums; or Flathead Tribes of Indians of the Pacific Coast,* (Toronto: William Briggs, 1907), p.189.

19 "Records of the Oblates of Mary Immaculate," by Ed. Peytavin, OMI, "Report on the Activities of 1886, Photocopy on file, SNA.

20 See Brian Thom *The Living and the Dead.* (MA Thesis, Department of Anthropology, U.B.C. 1995), Photocopy on file at SNA.

21 The Civilization Act's full name was "An Act to Encourage the Gradual Civilization of the Indians of this Province, and to Amend the Laws Respecting Indians, S.P.C. 1857."

22 Section 140 of the Indian Act.

23 Letter from Delvin to Vowell, 1896; Cited in Forest E. LaVioliette, *The Struggle for Survival: Indian Cultures and the Protestant Ethic in British Columbia,* (Toronto: UofT Press, 1973), p. 70.

24 Cited in Paul Tennant, *Aboriginal Peoples and Politics: The Indian land Question in British Columbia, 1849-1989,* (Vancouver, UBC Press, 1990), p.101.

25 See Cecelia Haig-Brown, *Resistance and Renewal: Surviving the Indian Residential School* (Vancouver: Tillicum Library, 1988).

26 Jean Barman, "Schooled for Inequality: The Education of British Columbia Aboriginal Children," in Jean Barman et al. ed., *Children, Teachers and Schools in the History of British Columbia,* (Calgary: Detselig Enterprises Ltd., 1995).

27 It is interesting to note that nearly a century before the 1858 gold rush, Spanish friars at Nootka Sound had developed similar strategies for acculturating the Aboriginal population of the West Coast of Vancouver Island. The Spanish determined that to expedite the adoption of Spanish culture Nuu-chah-nulth children had to be removed from the influences of their families. To facilitate this, the Friars transported a number of children south to San Diego, California and placed them in special residential schools. However, when European geopolitical power brokering resulted in Spain "ceding" the Northwest Coast to Britain in 1792, these children became forgotten tragedies of colonialism. Their fate remains a mystery to this day. John Kendrick, *The Men with Wooden Feet.* (Toronto: NC Press Ltd., 1985), Chapter 7.

28 St. Mary's was also the last residential school to close, graduating its last class in 1968. The school's dormitory housed *Stó:lõ* children from rural communities who attended Mission High School until 1984.

29 Jacqueline Gresko, "Creating Little Dominions Within the Dominion: Early Catholic Indian Schools in Saskatchewan and British Columbia," in Jean Barman, et al., *Indian Education in Canada, Vol. 1: The Legacy.* p.98.

30 Redford, pp. 15, 30, 38-41.

31 Anonymous Elder interviewed by Kun-Hui Ku, May 25, 1995. Transcript on file at SNA.

32 Jean Barman, "Schooled for Inequality: The Education of British Columbia Aboriginal Children," in Jean Barman, et al., *Children, Teachers and Schools in the History of British Columbia.* (Calgary: Detselig Enterprises Ltd., 1995).

33 "Cowichan Agency at Industrial School at Kuper Island. 1895-1897." Manuscript on file at British Columbia Archives and Records Service.

34 Wes Sam in conversation with Keith Thor Carlson, August 3, 1992.

35 Clarence Pennier (Chief of Scowlitz) in conversation with Gloria Morgan, December 22, 1994. transcript on file at *Stó:lõ* Nation Archives.

36 Steven Point, (Chief of Skowkale, Stó:lo Nation Chief's Representative) in conversation with Gloria Morgan, December 22, 1994. Transcript on File at SNA.

Stó:lō People
and the development
o f   t h e
B.C. Wage
Labour Economy

Keith Thor Carlson ■ John Lutz

INTRODUCTION

Few, would question the assumption that understanding *Stó:lō* culture and history requires an appreciation of the *Stó:lō* economy. What might not be so obvious is the argument put forth in this chapter which states that understanding the growth and development of British Columbia's modern wage labour economy requires an appreciation of the role played by Aboriginal people, and in particular *Stó:lō* men. What might also prove surprising to some is the extent to which the *Stó:lō* who participated in B.C.'s early post-fur trade wage labour economy were able to integrate new economic opportunities into their traditional economic and ceremonial life.

As background to these broader issues, this chapter begins by differentiating the traditional *Stó:lō* economy from the *Xwelítem* capitalist economy. It goes on to document how their unique traditional skills and the shortage of other labourers enabled *Stó:lō* men to initially dominate the labour and job markets. It shows that the wealth they acquired through these activities enriched their traditional economy and allowed the potlatch ceremonial to flourish. As time passed increased labour competition through immigration, racist hiring practices, and new technologies caused the *Stó:lō* to become marginalized from the new economy which, only a generation earlier, they had dominated. Christian missionaries and the Colonial government sought to assimilate

Stó:lō children, moving them away from their traditional seasonal economic lifestyle and replacing it with a *Xwelítem* style industrial mind set – work six days per week, ten hours

Many *Stó:lō* men profited from the construction of the C.P.R.

per day. To accomplish this they established "Indian Industrial Residential Schools" as discussed in the previous chapter.

Understanding this process enables one to appreciate the economic and social marginalization of many *Stó:lō* people today. Their communities continue to be plagued by extreme unemployment rates (50% - 80%); alcohol and chemical dependency; abuse; and so on. In recent years changes have begun to occur whereby, through the self-government process, the *Stó:lō* are regaining a meaningful role in the *Xwelítem* dominated economy while continuing to participate in their traditional social and economic activities.

1. THE EUROPEAN CAPITALIST ECONOMY AND THE *STÓ:LŌ* ECONOMY – A COMPARISON ■

We are all relatively familiar with the fundamental principles of a capitalist economy. In its most basic form, capitalism presupposes that people produce goods desired by others to sell or exchange at a profit. The capitalist economy is based upon hired labour and private ownership with the ultimate goal being to accumulate wealth.

In a capitalist economy wealth often takes the form of individually-owned property (such as a house or car), and prestige items (such as art work, jewellery, and fashion clothing). Of course, wealth can also take the form of monetary units such as Canadian dollars, which can be exchanged for other items. These forms of wealth all help determine a person's status. Generally, the greater a person's wealth the higher his or her status.

The pre-contact *Stó:lō* economy differed from the

You Are Asked To Witness

Upper class *Stó:lō* families inherited productive fishing spots.

European symbols of wealth and status;
Hatley Park, the second castle of Vancouver Island
Coal Baron Robert Dunsmuir.

European capitalist economy as did their concepts of property and wealth. The *Stó:lō* economy was intimately linked to social and ceremonial activities. Upper class families owned the most important *Stó:lō* property collectively. Examples of this kind of property included such things as highly productive berry patches, Fraser canyon fishing spots, and fish weirs. However, the *Stó:lō* did not consider that anyone owned resources such as salmon and land mammals. Lower class people could fish from less productive locations and pick berries at more remote patches. Similarly, names, while associated with individuals, were "owned" by families and carried with them rights to particular family-controlled resources such as fishing spots and berry patches. Such property was not bought and sold but rather was inherited or accessed through carefully arranged marriages.

In addition to family-controlled property, individual *Stó:lō* people "owned" special songs associated with their "spirit power." Other examples of private property, such as canoes, weapons, slaves, clothing, and tools, were acquired for reasons similar to those of the Europeans, namely to demonstrate wealth. However, whereas Europeans typically enhanced their status by simply accumulating wealth in the form of prestige items, the *Stó:lō* defined and enhanced their status primarily by giving

Elder Myra Sam collecting "swamp tea" leaves.

wealth away through a process of redistribution. In this way the prestige aspects of the *Stó:lō* economy were similar to the social status wealthy European philanthropists gained by giving their wealth away to charity.

The *Stó:lō* redistributed wealth in two main ways. The first and most elaborate manner was at a potlatch ceremony or a *stl'éleq*. Entire extended families pooled their accumulated prestige items (canoes, blankets, tools), to host a potlatch. The hosting family invited other upper class people from distant and neighbouring villages to

Caring for children.

attend and share their hospitality.

Vast amounts of wealth were given away at these ceremonies. The more given away, the more a family demonstrated not only its generosity, but primarily, its ability to accumulate large amounts of wealth. People understood that in order to acquire wealth the family must have worked hard. Redistributing wealth elevated and reinforced a high ranking family's upper class status. On these occasions, the upper class also validated their claims to inherited property resources by publicly describing the history of their family's control over particular fishing sites, and other properties. Lower class families, by comparison, found it difficult to accumulate wealth and host potlatches for they did not have access to productive fishing and resource collecting locations. In this way, their lower status was noticed by others and reinforced within the community. Elders explained that lower class people were "lazy people" who came from families that had "forgotten their history."[1] In other words, because they were unable to demonstrate that they had family rights to special resource collecting locations, they forfeited their rights to use valuable fishing and berry picking spots.

Aside from a potlatch, another manner of redistributing wealth was through extended family exchange networks. People from one village travelled to visit members of their extended family in distant villages to trade locally-obtained resources. For example, people from villages in the Fraser canyon brought dried salmon to trade for cranberries with relatives who lived near the Fraser delta.

A *Stó:lō* man dip netting for salmon.

You Are Asked To Witness

2 SEASONAL ASPECTS OF THE TRADITIONAL STÓ:LŌ ECONOMY ■

Many aspects of *Stó:lō* society were associated with seasonal activities. For example, while trout and other species of fish were available year round, they were generally not depended upon throughout the winter. Instead, the *Stó:lō* preferred to harvest great numbers of salmon during the late summer as the fish migrated to their spawning grounds. They then either wind-dried or smoked the salmon to preserve it for winter consumption. Likewise, they collected many berries, nuts, and tubers during the late summer and early autumn for winter use. During the winter months, after the previous season's hard work had been completed, most of the *Stó:lō* spiritual ceremonies including potlatches took place. In the spring, people harvested green shoots, nettles, and bulbs.

This simplistic summary of *Stó:lō* seasonal activities demonstrates how inseparable economic activity was from spiritual and social life. Everything had its proper time and place. For many *Stó:lō* the seasonal aspect of their traditional society continues relatively unaltered to this day.

Stó:lō economic activities, like social structures, are based upon the extended family. Parents, aunts, uncles, nephews, nieces, cousins, grandparents, great-aunts and uncles frequently operated as a collective whole. To promote the well-being of the extended family, they monitored and regulated family resources, pooled labour and equipment, and defended one another from hostile outsiders.

Within *Stó:lō* society an elaborate division of labour continues to exist. In traditional times, women were primarily responsible for the collection and processing of berries, nuts, bulbs, and tubers. They also cleaned and processed salmon caught by the men. Wealthy upper class families often acquired slaves, most of whom were female, who also assisted in these activities. Older women looked after the rearing and early education of children. Men who had acquired special spirit power and become especially skilled at hunting were referred to as *Tewít* – "specialist hunters." In *Stó:lō* society there were also health care specialists, approximately half of whom were women. Specially trained doctors called *Shxwlá:m* attended to people's emotional and spiritual requirements. Other types of doctors protected and healed the community in a variety of other ways, as doctors in specialized fields do today.

3 ABORIGINAL PEOPLE AND THE NEW WAGE LABOUR ECONOMY ■

The Fur and Salmon Trade Era

Stó:lō people began exchanging furs with European maritime fur traders in Georgia Strait in the 1790's. In 1827, the Hudson's Bay Company (HBC) established Fort Langley as a permanent trading post on the lower Fraser River. Aboriginal participation was essential to the economic success of the European fur and salmon trade. *Stó:lō* men hunted and trapped, while women cured animal pelts to exchange for European manufactured goods, available at Fort Langley. They also supplied Fort Langley with a huge quantity of salmon each summer. These trading activities were simply extensions of the exchange networks that the *Stó:lō* had established with other Aboriginal communities before the arrival of Europeans.

Height of Winter Ceremonies

Primary Spirit Quest Season begins

Gather green shoots

Early Salmon Runs

Beginning of Winter Dance Season

Main Potlatches

Gather Nuts

WINTER

SPRING

AUTUMN

Gather Nettles

Gather Bulbs

Gather Potatoes

Families relocate near Berry Patches.

SUMMER

Catch and Wind Dry Salmon

Gather Berries

Families visit Canyon

Stó:lō social and economic activities are associated with specific seasons.

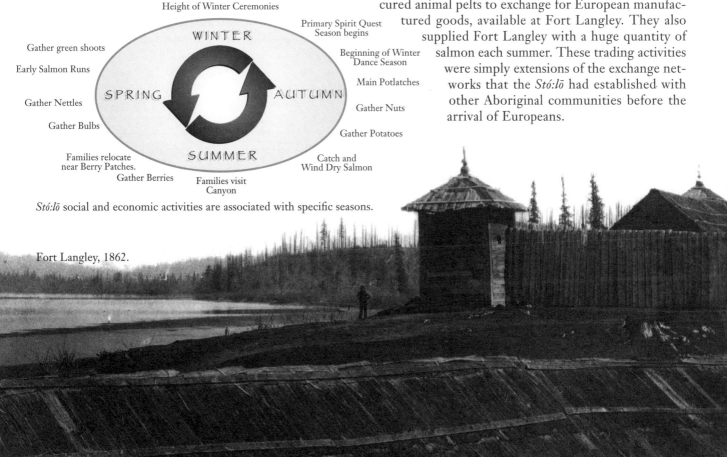

Fort Langley, 1862.

The men at Fort Langley expected *Stó:lō* people to dedicate a great deal of their time to the fur trade, and were disappointed when this did not occur. While the *Stó:lō* supplied the fort with some furs, they did not increase their hunting and trapping activities to accommodate the Hudson's Bay Company's demands. Trapping had always been a part of *Stó:lō* life, but the *Stó:lō* were not about to alter their lifestyle drastically to supply Fort Langley with furs. The European prestige goods that the *Stó:lō* exchanged for furs were desirable for re-distribution at status-enhancing potlatches, but they were not essential. The Hudson's Bay Company's profits were limited by *Stó:lō* people's reluctance to dramatically increase their beaver trapping. As a result, the HBC considered abandoning Fort Langley soon after it opened. However, Chief Trader James McMillan observed that while the *Stó:lō* were unwilling to trade heavily in furs, they were willing to extend their traditional salmon trading activities to the fort. In 1827 and 1828, the *Stó:lō* brought so many salmon to Fort Langley that McMillan's successor, Archibald Macdonald, shrewdly redirected trading activities to take advantage of traditional *Stó:lō* trade patterns. In August 1829 *Stó:lō* people provided Fort Langley with 7000 fresh salmon and the HBC hurriedly made plans to begin salting and exporting the fish to posts as far away as Hawaii.

American miners operating a gold dredge on the Fraser River, circa 1863.

Over the years, the export of salted salmon became Fort Langley's primary economic activity.[2] In addition to salmon and furs, the *Stó:lō* supplied the fort with cranberries, hazelnuts, and labour. Part of Fort Langley's official responsibilities involved supplying other more remote Hudson's Bay Company forts with farm produce. As farming required primarily short bursts of seasonal labour, it did not make financial sense for the HBC to send more full time European employees to the Fort. Instead, company officials found it convenient and profitable to employ *Stó:lō* people as seasonal labourers. These seasonal farming activities fit easily into the *Stó:lō* economic cycle. Consequently, the *Stó:lō* quickly became indispensable to the fort's operations. Seasonal work at Fort Langley became so profitable that upper-class *Stó:lō* families even began renting their slaves out to the fort as labourers.[3]

The Gold Rush

In 1858 the Fraser river gold rush dramatically altered the region's economy. When word first reached American towns in March 1858 that gold had been discovered in the gravel bars of the Fraser Valley, it caused a mass migration to the region. Around Puget Sound, "mills shut down, soldiers deserted their posts and sailors abandoned ship."[4] By April, news had spread to California causing convoys of ships loaded with gold seekers to head northward to the Fraser River. Between May 19 and July 1, 1858, nineteen steam ships, nine sailing vessels, and fourteen decked vessels transported 6,133 men from San Francisco to Victoria, while thousands more trekked northward along the coast on foot or in small private vessels. On a single day in July, over 2,800 miners arrived on two steamers in Victoria looking for smaller vessels to transport them to the Fraser River.[5] All told, over 30,000 miners arrived in *Stó:lō* territory between March and August 1858.[6]

Over 30,000 miners arrived in *Stó:lō* territory in the spring of 1858. The city of Yale, situated in the Fraser Canyon, sprang-up overnight.

Many Aboriginal people participated in the 1858 gold rush as independent miners.

Some *Stó:lō* people had been supplying Fort Langley with limited amounts of gold before 1858, but once they recognized the *Xwelítem* fascination with gold, many entrepreneuring *Stó:lō* became actively involved in mining. One witness described how all *Stó:lō* people living at the mouth of the canyon "moved down from Yale and camped on Hill's Bar (above Hope), about three hundred men, women and children, and they also commenced to wash for gold." Governor James Douglas reaffirmed this in a letter to London in early April 1858, stating that,

The search for gold and prospecting of the country had, up to the last dates from the interior been carried on by the Native Indian population, who are extremely jealous of the whites and strongly opposed to their digging the soil for gold. It is, however, worthy of remark and a circumstance highly honourable to the character of those savages that have on all occasions scrupulously respected the persons and property of the white visitors, at the same time that they have expressed a determination to reserve the gold for their own benefit...[7]

Governor Douglas also outlined how it was "impossible" to hire *Stó:lō* people as labourers, "as they are busy mining, and make between two and three dollars a day each man." This was several times the amount a skilled tradesman in Europe or the United States was earning at that time.

Within two years of the beginning of the gold rush, the gravel bars on the lower Fraser River had become exhausted, their supply of gold depleted. Many enterprising *Stó:lō* then found employment guiding, packing, and freighting supplies and people to new mines farther upstream. Miners and other newcomers highly valued traditional *Stó:lō* canoeing and orienteering skills, and some *Stó:lō* people took full advantage of the *Xwelítem*'s dependence on their knowledge, skill, and strength.

Road Construction Labourers

The construction of the Cariboo Road (which provided easy access to the gold mines in the interior of British Columbia through the Fraser Canyon), was a major engineering venture requiring many labourers. Being in the vast majority (by 1860 most of the 30,000 miners had moved out of *Stó:lō* territory), *Stó:lō* men earned money as road construction labourers. However, aside from menial tasks, *Stó:lō* men were also contracted to complete specialized tasks the *Xwelítem* newcomers were simply unable to perform. Such was the case in the construction of the Alexandra suspension bridge just upriver from Yale.[8] To transport the heavy cables up the treacherous canyon, a *Stó:lō* leader from Chilliwack known as "Captain John" organized a

Xwelítem mining activities often did irreparable damage to the environment. (Note the size of the miners on the hill side.)

The gold rush led to the building of the Cariboo Road. The *Stó:lō* provided a reliable labour force.

The Alexandra suspension bridge was built after *Stó:lō* people, working under contract for Captain John, transported the supplies up the perilous canyon.

crew and placed the giant cable spools on a platform between two large dugout freight canoes. When the canoes reached the head of navigation, the cable had to be reeled out in one long strand and slowly transported the remaining distance up the canyon over land. The *Stó:lō* crew placed the cable over their shoulders and, moving in unison, slowly 'snaked' the long heavy cargo to its destination.

Captain John's *Halq'eméylem* name was "*Swóles*", which means "getting rich." It was a fitting name given the fact that in a relatively short period of time Captain John's labour enabled him to save $2,000. With this money he was able to host a very impressive potlatch. By comparison colonial governor James Douglas' salary was only $1,000 that year.

Farming

Immediately following the gold rush, immigrant farmers from Britain, Continental Europe, and the United States began settling and cultivating land in the Fraser Valley. The *Stó:lō* had adopted the European potato generations earlier from the Hudson's Bay Company because it closely resembled their indigenous tuber crops. The potato required little care during its growing season and allowed the *Stó:lō* to participate in their seasonal activities. The *Stó:lō* showed little interest in agricultural pursuits that took them away from their traditional activities but

were willing to work as seasonal labourers on *Xwelítem* farms. Discussing the situation in 1879 the provincial Indian Commissioner wrote,

> The majority of the Indians on the Fraser River prefer working for the whites to cultivating their lands... During the fishing season these Indians earn from $1 to $2 dollars per diem which gives them a sufficiency of cash to supply themselves with all the necessities of life without resorting to the cultivation of the soil for a livelihood.[9]

As was the case for the earlier generation of *Stó:lō* people who worked at Fort Langley, it was easier and more profitable for them to work for *Xwelítem* farmers during planting and harvest season, than to cultivate crops of their own and compromise their involvement in fishing or other traditional activities. In the late 1800's, so few non-*Stó:lō* people were willing to accept farm labour jobs that the *Stó:lō* were able to demand lucrative wages for their labour. The money was then used to enhance their lifestyle as well as raise their social status through potlatching.

Canneries

Stó:lō participation in the newly introduced capitalist wage economy grew and diversified in the late-nineteenth century. Consistently, the majority of *Stó:lō* people elected to engage primarily in those activities that fit with their seasonal economic and social cycles. One new industry that particularly appealed to the *Stó:lō* in the late 1870s centred around the salmon canneries located near the mouth of the Fraser River.

Many *Stó:lō* people fished the early summer salmon runs to supply the canneries and fished the later runs to meet their own dietary and ceremonial needs. *Stó:lō* women provided the main source of labour inside the canneries where they worked for

Many of the *Stó:lō* found employment as seasonal farm labours.

You Are Asked To Witness

Stó:lō women

were essential

to the operation

of the canneries.

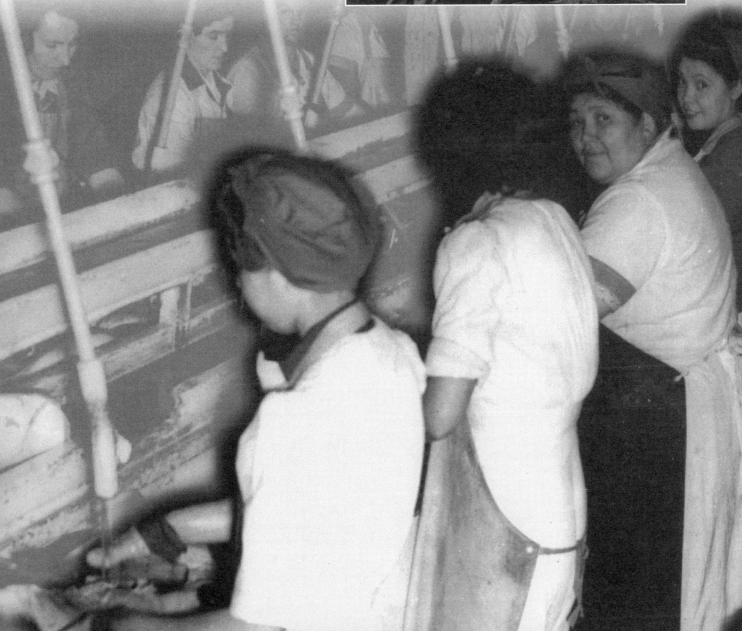

wages processing salmon caught by *Stó:lō* men. This division of labour was in keeping with the traditional *Stó:lō* division of labour.

Railroad Construction

Generally when people think about the construction of Canada's early railroads, they visualize Chinese immigrants toiling under horrendous working conditions. While this is an accurate image many people do not always realize that Aboriginal men also played a significant role in the development of the railway, working under identical conditions. Archival records indicate that nearly every *Stó:lō* adult male found employment in the construction of the Canadian Pacific Railroad (C.P.R.) between 1879 and 1885. B.C. Indian Commissioner I.W. Powell was told by one C.P.R. representative that over the course of the railway's construction "he had paid out nearly $300,000 for Indian labour alone." *Stó:lō* men supplied the C.P.R. with timbers for bridges and tunnels, worked as labourers laying down rails, and assisted in the masonry work reinforcing hillsides, among other tasks.[10]

Steam Ships/Paddle Wheelers

Long after the gold rush had ended *Stó:lō* men continued to be in high demand as pilots and deck hands on paddle wheelers and other steam ships carrying people and supplies between the growing *Xwelítem* communities along the banks of the lower Fraser River. In his reports, Indian Commissioner I.W. Powell described a situation in which *Stó:lō* deck hands could be obtained for $15 or $18 per month in 1883, whereas the following year the steamers were actually having difficulty attracting *Stó:lō* deck hands

for wages between $45 to $50 per month. This example dramatically illustrates the successful adaptation of *Stó:lō* people to the new economy. Economic opportunities were so great that *Stó:lō* men were able to demand relatively high wages for their skills.

Aside from actually working on the ships many of the *Stó:lō* accepted employment cutting fire wood for the steam boats and paddle wheelers. The big steamers burned up to four cords of wood an hour. At this rate of consumption is easy to imagine the constant requirement for more wood. There were "refuelling spots" all along the Fraser River, many of which were located on *Stó:lō* reserves.

Hop-picking

Hops became an important cash crop in the Fraser Valley in the late 1870's. Hop berries were essential ingredients in the growing beer brewing industry. From its inception, the *Stó:lō* men, women and children were central to the success of the hop industry as "pickers." They retained this position for seventy years, until they were replaced by automated picking machines in the 1940's.

Hops (*Humulus lupulus*), known as a flavouring for beer.

Like the canneries, hop-picking provided seasonal employment for entire *Stó:lō* families. The single-month picking season encouraged families to locate themselves right in the hop fields. Aboriginal people from all over the coast worked in the hop industry. As a result, the hop field gatherings, like the inter-village potlatch cere-

Hop yards provided the *Stó:lō* with an environment to continue practising traditional customs in a slightly modified context.

monies, enabled Aboriginal people from a broad geographic region to gather together for social, ceremonial, and economic activities. Families exchanged gifts, engaged in athletic competitions, and practiced spiritual activities. Running and canoe races, feasts, speeches, and information sharing were common and enjoyable features of the hop field gatherings.

Creating an Industrial Workforce:
Indian Residential/Industrial Schools

Government and church officials were interested in having *Stó:lō* people integrate themselves more fully into the new economy. They believed that if Aboriginal people did not assimilate into *Xwelítem* society, increasing contact with whiskey pedlars and other unscrupulous people would result in their physical extinction and/or social degradation. They reasoned that if *Stó:lō* people could be provided with certain skills and training, they would be better able to deal with the changes brought about by the arrival of *Xwelítem*. Foremost among the changes promoted was conversion to Christianity. Of almost equal importance was the teaching of basic academic and English language skills, specific job skills, and the development of an industrial worker's mind set (ie. acceptance

of a 10 hour work day, six days a week).

Xwelítem officials paternalistically hoped that during this process they could disassociate the *Stó:lō* from their traditional social and economic culture. The best way to accomplish this they believed was to establish residential/industrial schools where Aboriginal children could be institutionalized ten months of the year, and supervised 24 hours a day. The first such school to be established in British Columbia was St. Mary's, opened by the Oblate order of the Roman Catholic church in 1862 at what is now Mission. Operating until 1986, St. Mary's was also the last Indian residential school in B.C. to close. A second school, opened by the Methodists (later the United Church of Canada) was called *Coqualeetza*. Located in Chilliwack, it operated from 1880 and to the beginning of World War II.

The residential/industrial school curriculum emphasized two things, religious education and industrial training. During a typical day in a late nineteenth century Catholic residential school, boys and girls awoke at 6:00 am and attended church to pray. This was followed by breakfast and then Mass. The students then spent two hours studying English grammar and mathematics. Lunch was eaten at noon after which the boys were sent to work at either the farm, the carpenter shop, or the "cobbler shop". Girls worked the afternoon in the laundry or sewing rooms. At 4:00 pm all students received an hour of "religious instruction" before eating dinner. After the evening meal everyone received an hour of free playtime before "lights out" at 8:00 pm, after which no talking or reading was permitted. Each week students' chore schedules rotated between preparing meals, washing dishes, and cleaning dormitories, and other domestic tasks.

As this portrait reveals, life in residential schools was very regimented. Throughout the century-long operation of Indian residential schools within the Fraser Valley most *Stó:lō* parents remained opposed to the idea of sending their children away for ten months of the year. Aside from the terrible loneliness it was insulting to have their children told that traditional *Stó:lō* cultural practises were bad,

Portrait of the students at the Coqualeetza Residential School - Girls on the left and boys on the right.

immoral, or sinful. For these reasons many *Stó:lō* parents hid their children from school officials, while others worked hard to have their children accepted into regular public day schools which enabled them to return home each night. However, some *Stó:lō* parents began to encourage their children to attend residential school. It was done in the hope that their children might receive a "European" education and be better able to find meaningful employment. They also hoped that a residential school education would help them develop the skills necessary to be taken seriously by church and government officials, thereby making the graduates articulate advocates of their people's Aboriginal rights.

An additional tragic legacy of the residential school experience was the presence of teachers and officials who physically, sexually, and/or emotionally abused children. Moreover, children raised in an "institutional" environment were deprived of the love and nurturing of their parents. Even in cases where there was no overt abuse, and where teachers and school officials were kind, well intentioned individuals, such institutionalized settings did not provide children with the nurturing and loving experiences associated with a healthy home environment. Graduates of the residential school were simply never provided with the opportunity to learn how to become good parents. As a result residential school survivors later found it difficult to pass on parenting skills to their own children.[11]

By the early 1880's, virtually every *Stó:lō* family was participating in the capitalist work force, as well as living according to their traditional ways. While full-time permanent jobs were becoming increasingly available, few *Stó:lō* people availed themselves of these opportunities. They preferred seasonal employment which did not conflict with their traditional lifestyle. Women and children were regularly employed in the hop fields, in salmon canneries, and as farm and domestic labourers. Men likewise picked hops and caught fish for the cannery, but they also had a broader range of economic opportunities working as farm labourers, steam ship deck hands and pilots, and railroad labourers. The 1881 census shows that of the 524 *Stó:lō* men between the ages of 14 and 75, only 10 gave non *Xwelítem*-recognized occupation. Twenty seven responded that they were primarily fishermen or hunters. A few were cooks, boatmen, mill workers, and farmers, and 20 were recorded as carpenters. The vast majority of the men were listed as "labourers."[12]

4 THE BEGINNING OF *STÓ:LŌ* EXCLUSION FROM THE CAPITALIST ECONOMY ∎

By the end of the nineteenth century, many *Stó:lō* had successfully found a place within the new capitalist economy. This participation was compatible with their tradi-

tional lifestyle. In fact, the *Stó:lō* chose to enter the new economy in ways that benefited their position within traditional *Stó:lō* society. For example, lucrative wage labour and other capitalist economic opportunities had permitted people to host ever more elaborate potlatch ceremonies. Wealth that had previously taken a lifetime to accumulate could now be gathered in a few short years of seasonal labour. A shortage of *Xwelítem* labourers, in addition to the unique skills and knowledge possessed by the *Stó:lō*, enabled certain aspects of their society to flourish. However, this relative prosperity proved to be short-lived. With the dawning of the twentieth century, the *Stó:lō* experienced overt political and subtle social manipulation that stripped them of the privileged economic position they had assumed within the *Xwelítem* capitalist wage economy.

Increasing labour competition

As has been demonstrated, unprecedented economic growth followed the gold rush. Resource industries and agriculture were burgeoning and much of the province's central transportation infrastructure was being created. This provided the *Stó:lō* with many economic opportunities. However, after the completion of the initial large scale government "mega projects" like the Cariboo Road

Unable to return home to Asia, the Chinese were willing to work for very low wages after railroad construction was complete.

and the Canadian Pacific Railroad many of the high paying jobs disappeared. The case of the railway is particularly illuminating.

When railway construction ended not only were *Stó:lō* employees left without work but so were 15,000 Chinese labourers. Separated from their homeland and facing racism in Canada the Chinese were willing to work for half the rate demanded by the *Stó:lō*. Faced with such competition the *Stó:lō* found themselves being displaced from their cannery and farm hand jobs. As the following quotation from the local Indian agent explains, *Stó:lō* women, children and Elders were the first to feel the impact of the increased job competition:

"The poor Indian women and old men, their boys and girls, [who] used to make considerable money every summer picking berries" have been "ruined" by the "large numbers of Chinamen.[13]

Moreover, after the railroad was completed wave after wave of new *Xwelítem* immigrants flooded into the Fraser Valley from the east taking the more permanent jobs. By 1902, a government report explained that while

Less than a score of years ago [20 years], many Indians along the sea-coast of the province found profitable employment working as deck-hands, and at other such labour on the passenger and freight steamers plying to and fro; of late years however, white labour has almost wholly supplanted that previously employed.[14]

Whereas a generation earlier Aboriginal people were in the majority in British Columbia, by the turn of the twentieth century they comprised only 14% of the population. By 1911, 95% of the province's population was *Xwelítem*.[15]

Over the past century the provincial economy has become less dependent upon seasonal economic enterprises and those jobs that have remained seasonal have come to be dominated by recently arrived immigrant groups who accept low wages for their labour. For example, in the 1930's and 1940's *Stó:lō* agricultural labourers were displaced by inexpensive recently arrived Mennonite farmers and eastern European immigrants. More recently these seasonal agricultural jobs have been taken by another new set of immigrants, Indo-Canadians. When people arrive from impoverished regions of the world they are often willing to work for wages below those acceptable to local people simply because it represents an improvement over conditions in their country of origin. Lack of specific training and poor English language skills are other obstacles to meaningful employment faced by newly arrived immigrants. After they become settled and accustomed to situations in Canada, the second generation of immigrants move to higher paying jobs, and their original occupations are assumed by a new generation of immigrants. This continued immigration process suppresses wages in seasonal economic activities while ensuring a constant supply of new immigrants willing to accept low wages. As a result, it has marginalized the *Stó:lō* from an aspect of the Canadian economy that most conveniently accommodated their traditional economic, social, and religious activities.

Restrictive and Discriminatory Legislation

In the mid-to-late-nineteenth century the Canadian government passed a series of laws that, when combined, became known as the "Indian Act." Today, the Indian Act continues to regulate the lives of Canada's Aboriginal people. Its primary aim was to assimilate Aboriginal people into the expanding *Xwelítem* mainstream society. It sought

to accomplish this in a number of ways, one of which was banning the potlatch. As has been explained, the potlatch was central to Aboriginal economic and ceremonial life along the Pacific Coast. However, to some Christian missionaries certain aspects of the potlatch ceremony appeared incompatible with Christianity. Likewise, to some government officials the "redistributive" features of the potlatch appeared communistic, and therefore incompatible with capitalism. To address these matters, in 1884 the federal government declared the potlatch illegal. At first, this law was only loosely enforced, but by the end of World War One it was being enforced zealously.

The *Stó:lō* and other Aboriginal communities responded to this persecution in a variety of ways. Some decided to stop or drastically curtail their potlatch activity while others determined to hold onto their traditions and began hosting potlatches in secret, mostly at night. The combined impact of increased labour competition and assimilationist legislation succeeded in causing the scale of remaining potlatches to decline dramatically.

Government legislation also directly targeted the central feature of the *Stó:lō* economy – salmon fishing. As ever more *Xwelítem* settled in British Columbia, increased regulations and restriction were created to curtail Aboriginal participation in the salmon industry. In the 1890's, the government began issuing licenses to commercial fishermen and declared that the *Stó:lō* could no longer catch fish without a license. To the *Stó:lō* this seemed ridiculous. They had been catching and trading fish since time immemorial. Indeed, the early economic success of the Hudson's Bay Company's Fort Langley was based upon a *Stó:lō* commercial fishery. Not surprisingly, therefore, many *Stó:lō* fishermen chose not to pay for a license.

In 1913, the government passed legislation that even

Legislation suddenly made it illegal for the *Stó:lō* to continue selling fish.

Hell's Gate prior to the rock slide of 1913. Construction of the Canadian Northern Railway caused the slide, and nearly destroyed the Fraser River salmon runs.

between *Xwelítem* and the Aboriginal population, as well it created resentment and ill feelings between Aboriginal people and newly arrived Asian immigrants.

For the *Stó:lō* it had become apparent that they were facing unfair labour competition and had no control over the situation. Testifying before the special 1915 Royal Commission that sought to address Aboriginal grievances, Chief Selemslton of Sumas near Abbotsford explained,

We use to get our meat, ducks, fish out of this lake (Sumas) and on the prairie. We go out on the Fraser to catch our fish, and we get got out on the mountains on each side of this lake and get all the meat we want; but today it is not that way anymore… If I go out and take my gun there is always someone to round me up and have me arrested. If I go out and catch a fish the policeman comes after me with a gun. Every year that we use a net they come and take it away from us.

When the commissioners asked the local Indian agent if anything was being done to compensate the *Stó:lō* for the removal of their fishing and hunting rights, the Indian agent replied:

I have been instructed to supply those Indians with… the necessaries of life – the absolute necessaries [sic] of life in lieu of the fish that they were prevented from taking; in other words, when I visit Indians who are suffering from want I am supposed to supply that want to the extent of a little flour, tea, and rice… I am strictly instructed not to supply anything but the absolute necessaries [sic] of life.

From such testimony we learn that, whereas a generation earlier many *Stó:lō* had vast amounts of wealth, by the early decades of the twentieth century many lived in abject poverty. In the seventy years since the gold rush the *Stó:lō* had gone from dominating the new capitalist economy, and simultaneously participating fully in their traditional economy, to accepting government hand-outs in order to supply the "absolute necessities of life."

After the banning of the potlatch and the barring the *Stó:lō* from the fisheries, hop-picking became the single major economic arena in which the *Stó:lō* could still play a dominant role. The seasonal and communal nature of

further restricted *Stó:lō* people's involvement in the fishing industry. That year, construction of the Canadian Northern Railway caused a massive landslide in the Fraser Canyon at Hell's Gate. It was feared that the slide had decimated the salmon runs (to this day they have never recovered to their pre-slide size). In response, the government tried to rebuild the stocks by banning all Aboriginal salmon fishing in the Fraser River. *Xwelítem* commercial fishermen had their allocations reduced as well, but as the stocks recovered the government gave the *Xwelítem* increasingly larger portions of the runs to compensate them for their financial losses. *Stó:lō* fishermen never regained their pre-slide allocations. Recently, in 1995, commercial fishermen were allocated 94% of the Fraser River sockeye run and sports fishermen 3%. *Stó:lō* fishermen receive the remaining 3%.

Other legislative obstacles also confronted *Stó:lō* labourers. For example, new racial exclusion codes (negotiated between labour unions and industries) prevented Aboriginal people from participating in certain jobs they had long dominated. Two-tiered pay scales paid people of European extraction higher wages than Asian or Aboriginal people for the same work. Testifying before government officials in 1915, Johnny Lewis, a *Stó:lō* person from Sumas, explained that "we got run down so bad in money that we could not buy a boat or a net." Chief David Bailey from Coquitlam explained to the government commissioners that the *Stó:lō* could not get work because they "asked whiteman's wages, and the whiteman says it is a little bit too high, and the whiteman wants to give the Indians just the same as they pay the Chinaman, Japs and Hindus, and the Indians won't stand it." This racial manipulation of the economy accentuated the social and economic rift

You Are Asked To Witness

the hop field work provided an opportunity to continue traditional activities within a modified context – a context acceptable to the *Xwelítem*. Thus, the Agassiz and Chilliwack hop-yards became known among Aboriginal people as places where social gatherings and celebrations modeled after the potlatch could occur.

It is interesting that the *Stó:lō* were not squeezed out of the hop industry as they were from so many other economic fields. One reason is that hop picking was a hot, labour-intensive job. It required large numbers of labourers and, because of its short one-month duration, few *Xwelítem* or Asian immigrants were willing to engage in it. For the *Stó:lō*, the hop-picking season fit conveniently between the salmon-drying and berry-picking seasons. Because of the social aspects attached to the hop-picking industry entire *Stó:lō* extended families arrived at the fields and divided the labour. Typically, older women prepared meals and continued the education and nurturing of young children, while their adult children and grandchildren picked hops. Because of the racist "Chinese head tax," Chinese men found it very difficult to bring their wives and families to British Columbia. For this reason most Chinese living in

Hop yards were one of the last refuges for *Stó:lō* participation in the labour economy. Mechanization finally drove the *Stó:lō* out in the 1940's.

British Columbia were single men who did not have the necessary family social networks to engage in short economic activities such as hop-picking, which required cooks and other support people.

Changing Technology

In the 1940's, the *Stó:lō* faced yet another impediment to meaningful involvement in the capitalist economy: technological innovations that enabled people who owned hop fields to pick hops with machines. This made *Stó:lō* labour redundant. It became almost impossible for the *Stó:lō* to find employment that would accommodate their traditional, seasonally regulated lifestyle. This accentuated the vaguely defined cultural depression (a legacy of two centuries of rapid depopulation and increased social and economic marginalization), which had become a characteristic of many *Stó:lō* people's lives. Social problems increased and unemployment became a chronic problem. To this day, it is not uncommon for over 50% of the people living in *Stó:lō* communities to be unemployed, or under-employed.

Sumas Lake before it was drained.

Sumas Lake after it was drained.

5 THE CONTEMPORARY *STÓ:LŌ* ECONOMIC SITUATION ■

In the past twenty years, the economic situation of the *Stó:lō* has significantly improved. One reason is the persistent determination of *Stó:lō* leaders to act as advocates for their communities in dealings with the federal and provincial governments. Legislation banning the potlatch and other spiritual ceremonies was lifted in 1951. With each succeeding year, a growing number of *Stó:lō* people are again participating in such activities. New economic opportunities in heritage tourism, such as the *Xá:ytem* Longhouse Interpretive Centre in Mission, are once again providing the *Stó:lō* with meaningful seasonal employment. Self-government agreements and the transfer of authority from the federal and provincial governments concerning health and social services, child welfare, housing, education, and advisory services, among others, have provided not only job opportunities, but also a sense of pride and renewed hope for the future, as the *Stó:lō* assume increased responsibilities for their lives. Likewise, tentative steps are being taken to restore historic *Stó:lō* commercial fishing rights.

The 1991 Canadian census shows that 32% of the *Stó:lō* over the age of 25 living on reserve are officially "unemployed." The unemployment rate for men is 32%, while for women it is 50%. Interestingly, *Stó:lō* employment trends continue to follow the pattern established in the previous century, that is, many *Stó:lō* look for seasonal employment that will permit them to participate in their traditional seasonal social, religious, and economic activities. For example, the top five occupations for *Stó:lō* men living on reserve are salmon fishing (47%), forestry/logging (18%), construction trades (14%), farming (8%), managerial/administration (7%), and processing (7%). Of these, only managerial and administrative jobs are not seasonal.

Income levels for the *Stó:lō* (while below national averages) are improving in relation to other Canadians. *Stó:lō* men living on reserve who work full time earn, on average, $28,000. For *Stó:lō* women living on reserve, the average income is $17,000. The average yearly income for *Stó:lō* men engaged in only seasonal employment is just under $12,000, whereas for women it is just under $6,000.

The most recent generation has likewise witnessed a marked improvement in education levels among the *Stó:lō*. In 1991, 8% of the *Stó:lō* population were university graduates or currently enroled in university. 44% of the population were either graduates or currently enroled in other post-secondary institutions such as trade schools or diploma programs. An additional 15% of the *Stó:lō* had graduated from high school but not gone on to further education. An alarming 32% of the adult population has not graduated from high school. By comparison, only 5% of other Canadians achieve a university education, yet roughly 80% graduate from high school.

Currently, economic development and job creation are among the top priorities of the *Stó:lō* Nation chiefs. As one *Stó:lō* community leader recently expressed,

We need to provide meaningful employment opportunities for our people. To do that we need to implement the objectives of the *Stó:lō* Nation – namely to practice traditional culture, to re-establish healthy communities, and to restore self-government. Our people need to realize that collecting welfare is not an Aboriginal right, and it is not healthy. Once we regain a meaningful role in how the resources in our territory are developed we will have an economic base which can provide meaningful economic opportunities and employment.

Recommended Further Readings:

Knight, Ralph, *Indians At Work: An Informal History of Native Labour in British Columbia*, 1858-1930, Vancouver: New Star Books, 1978.
Newell, Diane, *Tangled Webs of History*, Toronto: University of Toronto Press, 1994

Footnotes

1 Interview with Addeline Lorenzetto and Wilson Duff, 1952.
2 Mary K. Cullen, *The History of Fort Langley,* 1827-96 (Minister of Supplies and Services Canada, 1979) p. 96.
3 See Carlson and McHalsie, forthcoming in BC Studies.
4 Margaret Ormsby, *British Columbia: A History* (Vancouver: The MacMillan Company, 1958), p.138.
5 G.P.V. Akigg. *"The Fraser River Gold Rush."* In: The Fraser's History from Glaciers to Early Settlements. Papers from a seminar presented at the Annual Meeting of the British Columbia Historical Association on May 27, 1977. Burnaby, B.C. p.32.
6 Elwood, Evans **"The Fraser River Excitement, 1858,"** unpublished manuscript. BCARS.
7 James Douglas, to Home Government, April 6, 1858, Colonial Correspondence. BCARS.
8 The original Alexandra bridge proved inadequate for modern traffic and was replaced by a bigger bridge of the same name. Interested people can still visit the original and walk across its deck by stopping at the rest site just upriver of the new Alexandra bridge and following the trail to the river.
9 I.W. Powell in Canada, Sessional Papers, 1886, Vol. 4, Pp. 87-8, 118.
10 I.W. Powell, in Canada, Sessional Papers, 1886, Vol. 4, Pp.87-8, 118.
11 For additional information on residential schools in *Stó:lō* territory see chapter ?? this volume.
12 Canada, Manuscript Census. New Westminster District, copy at *Stó:lō* Nation Office.
13 P. McTiernan in Canada, Sessional Papers, 1885, p.105.
14 A.W. Vowell, in Canada, Sessional Papers, 1902, No. 27, Pp.288-9.
15 Dianne Newell, *Tangled Webs of History; Indians and the Law in Canada's Pacific Coast Fisheries* (Toronto: University of Toronto Press, 1994), p.67.

Stó:lō Soldiers, Stó:lō Veterans

Dedicated to the memory of Wesley Sam, 1919-1994

Keith Thor Carlson

INTRODUCTION

The experiences of *Stó:lō* soldiers in the Canadian Armed Forces during the Second World War can be a vehicle for understanding significant historical and anthropological issues. Very little has been written about the role of Aboriginal servicemen in the Second World War, and even less relating to the official government treatment of Aboriginal veterans since 1945. Throughout Canadian history Aboriginal people often chose to participate in "European wars" for reasons unappreciated by Canadians of European decent. Relatedly, stereotypes of the "Indian warrior" have driven government recruitment practices and influenced the way Aboriginal soldiers have been treated by the military establishment. These stereotypes have also clouded public perceptions of Aboriginal military personnel, and affected the way in which returning Aboriginal veterans have been received by their own communities.

This chapter looks at official Canadian policy towards Aboriginal people during World War II, as well as the government's treatment of *Stó:lō* veterans after the war. The experiences of returning *Stó:lō* veteran "warriors" as they attempted to reintegrate themselves into civilian life and their Aboriginal communities after the war, will also be discussed. Finally, this chapter discusses the way the wartime experience of *Stó:lō* veterans both positively and adversely affected their position within *Stó:lō* society.[1]

Wes Sam, *Stó:lō* Veteran of WWII sharing stories about the role of Aboriginal veterans in bringing about changes to the Indian Act.

1 ABORIGINAL SOLDIERS IN CANADIAN HISTORY ■

Aboriginal soldiers have played a significant role in Canadian military history for over 200 years. In the 1700's and 1800's Aboriginal people from what is now eastern Canada often acted as military allies for the British against the French or vice versa. Typically, these conflicts originated in European issues which had little to do with North America, let alone Aboriginal people. Yet, when non-indigenous politics and military feuds spilled over from Europe into North America, Aboriginal people often chose to participate. They participated not because they cared about or even understood the original European cause of the dispute, but because the interests of the British or French governments happened to parallel or compliment their own.

Many people are familiar with the story of how the Iroquois sided with Britain against the French in Quebec in the 1760's. Many more, no doubt, have heard the history of how the renowned Aboriginal leader Tecumseh united the Tribes of the Upper Mississippi and Great Lakes region to fight as allies of the British against the Americans in the War of 1812. Tecumseh did not necessarily side with the British because he agreed with overall British policy against the Americans. Rather, Tecumseh recognized that unlike the American government, the British were not encouraging settlers to move into the region used by Aboriginal people and fur traders. The British became a convenient, if somewhat temporary, ally as long as their interests coincided with those of Tecumseh and his people. Similar alliances were formed between various Aboriginal communities and the French, Spanish, Russian, and later the American and Canadian governments at different times in various parts of the continent.

After 1812, the significance of Aboriginal allies for North American military and political disputes declined. The annexation of French, Spanish,

Tecumseh united diverse Tribes to fight as allies of the British against the Americans in the War of 1812.

Dutch and later Mexican territories into either the United States or British North America (Canada) ultimately ended international conflict on the continent. Carefully defined and accepted international borders reduced the need for Aboriginal allies. Likewise, rapid Aboriginal population decline, primarily resulting from introduced disease, and a simultaneous population explosion among the *Xwelítem* (non-Aboriginal) population reduced the relative military strength of Aboriginal communities vis à vis European powers. British, Canadian and American legislation undermined Aboriginal unity thereby making Aboriginal communities less powerful, and therefore less valuable as allies (or dangerous as enemies). Over time, those Aboriginal people who decided to participate in either the Canadian or American military ventures did so increasingly as individuals rather than as part of an autonomous allied Aboriginal community.

Stó:lō WWII veterans Benny Joe, Wes Sam, Joe Alex and Harold Wells at the dedication of the *Stó:lō* veterans memorial on the Coqualeetza Grounds in Sardis, November 11, 1993.

2 ABORIGINAL PARTICIPATION IN WORLD WAR I & II (1914-1918 & 1939-1945) ■

The involvement of Tecumseh and other Aboriginal leaders in Canada's early military campaigns clearly shows that when Aboriginal people chose to participate they did so for reasons unappreciated by their European friends and allies. Similarly, individual Aboriginal soldiers in the First and Second World Wars chose to participate for reasons often unappreciated by mainstream Canadian society. Before looking at specific histories of individual *Stó:lō* service men it is useful to set the scene by examining actual Canadian government policy.

World War I (1914-1918) established a number of precedents concerning the involvement of Aboriginal people in Canada's military. During the first half of "the Great War," the Canadian government refused to accept Aboriginal volunteers. The official justification for this was based on the paternalistic grounds that Aboriginal people needed to be protected from the "savage" German army. At that time, the Canadian government had determined that German soldiers had such a low regard for "non-white" people that they could not be trusted to provide Aboriginal prisoners of war with all the "privileges of civilized warfare."[2] Later in the war, when manpower shortages became critical, such concerns were set aside and Aboriginal volunteers were welcomed at recruitment centres. Yet, while other Canadian men were being conscripted and forced to serve in the military, Aboriginal men were given the option of deciding for themselves whether they would serve or not. Parliament determined that, as "wards of the government," Indians could not be compelled to fight in an overseas war.

Raymond Bobb

Given this precedent, one would assume that Aboriginal people would have been exempt from compulsory military registration or service in any and all future overseas wars. Indeed, correspondence from the Department of Indian Affairs dated at the beginning of the Second World War indicates that the federal government intended to follow the WWI precedent of exempting Aboriginal people from conscription. However, when the Canadian government declared war on Nazi Germany in 1939 few politicians gave any thought to the effects the war would have on Canada's Aboriginal population. National attention was focused on the "bigger issue" of defeating Fascism. This preoccupation caused much bureaucratic confusion – confusion that resulted in hardships for Canada's Aboriginal population.

To prepare the country's defence, in August 1940, the Canadian Parliament passed the *National Mobilization Act*. This legislation required all adult Canadians to register for potential military service, and was designed to help the government coordinate the nation's manpower resources. Because of the precedent set in WWI, Aboriginals were the only people in Canada exempt from the registration. However, it appears that one hand of the federal government was unaware of what the other was doing, for at the time the *Mobilization Act* was enacted, the government passed companion legislation making it illegal for employers to pay their civilian employees unless they could produce their *Mobilization Act* "registration card." This measure was intended to ensure that all civilians registered under the *Mobilization Act*, and were "on the list," should conscription become necessary. Registering also required men to serve one month of basic military training with their "Home Militia." Thus, conflicting policies inadvertently resulted in Aboriginal peo-

Stó:lō veteran Wes Sam during ceremony of November 11, 1993.

ple being unable to collect their civilian pay cheques unless they registered for the draft. Many Aboriginal people protested this fact, leading a top official in Ottawa to clarify that Indians were exempt from having to register.[3] Yet, for unknown reasons, this information was never adequately communicated to either the police or private sector employers. As a result, Aboriginal people lost their jobs and were arrested by overzealous police officers for not possessing Registration Cards.[4]

Responding to ever-increasing complaints, the government decided the simplest solution was to "register" Aboriginal people so they could continue working in the civilian workforce. However, Aboriginal men were assured that they would be exempt from the otherwise compulsory 30 day Home Militia basic training process. Likewise, they were also promised that their registration would not lead to compulsory military training and service should the government ever decide to conscript people. For whatever reason, the first part of this message (exemption from training and service) was once again ineffectively communicated to individual Indian Agents and Aboriginal communities. As a result, by 1941,

Stó:lō people working in the salmon cannery industry.

even though they did not have any of the privileges of citizenship (ie., Aboriginal people could not vote, purchase alcohol, or attend university) many Aboriginal people had been compelled to complete the 30 day basic training as though they were Canadian citizens.[5]

By the time officials in Ottawa improved their communication strategies to inform local officials that Aboriginal people did not have to register, many Aboriginal men had already completed basic military training. As a result, the government decided that the only way to be fair to everyone was to compel all remaining Aboriginal men to also attend basic training. Shortly thereafter in January 1941, the National Mobilization Act extended the mandatory training period from 30 days to four months. After completing their training, men automatically became part of the "Home Service Militia." In late 1944, the government reneged on its promise to Aboriginal leaders and enacted conscription legislation allowing them to draft Aboriginal people for compulsory active duty.[6] In other words, Aboriginal men who had been repeatedly assured they would not have to serve in the forces, and who had only registered in order to collect their civilian pay cheque, suddenly found themselves being drafted and eligible for overseas fighting.

At this point a number of Aboriginal communities throughout Canada redoubled their efforts to remind the government of the WWI exemption precedent. They also reminded the government of the earlier promises made during the war in progress. They argued that Aboriginal men should be allowed to make the choice to participate, and not be forced. One Aboriginal man from Quebec named Shortfence actually took the government to court, arguing that as a non-citizen he should have been excluded from conscription. The government lawyer countered that while Aboriginal people were not full Canadian citizens, they were "subjects" of His Majesty the King, and therefore they were obliged to comply with the draft. After listening to the arguments, the court determined that only those Aboriginal people whose treaties with the federal government explicitly exempted them from compulsory military service would be exempted from the draft. Recognizing that there were two ways of recording history, the court included with this group all Aboriginal communities whose oral traditions stated that it was their understanding that during the treaty making process, their leaders had secured

military exemptions, even if the treaty document itself was unclear on the matter. As a result of this legal decision, all Aboriginal people from "Treaty groups 3, 6, 8, and 11" (much of Ontario and the prairie provinces) were excluded from the draft. All other Aboriginal people were considered to have surrendered any special rights of exemption to the government through their treaties. Interestingly, no mention was made of Aboriginal people in B.C., who had never signed treaties.

3 DISCRIMINATION WITHIN THE ARMED FORCES ■

The above discussion of Canadian-wide developments should be considered against the specific British Columbian and *Stó:lō* experiences. To this day, the vast majority of B.C.'s Aboriginal people have never signed treaties alienating any of their title or rights. Therefore, it would appear that Aboriginal people living in British Columbia, by the court's definition, should have been included among those groups exempted from military service. However, this never occurred, and it is little wonder,

Stó:lō WWII veterans (left to right) Dan Francis, Archie Charles, Moody Michelle, Clarence Morgan, Mr. Kelly, Alfred Myra, Benny Joe and Wes Sam at 1993 Remembrance Day Ceremonies.

given the fact that a decade prior to the war, in 1927, the Indian Act had been amended making it illegal for a lawyer to work for an Aboriginal person or organization pursuing matters of Aboriginal rights and title. This law was not repealed until 1951, largely as a result of the effective lobbying of Second World War Aboriginal veterans.[7]

Being compelled to register and enlist for active duty did not mean that Aboriginal enlistees would be provided with all the choices available to non-Aboriginal servicemen. Up until 1943 the Royal Canadian Navy accepted only people who were of "pure European Descent and of the White Race."[8] Naval Officials felt that "The confined living spaces... [on board ship] do not lend themselves to satisfactory mixing of the white races with Indians."[9] When the war broke out The Royal Canadian Air Force had an even more racially restrictive policy which required that all recruits "be British subjects and of pure European descent."[10] This policy only officially reversed in 1941. However, through the entire conflict it remained an unwritten rule that Aboriginal people were not welcome in any branch of the armed forces except the Army.[11] *Stó:lō* veteran Wes Sam explained that, "When I joined up I wanted to get into the air gunners. A lot of my white friends got into the air gunners and that's where I wanted to go too, but when I tried out I was rejected. All my white friends were accepted, but I was rejected. So I thought I'd try to get in through the back door, and I went to another recruitment office in Vancouver. They told me 'try the army.' So I did, and the army accepted me so fast I never even got to go home and visit my family – straight to the barracks."[12] These bigoted policies move from being simply distasteful to deplorable when one considers that a serviceman's chance of being killed or wounded was far greater in the Army than either the Navy or the Air Force.

Harold Wells, *Stó:lō* veteran of WWII

4 STÓ:LŌ ORAL TRADITIONS: PERSONAL REASONS FOR ENLISTING ■

Through the written archival records we learn that government policy was very confused when it came to dealing with Aboriginal people during the Second World War. Bureaucratic confusion had a great and sometimes devastating impact on individual Aboriginal people. To more fully appreciate this impact, it is useful to review the individual oral histories of various *Stó:lō* veterans. By listening to their voices we can come to appreciate the personal impact of government policy. Their stories also illustrate the creativity and resourcefulness of *Stó:lō* people faced with frustrating and threatening government policy.

More than 100 young *Stó:lō* men and at least one *Stó:lō* woman served in the Canadian military during World War II.[13] The factors which motivated individual *Stó:lō* people to enlist were just as varied and complex as those which had influenced men like Tecumseh two hundred years earlier. Some *Stó:lō* veterans, like Charlie Fisher, remember enlisting because, "I couldn't get work and I needed a job to feed my wife and son."[14] More commonly, *Stó:lō* veterans mentioned that they were led to believe that if they did not enlist on their own they would inevitably be drafted. In addition, they were told that volunteers were provided placement options that draftees were not. In other words, because they were not even aware that they had the option of not serving in the military they were effectively denied their rights in more ways than one. *Stó:lō* veteran Harold Wells explained how this was the case for him:

M y older brother got notice to appear [at the recruitment office]. He decided he wouldn't volunteer for active service, so they sent him up to Vernon [B.C.], where they had a separate camp for guys who wouldn't volunteer.... He spent four months there. The only thing was, he said they never let him out. All the time you were there, [they] wouldn't give you weekend leave or anything like that. He finally decided the only way he could get out of there was to volunteer for active service. So that's what I did too.[15]

Fear of being drafted and assigned an undesirable position was the most common reason for enlisting, but it was not the only one. Some *Stó:lō* veterans remember being enticed by captivating tales describing life in the military (and in particular Europe) as a "life without racism." Such stories were particularly appealing to young men who had grown up in an environment rife with racial discrimination. *Stó:lō* veteran Wes Sam recalled being greatly influenced by such stories told to him by older Aboriginal servicemen who had returned home on vacation or leave. When asked if racial discrimination and government injustice towards Aboriginal people before the war discouraged *Stó:lō* men from enlisting, Wes Sam explained:

Those things become history.... Those *Stó:lō* soldiers brought back stories of their experiences from over there in Europe. And when the government changed the law of the lands, [allowing Aboriginal people to become Canadian citizens in 1951] it was because of the knowledge of these veterans. Because the ordinary person in the *Stó:lō* communities, they did not know they were in poverty. They did not know that they were not treated right [by mainstream society and the government]. They did not know that they were discriminated against. When you don't know those things you learn to accept. When you moved from your Canadian country and went to Europe it was an entirely different experience for a Native person.

Question: Is that why Stó:lō people were so eager to join?

Yes. When that knowledge was obtained by the first Native veterans [to arrive in Europe] they sent the word back to their villages: "Oh, what a great place this is! We never felt so good in our life. – We were treated like any other person – Equal to all people who wear the Canadian badge." "Back home," they said, "people look down on you...." As soon as the veterans returned home, and started telling the other people... the stories of how wonderful that life was over there; how we could be treated so well – it was a wonderful experience. And the veterans said, "We could change that. We could have that right in our own land if we wanted to." So it was a new concept of life. They said that's what they were trying to do.[16]

5 LIFE AFTER THE WAR: LOST VETERAN'S BENEFITS: ■

The brief historical description of Canadian government policy towards Aboriginal people during the Second World War presented earlier is a story of the insult suffered by Aboriginal veterans confronted by racist enlistment policies and the marginalization of Aboriginal rights. To this insult, injury was later added when returning Aboriginal service men failed to receive the same veteran's benefits as their non-Aboriginal comrades-in-arms.

All returning veterans were entitled to certain benefits at the end of the war. Among these were financial assistance for education and job training, inexpensive life insurance, $6,000 loans towards the purchase of property, and a $2,320 cash grant towards the purchase of farming or fishing equipment.[17] Each veteran should have been informed of his right to these benefits upon returning to civilian life. However, surviving *Stó:lō* veterans are unanimous in stating that they were never appraised of their entitlement to such benefits, let alone received any. To understand how this could have occurred, we must again consult the official government archival records.

It appears that after the war ended Aboriginal veterans became the victims of an interdepartmental rivalry between the Department of Indian Affairs and the Department of Veterans Affairs. Veteran's benefits were under the jurisdiction of the Department of Veteran's Affairs. However, the Department of Indian Affairs successfully demanded that all government programs relating to Aboriginal people be administered through their offices. As a result, responsibility for informing Aboriginal veterans of their benefit entitlements fell to individual Indian Agents. Apparently, the Indian Agent working among the *Stó:lō* never made this a priority.

Thus, while non-Aboriginal veterans were upgrading their education and starting businesses as farmers or fishermen with government assistance, *Stó:lō* veterans were scrambling on their own to adjust to civilian life. They had expected that the noble principles they had fought for in Europe and Asia would be applied in their home communities in Canada. When this proved not the case they were bitterly disappointed.

One *Stó:lō* veteran explained that upon returning home from the war, he applied for a job as a foreman on the railroad. He assumed that his pre-war experience working for the same company as a labourer, coupled with the administrative training he had received in while in the military qualified him for the job. His potential employer apparently thought so too, but decided to deny him the position regardless. The railroad official justified his decision stating that "white people simply won't work under an Indian." Economically marginalized, he was forced to accept low-paying menial employment for which he was vastly overqualified.

Another *Stó:lō* veteran told a similar story of racial discrimination. Like many Aboriginal soldiers who had been impressed with the lack of overt racism and the unusual extent of social integration they experienced during the war, this particular *Stó:lō* veteran had been persuaded to "give up his [Indian] status" at the war's end and become an "enfranchised" Canadian citizen. However, when he tried to buy a house and move into a predominantly

Map of Canadian Indian Treaties

Stó:lō veterans explained, the motivating factors behind every *Stó:lō* soldier's decision to enlist were diverse and complex. It is interesting, however, that none of the surviving *Stó:lō* veterans ever mentioned that they joined the army because they saw themselves as a "warrior," or because they wanted to

"white" residential suburb he discovered that being a Canadian citizen and veteran did not necessarily entitle him to all the social benefits of equal citizenry. He was told by a real estate agent that his presence would adversely affect his *Xwelítem* neighbour's property values. As such, he was not welcome. Sadly, when this newly enfranchised citizen tried to return to his reserve he was informed by the local Indian Agent that according to Canadian law, as specified in the "Indian Act" prior to 1951, non-Indians were not legally entitled to live on reserve. His Canadian citizenship had become a burden with few benefits. Socially ostracized this young veteran and his *Stó:lō* family were left with no other option than to move into a "shack" on the outskirts of town.

Enfranchised *Stó:lō* veterans were not the only ones told they were not welcome on their home reserve. Many returning *Stó:lō* veterans who retained their Aboriginal status also found themselves ostracized by members of their home villages because they were seen as having rejected their *Stó:lō* culture when they joined the army. They were criticized by some for having tried to "become White:"

> When we returned we were not accepted by the people in our own communities. We stopped going to Indian gatherings for many years because we were vets. We were not accepted, they rejected us.... They never liked us because we were more systematic and thoughtful. The military trained us to think critically and accept discipline. The Indian who stayed behind looked at us as if we were different.... Upon our return the people of our reserves just pushed us aside.... The other *Stó:lō* people who stayed behind and didn't enlist, well they thought we were strange because we were more military minded.[18]

As Harold Wells, Wes Sam, Charlie Fisher and other

be a "warrior." It should be noted that in *Stó:lō* society the most highly respected people are known as *sí:yá:m*.[19] By definition a *siyá:m* is wise and gentle. Traditionally, violence was a last resort if all other avenues of dispute resolution failed, and even then, it tended to be defensive rather than offensive. A *siyá:m* was not a warrior, but a diplomat. By way of contrast, warriors in traditional *Stó:lō* society were referred to as *stómex*, a term which implies "short tempered and likes to fight."[20] *Stómex* people were aggressive. If *stómex* warriors received any respect from the community, it was usually derived from the fear they instilled in people. To the extent that they helped defend their communities, and brought wealth to their families through raiding other villages, they were appreciated. But the oral records indicate that *stómex* warriors were never accorded the respect accorded to a *siyá:m*. Indeed, by the late nineteenth century – when raiding was no longer practised – aggressive *stómex* warriors found themselves essentially unvalued by their communities. Yet, for most *Xwelítem* people, particularly military officials, every "Indian enlistee" was viewed as a potential warrior. Hollywood images seem to have been accepted as accurate ethnographic descriptions by the officials at the recruitment office. These officials assumed that Aboriginal men's "warrior" heritage would make them excellent soldiers.

Such stereotypical assumptions on the part of Canadian government officials proved insulting to many *Stó:lō* enlistees. They were also potentially harmful. For example, as *Stó:lō* veteran Wes Sam explained, when he enlisted everyone in the Army expected him to be a "great shot, and a good tracker and to have a [mystical] sixth sense, just like Indian warriors in the movies."[21] The military establishment as well as other rank and file soldiers expected Aboriginal soldiers to be especially brave and adept at warfare. *Stó:lō* soldiers were encouraged to become "snipers" and to fill other "special roles," where they could kill enemy soldiers by surprise. Considered from a *Stó:lō* perspective, the Canadian Army expected

Stó:lō soldiers to act "stómex." Thus, for a Stó:lō soldier to live up to the expectations of his Xwelítem comrades, and thereby gain their respect in a war-time setting, he would have had to compromise some of his Stó:lō values. It is not difficult to imagine how after having accepted the role of a "warrior" during his time in the military, a returning Stó:lō veteran would have a difficult time reintegrating himself into Stó:lō society.

The experience of one Stó:lō veteran is particularly enlightening. Due to the sensitive and personal nature of the story, his identity has been disguised, and he will be referred to as "Tonto" – the supposedly flattering "nickname" bestowed upon him by his non-Aboriginal "buddies" in the army.[22]

Tonto came from a respected Stó:lō family – one regarded as siyà:m. Surviving family members explain that Tonto decided to leave his young wife and join the army because the 1930's depression had been particularly hard on Stó:lō families, and he needed employment. Before enlisting, Tonto had established a reputation as an accomplished hunter ("tewít" in the Halq'eméylem language) and because he was familiar with a rifle he was quickly assigned to the infantry as a sniper. The other men in Tonto's unit always complimented him on being an excellent shot and a loyal companion, just like his namesake on the "Lone Ranger" radio program. According to people who knew Tonto, he appeared to have been flattered by the attention and respect he received from his Xwelítem friends in the army. Tonto was not accustomed to "white people" looking up to him or appreciating his particular skills and abilities. To earn their respect and friendship, Tonto appears to have begun to change his behaviour, to comply with what he thought his comrades expected from "Tonto, the Indian warrior."

By the end of the war, Tonto's success as a sniper had turned him into an acknowledged Canadian hero. His companions boasted that his "Indian skills" had made him the perfect soldier. He was eager for battle and had shot and killed over 20 Nazi soldiers. When Tonto returned from Europe after the war, he was given a hero's welcome by Xwelítem communities in the lower mainland and Fraser Valley. Family members even remember the Mayor of Vancouver giving him the keys to the city. When the excitement of the victory over Nazi Germany subsided, and people began returning to their peace-time routine, Tonto ultimately found himself living back on his home reserve. However, instead of being treated like a

Remembrance Day Service,
November 11, 1993.
Mrs. Ethel Fisher lays cedar boughs
in memory of her late husband Charlie.

You Are Asked To Witness

Sí:yá:m remain highly respected leaders, respected because of their wisdom and gentle nature.

heroic warrior by the *Stó:lō*, he was viewed with suspicion. It seems that in their minds, the war had transformed him into a *stómex* warrior, and, as explained earlier, by 1945, *stómex* warriors no longer had a respectable place within *Stó:lō* society.

Elders explain that people were afraid of Tonto after he came back from the war. One Elder expressed his feelings this way: "[Tonto] was a killer, I didn't like to be around him." It appears that *Stó:lō* people did not know how to relate to a person who had achieved his status in mainstream Canadian society by being aggressive and killing people. Even if he had killed Nazis in what most other Canadians considered a "just war," he had still acted in a *stómex* manner not easily accepted by many *Stó:lō* people.

As time passed Tonto started drinking heavily, possibly to help him avoid having to deal with the fact that so many people from his home community did not like being around him. His wife eventually left him, leaving Tonto to live the remainder of his life forgotten by the mainstream Canadian culture which had made him a "warrior hero," and socially marginalized within *Stó:lō* society. Ultimately, in the 1970's, Tonto died a tragic alcohol associated death.

Unfortunately, Tonto's experiences were not uncommon. When asked whether he thought *Stó:lō* veterans were as discouraged about the continued presence of racism in Canadian society after the war as African-Americans veterans were upon their return to civilian life in the United States, *Stó:lō* veteran Wes Sam replied: "More so. You got it from your own Native people."[23]

Wes Sam explained that:

The tragic part is, our own people, looked down on us. They said, 'why did you have to go and join – it wasn't your fight....' After we came back from overseas many of us fell back into the little cracks and holes in our own villages – into obscurity. And that hurt a lot of the old veterans. They never did come forward. They never did attend big gatherings. The people of authority among our own people didn't want them to be recognized that way. That's what hurt us as veterans – myself as a veteran.[24]

Stó:lō soldiers were not warmly received in their *Stó:lō* communities after the war because "it wasn't their fight." Like the nineteenth century *stómex* warrior who raided distant communities a century earlier, often simply to acquire wealth, the WWII *Stó:lō* soldier had gone and fought against people, sometimes civilians, who had done nothing to directly harm *Stó:lō* or even Canadian people. It was not immediately apparent to all *Stó:lō* people that enlisting in the army, and fighting Germans or Italians in Europe was an indirect means of defending their home community. Had Germany attacked the Fraser Valley, and *Stó:lō* men fought to protect their families and communities, it would have been easy to regard the soldiers as respected *sí:yá:m* But because many *Stó:lō* soldiers had sought to live up to their non-*Stó:lō* comrades' expectations of an "Indian warrior," they had behaved in a way which was interpreted as distasteful, and even dangerous, by members of *Stó:lō* society.

6 STÓ:LŌ VETERANS HELPING AND HEALING COMMUNITIES: NEW OPPORTUNITIES ■

As time progressed, an ever increasing number of *Stó:lō* people came to appreciate their World War II veterans. In a manner similar to the *stómex* who relied upon special training, wisdom and spirit power to assist his people, veterans could use the special organizational skills, education and training they acquired while in the armed forces to assist their communities deal with the assimilationist policies of the Canadian government. They began working to help their communities achieve a more fulfilling and respectable position within the broader Canadian society.

Stó:lō veteran Wes Sam explained that the Aboriginal veterans

Weren't satisfied with the way they were treated once they [returned to Canada and] became Canadian here again. They said, "all right, this is what I done for Canada, and this is what you brought back. This is not right!" For me, as a soldier who was over there... I wanted to be treated just like every other Canadian, but I guess between our Indian leaders and the government of Canada (the Department of Indian Affairs) they made it very difficult for Indian soldiers, for veterans, to be heard. So we, as veterans, as Native people, mentioned this to our Legions. The [Royal Canadian] Legion took all this thing into hand. They used their organization to change the laws of the land [remove the most racist and assimilationist clauses in the Indian Act such as the provisions which prevented Indians from being citizens, and prevented them from voting or purchasing alcohol, or hiring a lawyer etc.[25]... In the churches and the Legions there were veterans, you know, Native and non-Native – so these organizations delved into a little research program to find out about Native people's participation in the Second World War, and with that knowledge they went to the government of Canada...

So, the changing of the laws of the land took place by 1952. They start to break down the barriers recognize, to recognize that all Canadians will be equal, all Canadians. Up to this time, the laws of the land did not allow a native person to go to high school, did not allow him to become a lawyer, did not allow him to take any part in education that would hinder the Department of Indian affairs style of looking after. So, it was very simple for them. It was their law – it sure wasn't ours. But us veterans wanted to change that law. Through the aid of organizations such as the Legion and church groups the Indian Act was changed....

"In 1952 there was a major shake-up, I guess you could call it that, to the administration of native people, of the old law that we had. It was a step towards making available to the native people the rights that had been enjoyed by other Canadians for a long long time: The right to chose where you want to live, or be whatever you want to be. If you want to become a nurse, that's what you train for, or a doctor, lawyer, or whatever it might be, you finally got the right to higher education. We didn't have those rights prior to World War Two. There was no way that we'd ever have been able to obtain that kind of training or education then. They controlled it, the Department of Indian Affairs controlled you. If they wanted to, they made you sign a paper. If you want to go to University you had to sign a paper taking you off the list of Indians, put you on like any other Canadian. 🗿

As the years went by, Aboriginal veterans increasingly played key leadership roles in defending their communities' interests. For example, in 1969 when the federal government proposed that all Aboriginal people be stripped of their collective Aboriginal rights WWII veterans played

Although aggressive and feared *Stómex* warriors were respected because they helped protect their home village and because their raids brought wealth, but as time progressed, warriors became less needed and overly aggressive men were looked on with fear.
(Paul Kane, 1863)

key roles in organizing an effective opposition. Their leadership caused the government to rethink and then reverse its position. Likewise, in the early 1970's, when the federal government attempted to deny *Stó:lō* people the right to use the Coqualeetza Property in Chilliwack (which had formerly been set aside as an Indian Residential School and Indian hospital) it was *Stó:lō* veterans who organized and led the occupation of the site. Their leadership ultimately convinced the government to declare the property a collective reserve for the use of all *Stó:lō* people.

Stó:lō veterans of WWII found opportunities to make their war-time skills and experiences useful and appreciated. People recognized this, and acknowledged that their military service was in many ways beyond their control, and therefore they were not to blame for having "acted white" or appearing *stómex*. As a result of these changes of attitude, in 1993 the *Stó:lō* Tribal Council organized and hosted a special Remembrance Day ceremony to specially honour the life-long contributions of their veterans. At the ceremony they emphasised not so much the *Stó:lō* veterans' military contributions, but their post-war contributions to their communities.

7 CONCLUSION ■

In many ways the story of the *Stó:lō* veteran is a reflection of the broader Aboriginal experience in Canada. *Stó:lō* veterans' participation in World War Two was largely the result of governmental bungling. Though disenfranchised, *Stó:lō* men were compelled to join the Canadian war effort. Upon their return, *Stó:lō* veterans were abandoned by the military establishment that had embraced them as potential "warrior soldiers." Not only were *Stó:lō* veterans denied benefits accorded to other veterans, they were again racially marginalized. As Canadian veterans they shared the legacy of "shell shock," or what is now called post-traumatic stress syndrome. As *Stó:lō* veterans they were confronted by special cultural dilemmas. They were criticized for acting too "white" and thinking they were better than other *Stó:lō* on the one hand, and of acting too much like traditional *stómex* warriors on the other. Their overcoming of these obstacles stands as testimony to their dedication to principle and their commitment to their communities' welfare.

Stó:lō veterans received the recognition they so long desired at the first *Stó:lō* Remembrance Day ceremony in 1993.

Footnotes

1 I am indebted to Ed Labinsky, Pauline Joli de Lotbiniere, and Robert Scott Sheffield (past graduate students from the Universities of British Columbia and Victoria) for their assistance in documenting and researching issues pertaining to *Stó:lō* veterans.

2 James W. St. G. Walker, "Race and Recruitment in World War One: Enlistment of Visible Minorities in the Canadian Expeditionary Force," *Canadian Historical Review,* Vol.LXX, 1989.

3 MacInnes to all Inspectors, Indian Agents and the Indian Commissioner for British Columbia, August 6, 1940, (RG 10, c-8514, file # 452-26; Chief Registrar to McGill, August 3, 1940, RG 10, c-8514, vol.6770, file #452-26, (Microfilm copies at *Stó:lō* Nation Archives – SNA). See also Robert Scott Sheffield, *"...In the Same Manner as Other People": Government Policy and the Military Service of Canada's First Nations People,* (University of Victoria, Unpublished M.A. Thesis, 1995) Chapter 3.

4 Sheffield, p.54.

5 Correspondence Outward, McGill, August 20, 1940, RG 10, c-8514, vol. 6770, file 452-26), (Microfilm copy at *Stó:lō* Nation Archives).

6 Sheffield, p.103

7 See Chapter 5 this volume.

8 Maclauchlan to Camsell, March 18, 1941, cited in Sheffield, p.23.

9 Ibid., p.23.

10 Directorate of History, National Defence Headquarters, 75/347, April 4, 1939. (Microfilm copy at SNA).

11 Sheffield, p.28-30. Sheffield also shows that at least initially the army was even reluctant to accept Aboriginal people due to poor health conditions and inferior residential schools education levels.

12 Wes Sam in conversation with Charlie Fisher and Keith Thor Carlson, September 23, 1993. (Fieldnotes on file at SNA).

13 At least four *Stó:lō* men enlisted in the United States Armed Forces during WWII. Apparently, those who joined the U.S. services did so because they were living in the States participating in a modified version of their traditional seasonal rounds at the time. One *Stó:lō* woman is also known to have participated in the Canadian Armed Forces.

14 Charlie Fisher in conversation with Wes Sam and Keith Thor Carlson, September 23, 1993. (Fieldnotes on file at SNA).

15 Herald Wells in conversation with Scott Sheffield, May 11, 1995, Hope B.C. (Tape on file at SNA).

16 Wes Sam in conversation with Pauline Joli de Lotbiniere, May 12, 1993. (Tape on file at SNA).

17 "Department of Veteran Affairs Benefits," A document published by the Canadian Senate Committee on Aboriginal Affairs, Senate of Canada, 140 St. Wellington St., Ottawa Ontario. This document outlines the benefits all veterans are/were entitled to.

18 Charlie Fisher in conversation with Wes Sam and Keith Thor Carlson, September 23, 1993. (Fieldnotes on file at SNA)

19 See Chapter 5 this volume.

20 Sonny McHalsie in conversation with Keith Carlson, June 19, 1995. (Tape on file at SNA).

21 Wes Sam in conversation with Keith Carlson, Soowahlie, B.C., July 1992. (Fieldnotes on file at SNA)

22 When asking for direction on how to discuss the personal history of people who were sometimes not well liked or perhaps misunderstood by their community in the past, Elder Frank Malloway suggested that it was not appropriate to bring up something that might hurt or embarass their living family members: "its past history, its past history, it shouldn't be talked about, you know." Frank Malloway in conversation with Heather Myles and Tracy Joe, Yakweakwioose, June 17, 1996. (Taped copy and transcript on file at SNA). See Chapter 1, this volume.

23 Wes Sam in conversation with Keith Carlson and Pauline Joli de Lobiniere, Soowahlie, May 14, 1993. (Transcript on file at SNA).

24 Wes Sam in conversation with Pauline Joly de Lotbiniere. Soowahlie, May 12, 1993. (Transcript on file at SNA).

25 See Chapter 5 this volume.

the Aboriginal Right *to* Fish

Laura Cameron

INTRODUCTION

The subject of Aboriginal fishing rights raises several critical issues pertaining to human rights, constitutional and criminal law, as well as the history of the Canadian justice system. The term Aboriginal means people who have existed in a place from time immemorial.[1] It asserts nothing about race. If a people who have occupied a place from time immemorial happened to have green eyes and red hair, they would still, of course, be Aboriginal inhabitants. The basis of the *Stó:lō* claim to Aboriginal fishing rights rests on their original control of fish resources in their traditional homelands and homewaters.

1 Ernie Crey, an Aboriginal fisherman active in Aboriginal fisheries management explains that,

> **a**s a member of the Cheam Band, which is one of more than 20 Indian band communities that make up the nation of the *Stó:lō* people, my history tells me that salmon is the reason I am here. We are salmon people. The history of the salmon in this part of the world is my own people's history. The salmon, and the Fraser River, define who we are. We take our name from the word that we give the river: *Stó:lō*. Our history tells us that at the beginning of the world, salmon was given to the *Stó:lō* by *Xä:ls*, the creator and great Transformer. He taught us how to survive by maintaining a good relationship with salmon. He taught us how to fish for salmon, how to cook it, and how to look after it.[2]

The rights of Aboriginal people are recognized in *Canada's Constitution Act of 1982*. Aboriginal people are guaranteed the same individual rights that all Canadians enjoy, but are also entitled to certain additional collective rights, held in keeping with their existence and culture. Treaties, officially negotiated government to government, may seek to end, or extinguish, collective rights.

The *British Royal Proclamation of 1763* affirmed pre-existing common law rights, followed by Crown authorities in most of the areas east of the Rocky Mountains, that Aboriginal people hold continuing rights to their lands, except when they voluntarily decide to surrender them to the Crown through treaties. Only then are those rights extinguished. "If at any Time any of the Said Indians should be inclined to dispose of the said Lands, the same shall be Purchased only for Us, in our Name, at some public Meeting or Assembly of the said Indians."[3] The Crown has made over eighty treaties with the vast majority of Aboriginal groups in Canada since 1763, promising certain benefits and compensation in return for the extinguishment of Aboriginal title to lands desired by the Crown. Later, we will explore the significant fact that the Crown failed to negotiate treaties with Aboriginal

groups living in the area named British Columbia.

Part of the Constitution, *The Charter of Rights and Freedoms*,[4] states that:

Section 25

The guarantee in this Charter of certain rights and freedoms shall not be construed so as to abrogate or derogate from any aboriginal, treaty or other rights of freedoms that pertain to the aboriginal people of Canada including,

(a) any rights or freedoms that have been recognized by the Royal Proclamation of October 7, 1763; and

(b) any rights or freedoms that now exist by way of land claims agreements or may be so acquired.

Aboriginal rights also are recognized elsewhere in the Constitution Act of 1982:

Section 35

(1) The existing aboriginal and treaty rights of the Aboriginal peoples of Canada are hereby recognized and affirmed.

(2) In this Act, "Aboriginal peoples of Canada" includes the Indian, Inuit and Metis peoples of Canada.

Section 35 does not define what "Aboriginal rights" are. The Aboriginal population has long defined these rights for themselves. However, the legal interpretation of Section 35 has largely fallen within the domain of the courts.

Those who make legal judgments on Aboriginal rights are often asked to understand the past in many different ways. They may easily accept evidence from dominant culture, such as letters between colonial officials. However, they may also be asked to accept and listen to evidence which may be unfamiliar to them in form and content, such as oral tradition which is passed from generation to generation. By ruling on such evidence, judges decide not only what happened in the past, but they simultaneously influence future interpretations of the law.

Aboriginal people have continued to assert their Aboriginal rights to fish, even though, as the former Assembly of First Nations leader for B.C. Chief Joe

Mathias states, "through an array of federal and provincial legislation, Indian people were prohibited by law from even trying to protect our rights."[5]

After exploring Aboriginal fishing rights in their historical context, we will look at recent legal decisions that are remaking Canadian law.

2 TRADITIONAL ABORIGINAL FISHING IN BRITISH COLUMBIA ■

The Fraser River is one of the world's great salmon producing rivers. Depending on season and cycle, several species of salmon – pink, chum, coho, sockeye and chinook – continue to make their way from deep-sea habitats to their spawning grounds in the Fraser River system. Salmon has always been the principle source of food for Aboriginal people living along the rivers of the Pacific northwest coast. The enormity of the salmon harvest on the Pacific coast and the coastal rivers can perhaps be better appreciated with some figures. Scholars estimate that there were between 10,000 - 30,000 *Halq'eméylem* speakers in the century prior to *Xweitem* colonization.[6] According to rough estimates regarding nutritional needs and other available food, 220 kg of fresh salmon were consumed per person annually,[7] for an upper limit of 88 million kg of salmon consumed per year in the B.C. area.

But salmon were never exclusively used for personal consumption. Besides its importance for social and ceremonial purposes, salmon was an important trade item in both local and external exchange networks. When the Hudson's Bay Company established Fort Langley in 1827, the *Stó:lō* maintained their fishing customs and practices, but saw in the company trade a new opportunity from which they could benefit. The *Stó:lō* became major players in the cured salmon trade with the Sandwich Islands (Hawaii).[8]

As the commercial fisheries and canning operations expanded dramatically in the late nineteenth century, the harvesting expertise and cannery labour of *Stó:lō* and other

Salmon fishing along the Fraser River.

Aboriginals was absolutely critical to the industry.

Management of the Aboriginal fisheries was necessary because salmon, with their varying spawning cycles, could not be caught anytime, anywhere. The *Stó:lō* developed ways to cope with shortages as well as gluts. They developed diverse strategies to capture fish: dip nets, trawl nets, harpoons and a variety of fish traps. Different methods allowed them to exploit the fish resource at varying times and places. Weirs, fence-like fish traps which could be opened or closed, were built across wide slow moving rivers, and managed communally. The tremendous harvests were preserved on drying racks or smoked. Certain groups specialized in particular catches and these items were exchanged with other villages. Ernie Crey relates that "for the First Nations, the right to harvest salmon has always carried with it moral and spiritual imperatives of stewardship and conservation, whether the salmon was harvested for social, ceremonial or economic reasons.'" Because of their management of the salmon resource, Northwest Coast Aboriginal communities could support

Salmon weir located on the Cowichan River. "Salmon crowded into the enclosure and could be scooped or speared".

higher population densities than most non-agricultural peoples throughout the world.[10]

European Laws and Aboriginal People

Before Union with Canada in 1871, the B.C. fisheries were largely unregulated by colonial governments. The *Stó:lō* fisheries continued to harvest and manage fish for trade as well as for food and ceremonial purposes. With Union came the renewed expectation that treaties would be signed with Aboriginal people along the Pacific coast.

Governor James Douglas had already arranged treaties (known as the Douglas Treaties) with 14 'tribes' on a small portion of Vancouver Island between 1850 and 1854. In each instance where land was surrendered to Euroamericans, Aboriginal people were authorized to "carry on (their) fisheries as formerly."[11]

East of the Rocky Mountains, the making of treaties was an established practice of the British Crown. The Royal Proclamation of 1763 affirmed that "the several Nations or Tribes of Indians with whom we are connected and who live under our protection should not be molested or disturbed." Nevertheless, until the B.C. Treaty Commission was formed in 1993,[12] government authorities in B.C. had refused to recognize Aboriginal rights to land and resources and acted to ensure that no other treaties were arranged with the Aboriginal people along the Pacific coast. The treaty-making process broke down partly because the Crown and the Colony were in dispute as to which official body should compensate Aboriginals for lands surrendered. Besides the Douglas Treaties, no other treaties were negotiated to protect or extinguish Aboriginal rights in B.C. (except for a portion of northeastern B.C. covered by Treaty 8).

With the Constitution Act of 1867, Parliament was given legislative jurisdiction over "Indians and Lands reserved for the Indians." *The Enfranchisement Act 1869* was an attempt to quickly assimilate Aboriginals into *Xwelìtem* society. Originally the Act allowed for Aboriginal people to voluntarily give up their status as "Indians." The government was also authorized to replace Aboriginal traditional leadership with elected councils. The "so-called" *Indian Act*, remodelled many times since its foundation in the 1857 "Civilization Act," gave Ottawa the authority to administer the lives of Aboriginal people (those officially registered as "Indians"). The Indian Act was originally intended to assimilate Aboriginals into mainstream culture and force them to live under the protection and supervision of the federal government, while being schooled in the ways of "civilization." Traditional sacred and ceremonial practices such as the potlatch and winter dance were made criminal offenses. As Chief Joe Mathias states, "very obviously, the Indian Act was making it a criminal offense to practice the most sacred element of our culture and our religions. It struck at the very heart of our survival as races and nations of people. Its stripped us of a fundamental political institution."[13]

3 THE CREATION OF THE INDIAN FOOD FISHERY ■

The federal government also attempted to control the social and economic destinies of Aboriginal people through the Fisheries Act, although general provincial legislation would also affect the *Stó:lō*. When the fish canneries were established after 1871, Aboriginal people were integral to this industry's success. Ernie Crey explains that

Stó:lō people fished for the Fraser River canneries and worked on the canning lines. So did Musqueam people, Tsawwassen people, Nuu-Chah-Nulth people, Kwagewlths, Nisga'a people and Tsimshians. The canneries needed us. We knew how to fish, where to fish, and what to fish with.

But we were still pretty independent. We could sell to whoever we wanted to. When it was time to go home and fish for the winter, and for the smokehouse, we'd get up and go. If one cannery wasn't paying us what we wanted, we'd sell to another cannery.[14]

Regulation of fishing practices began in 1878 when Ottawa banned the use of salmon nets in freshwater. As the Aboriginal population began to decline and the immigrant population started to swell in the late 1880's, competition between Aboriginals and *Xwelítem* for salmon came to the attention of the Canadian state. In 1886, the number of canneries had dramatically expanded as well as the number of commercial fishers working on the Fraser River. When over-fishing became apparent in this naturally low-cycle salmon year, Aboriginal fishing in the headwaters of the Fraser was targeted for blame.[15] Continuing a national pattern begun in the Maritimes, the state soon acted on this political opportunity to assume control and management of the fishing industry

and limit Aboriginal access to fish.

The *Stó:lō*, who fished on the Fraser River between the coastal commercial fishery and the salmon spawning grounds, were now viewed as competitors to *Xwelítem* commercial interests. In 1888, federal authorities passed legislation which stated that the Aboriginal fishery was to provide food only for personal consumption. "...Indians shall, at all times, have liberty to fish for the purpose of providing food for themselves but not for sale, barter or traffic, by any means other than with drift nets, or spearing."[16]

Thus, federal policy instituted the idea that fishing for food was separate from any other use of fish, including trade. Without negotiation or consultation, the government had created the concept of the Indian food-fishery. "If an Indian wanted to fish for food, that was all right, but he couldn't trade his salmon and he couldn't sell his salmon. Suddenly the salmon belonged to the Queen. The fishery wasn't controlled by the Indians anymore."[17]

The licensing system introduced by the 1888 Fisheries Act would also curtail independent Aboriginal commercial fishing. The Act made it an offense to fish commercially without a license. Because most of the licenses would be issued to the canneries, the majority of Aboriginal people wanting to sell their fish would have to work for the canneries. The government policy thus acted to capture a cannery labour force composed of Aboriginal men and women. To the detriment of the entire fishing industry, the Fisheries Act worked to transform Aboriginal fishery managers into labourers, thus undermining the resource management expertise of Aboriginal fishers.[18]

4 RESISTING THE FISHERIES ACT ■

As Crey states, "from 1888 onward, the great tribal fisheries of the Fraser River watershed were under attack. Fisheries officers were sent throughout the interior to tear down our fishing weirs, to dismantle our traps, and to keep us away from the river." In 1894, *Stó:lō* chiefs, including Chief John Sualis of Soowahlie, protested against the licensing system by petition.

> . . . We are troubled when we are told that we must no longer catch our fish in the way we have always caught them, viz., the long net anchored along the sides of our streams and rivers. We are also told that certain seasons we may catch Salmon for our own use, but not sell them to white people. We think this very unjust, for there are times when the sale of Salmon would bring to us little things which we could not otherwise have. And when the Salmon are in season, why should the Indians be compelled to pay licenses for catching and selling what belongs to them?[19]

The Fisheries Policy of 1894 required Aboriginal nets to be tagged with special markers. In testimony to a federal-provincial government commission in 1915, Chief Selesmlton (Ned) of the Sumas Band at Kilgard indicated his people's dissatisfaction with the tagging system and the fisheries regulations in general.[20]

Q. Do they do any fishing for the canneries?

A. Once in a while we go down but we have to buy a license.

Q. Have they got any gasoline boats?

A. We have no gasoline boats - we have rowboats and canoes.

Q. So that when you go down to the canneries you work on a cannery license.

A. We hardly ever go down. We used to buy our own license, but we don't do it now.

Q. Why did they stop that?

A. Because we don't make nothing anymore.

Q. Is there any interference in getting their fish supply?

A. That is where the trouble is; when we try to get our fish for the winter we are stopped.

Q. How does the trouble come about?

A. Because the white people own the fish and they are taking care of the fish and they have game and fisher inspectors after us all the time.

Q. But under the law can't they get all the fish they want?

A. No, they don't get enough that way.

Q. Why does the Inspector of fisheries get after you?

A. The reason we don't get enough fish during the season is when we go out and set our nets we have to stay right with it all the time - if we pull a fish out of the lake [Sumas Lake] the fishery inspector takes the net away from us.

Q. I understand that you get a tag and that is attached to the net, and do you mean to say that when that net is set with the tag attached to it that the fishery inspector comes and takes that net away?

A. Sometimes we lose those tags.

Q. So that is it, when there is no tag on the net he takes it away?

A. Yes.

Q. Well, the Indian must keep his tag because if the fishery inspector finds a net without a tag on it he thinks it is a poacher - you must therefore look after your tag and see that it is attached properly to your net?

A. The tag is stolen from the net.

Q. Who does that?

A. I don't know.

Indian agent Byrne: They must be whitemen or half-breeds who does that and puts them on their nets.

Aboriginal people continued to assert their rights to fish and sell their catch despite provincial and federal opposition. After the Hell's Gate disaster in 1913 when salmon runs were devastated by rock slides caused by railway construction in the Fraser Canyon as well as by commercial over-fishing, the government curtailed Indian "food fishing" in the Fraser

River. They also took this opportunity to attempt to eliminate the Aboriginal "food fishery" altogether. Although the government ultimately relented, the "food fishery" became licensed in 1917 and subject to the same place, time, and gear restrictions as the commercial fishery. And not only would Aboriginal people be charged for selling their "food fishery" fish, the buying of these fish also became illegal.

In 1916, Aboriginal people in the province united under an organization called the Allied Tribes of BC to press Aboriginal claims for land and resources. They tried to open negotiations with the province and the federal government. However, in 1927, just before the Allied

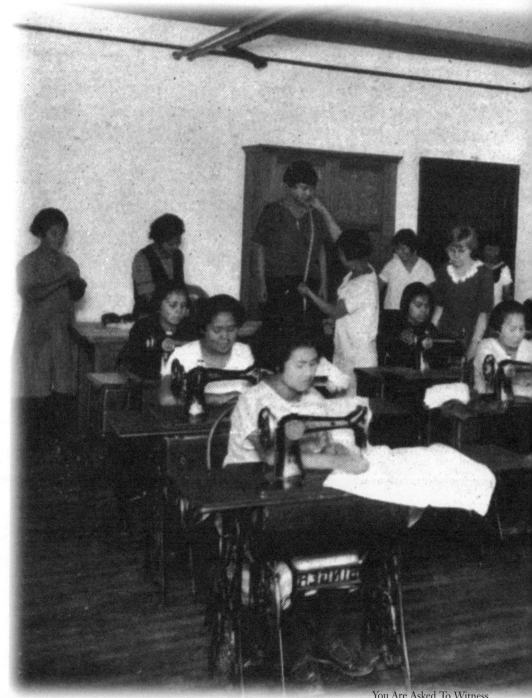

You Are Asked To Witness

Tribes went to Ottawa to press their claims, the federal government inserted a provision in the Indian Act which prevented Aboriginals from obtaining legal assistance to continue their legal battles.

According to the Indian Act, R.S.C. 1927, s. 141:

Every person who, without the consent of the Superintendent General expressed in writing, receives, obtains, solicits or requests from an Indian any payment or contribution of promise of any payment or contribution for the purpose of raising a fund or providing money for the prosecution of any claim which the tribe or band of Indians to which such Indian belongs, or of which he is a member, has or is represented to have for the recovery of any claim or money for the benefit of the said tribe or band, shall be guilty of an offense and liable upon summary conviction for each such offense to a penalty not exceeding two hundred dollars and not less than fifty dollars or to imprisonment for any term not exceeding two months. ☙

The provision remained on the books until 1951.

B.C. Aboriginal people also suffered within the Canadian justice system, being disqualified to vote federally until 1960. But renewed Aboriginal challenges to the legal system were beginning to make waves. When new fisheries regulations in 1968 closed the Fraser River to the "food fishery" from Mission Bridge to Lytton for almost the entire month of July, many *Stó:lō* were arrested and had their nets confiscated when they continued to fish. Although the new regulations were apparently intended to protect the Stuart Lake sockeye run, Aboriginal people noted that during the "closure" the commercial salmon fishery at the mouth of the Fraser River was permitted to remain open.[21] The conservation measures protected industry revenues, not Aboriginal fishing.

Fraser Valley Aboriginal leaders sent a brief to the federal government outlining their claims to Aboriginal fishing rights, which they stated were authorized by the Royal Proclamation of 1763.[22] After two years of protests from the *Stó:lō* over the July closure, the government allowed one 24 hour opening in the three-week closed season of 1968. At the time, Genevieve Mussell, a former *Stó:lō* chief and a leader in the protests, stated that "Indians fear they will lose all their fishing rights if there is not some definite recognition of an aboriginal right to the Fraser's fish resources."[23] Although Aboriginals would continue to be arrested for fishing against regulations, no longer would they do so quietly.

The justice system has begun to play an important role in clarifying the rights, rules, and responsibilities involved in the relationship between Aboriginal groups and government. Recent

Coqualeetza Residential School.

legal decisions have played a critical role in bringing the Department of Fisheries and Oceans and the Province of British Columbia to enter into negotiations with Aboriginal people regarding fishing rights. The legal issues are complex and require an understanding of history as well as law.

The following case summaries, beginning with the Calder decision in 1973, provide a brief introduction to a challenging subject. A review of the levels of Canada's judicial system will help us track trial decisions to higher courts of appeal.

SUPREME COURT OF CANADA
It is the highest court of appeal

B.C. COURT OF APPEAL
Hears matters that have been appealed from lower court decisions (not a trial court).

SUPREME COURT OF BRITISH COLUMBIA
Acts as the trial court for serious criminal cases.
Tries civil matters dealing with sums over $10,000.
Acts as the appeal court and certain
provincial court decisions, and for judicial review.

PROVINCIAL COURT
Criminal division tries most criminal matters.
Family Division is the trial court for many family matters and offenses committed under the Young Offenders Act.
Small Claim Division deals with most civil matters dealing with sums under $10,000.
Traffic Division deals with traffic violations.

Calder v. The Attorney General of British Columbia

In 1969, the Nisga'a Tribal Council decided to take the provincial government of British Columbia to the Supreme Court of B.C. The Nisga'a wanted the Court to declare that their Aboriginal title to the Nass Valley had never been lawfully extinguished. The court ruled against the Nisga'a, accepting the province's argument that the Royal Proclamation of 1763 did not apply to British Columbia, and thus did not create Nisga'a title to the Nass Valley. The Court also concluded that even if the Nisga'a did at one time have title, colonial land legislation had implicitly (not expressly, not plainly) extinguished that title before union with Canada in 1871. The Court accepted the province's argument that continuing Aboriginal rights were inconsistent with the colonial government's policies (such as creating Indian reserves and enacting laws which provided licenses for the exploitation of natural resources), and therefore these policies implicitly extinguished Aboriginal rights. The British Columbia Appeal Court upheld that decision, stating that Aboriginal rights exist only if the government recognizes them.

In 1973, the Calder case went to the *Supreme Court of Canada*. Of the seven judges (one of whom decided against the Nisga'a on a technical matter), three ruled that the Proclamation extended to B.C. and legally affirmed pre-existing Aboriginal title. Title had not been clearly and plainly extinguished, and thus the Nisga'a continued to hold title to their land. The three other judges ruled that the Proclamation did not apply to B.C. that the Nisga'a title had been implicitly extinguished. Nonetheless, they accepted the argument that Aboriginal title had once existed.

The province and the Nisga'a were thus tied three-three. In practical terms of land ownership, the lower court decision was upheld. However, the fact that six Supreme Court judges had accepted the concept of pre-existing title led to a revised federal policy on Aboriginal claims. Canada's highest court had declared that when the colonial government of B.C. was formed in 1858, the Nisga'a had a legal right to their territory.[24] The split decision on extinguishment raised the possibility of unextinguished title in Canada. In instances where Aboriginal rights had not been clearly extinguished, the federal government was now willing to negotiate modified modern treaties called comprehensive claims agreements.

In most of the comprehensive claims put forward in British Columbia, Aboriginal fishing rights were emphasized.[25] Although the federal government administers Indian Affairs policy, the province controls the land and most resources required to satisfy Ottawa's responsibilities to Aboriginal people.[26] Unlike every other province and territory in Canada, B.C. alone has refused to recognize Aboriginal land rights which would form the basis of comprehensive treaty negotiations. The B.C. government's continued refusal to recognize Aboriginal rights took pressure off Ottawa to negotiate treaties with B.C. Aboriginal people, although with the 1993 formation of the B.C. Treaty Commission this indicates that the province has changed their position.

Regina v. Sparrow

In the spring of 1984, Ron Sparrow went fishing in the Fraser River estuary. As a member of the Musqueam band (*Stó:lō* in heritage), Sparrow was licensed to fish for food. However, under the Fisheries Act Sparrow was restricted to using drift nets no longer than 46 meters. Sparrow's net was 82 meters in length and he was therefore charged with illegal fishing. Attempts to defend Sparrow's action led, six years later, to the first Supreme Court decision concerning Section 35(1) of the Constitution Act, 1982.

Sparrow admitted that his food fishing license did not permit him to fish with such a long net. However, he defended his action by arguing that he was exercising an Aboriginal right to fish. He said that the net limit restriction was a violation of Section 35(1), which recognized and affirmed existing Aboriginal and treaty rights.

Sparrow was convicted in Provincial Court. Citing the Calder decision, Judge Goulet ruled that an Aboriginal right could not be claimed unless it was supported by a formal treaty. The Musqueam were without a treaty regarding fishing rights and thus Section 35 did not apply. The County Court dismissed Sparrow's appeal for similar reasons.

Sparrow took his case to the B.C. Court of Appeal where the court ruled that the findings of the lower courts were flawed. The B.C. Appeal Court ruled that Section 35 is to be understood as a guarantee of Aboriginal rights: rights that could not simply be extinguished through government regulation. Furthermore, after necessary conservation measures, the Aboriginal food fishery is entitled to priority over any other group which harvested fish, such as the commercial or sports fisheries. A new trial was ordered to decide if government regulations had conflicted with Aboriginal rights. Both Sparrow and the government appealed this verdict.

In 1990, Sparrow went to the Supreme Court of Canada. The Supreme Court ruled that Section 35's phrase "existing Aboriginal rights" must be interpreted flexibly in order to permit their evolution over time. Aboriginal rights are not frozen in time, but must be interpreted in a contemporary setting. The Court stressed its obligation to deal with Section 35 liberally and generously, recognizing that the provision was intended to affirm those rights.

The Court also recognized the federal government's fiduciary relationship with Aboriginal people. Fiduciary means that the government is not supposed to act against Aboriginal interests, but rather must act to preserve and protect Aboriginal rights. Ottawa is thereby obliged to justify any government regulations, such as those in the Fisheries Act, that interfere with Aboriginal rights.

The Supreme Court rejected the government's claim that fisheries' regulations had extinguished Aboriginal rights to fish for food. Although the government had increasingly restricted Aboriginal fishing since 1878 to the use of certain equipment in particular times and places, nothing in the Fisheries Act demonstrated an intention to extinguish the Aboriginal right to fish. The Court ruled unanimously that mere regulation is not extinguishment. Furthermore, the Court ruled that "the test of extinguishment to be adopted, in our opinion, is that the sovereign's intention must be clear and plain if it is to extinguish an aboriginal right." Implicit extinguishment was insufficient.

Finally, the Supreme Court affirmed the priority of Aboriginal food fishing. After valid conservation measures are taken to sustain the fish resource, Indian food fishing must get top priority ahead of any other user group. The Court found there were further questions to be considered such as the validity of the government's net restriction. The case was returned to the trial court.

Delgamuukw v. The Queen

Like the Calder case, Delgamuukw, (the case named for a hereditary chief of the Gitksan), did not focus on the Aboriginal right to fish. However, as in Sparrow, the judges addressed the critical issues of Aboriginal rights and extinguishment.

In 1987, the hereditary chiefs of the Gitksan - Wet'suwet'en of the Skeena and Bulkley Rivers went to the Supreme Court of B.C. to claim ownership and jurisdiction over 57,000 square kilometres of their traditional territories and resources in northwestern British Columbia. They held that their right to these places had never been extinguished by the British Crown or Canada. Central to their argument was their contention that prior to contact with "Whites," they had managed their territorial resources and governed themselves according to the laws and practices of a sophisticated society. They argued that their systems of belief and government have continued to exist to present day, and claimed damages for the loss of all resources and lands since the establishment of the Colony of British Columbia.

The trial lasted three years. In 1991, the claim was dismissed completely by the B.C. Supreme Court. Chief Justice Allan McEachern ruled that Aboriginal rights exist only "at the pleasure of the Crown" and may be extinguished when the intent of the Crown to put an end to them is clear and plain. And he concluded that Aboriginal rights to land in the Colony of British Columbia had been extinguished by pre-Confederation laws regarding colonial ownership of land. He ruled that Aboriginal rights, including fishing rights, were only subsistence rights before European contact, and could not evolve to include a commercial aspect. He stated that the lives of Aboriginal people were "nasty, brutish and short" prior to European contact. For Justice McEachern, the Gitksan and Wet'suwet'en had the right only to "live in their villages and to occupy adjacent lands for the purpose of gathering the products of the lands and waters for subsistence and ceremonial purposes."

In June 1993, the B.C. Court of Appeal, found that Aboriginal rights in the territory had not been extinguished by pre-1871 enactments. However, the court ruled that Aboriginal rights to the claimed territories do not entitle them to jurisdiction or ownership. The nature and scope of the plaintiff's unextinguished Aboriginal rights, such as their rights to fisheries, were left for future determinations. As of August 1996, an appeal to the Supreme Court is proceeding, as negotiations between the Gitksan and Wet'suwet'en and the B.C. government have broken off.

R v. Vanderpeet

In September 1987, Charles Jimmie and Stephen Jimmie caught some sockeye salmon in the Fraser River near Yale. The salmon was caught legally, because each possessed valid Indian food Fish Licenses. Charles Jimmie took the fish back to his reserve in Chilliwack where he lived with Dorothy Marie Vanderpeet. Mrs. Vanderpeet is a member of the Tzeachten Band of the *Stó:lō* Nation. Later that day, Vanderpeet sold ten of the fish to a non-Aboriginal for $50. Vanderpeet was charged with unlawfully selling fish.

A.R.T. - Fishing + Hunting

Court rulings 'hammer' natives

Commercial fishers hail decisions as long needed

GORDON HAMILTON
Sun Business Reporter

A court ruling denying the aboriginal right of native Indians to sell salmon is being hailed as a victory by the commercial fishing industry, while Indian groups say they will fight the battle another day.

And on the Fraser River, the ruling — although a disappointment — has changed nothing for Indian fishers, says Ernie Crey, of the native-run Lower Fraser Fishing Authority.

"Life goes on," Crey said Monday, noting that Sto:Lo Indians along the lower Fraser have been catching and selling fish since the 1880s.

"In the past the court and the department of fisheries . . . have prohibited the sale of Indian-caught fish. Notwithstanding that we have caught and sold our fish."

A panel of five B.C. Court of Appeal judges ruled 3-2 Friday to uphold an earlier lower court conviction against Sto:Lo member Dorothy Marie Van der Peet for selling Fraser River salmon.

"It's the clarification we have been looking for for a long time," said Mike Hunter, president of the Fisheries Council of B.C.

"It makes clear there is an aboriginal pot of fish (for food, ceremonial and social purposes) and a commercial pot of fish. Don't confuse the two."

The question now is what new Fisheries and Oceans Minister Ross Reid intends to do, said Crey.

The federal government announced last week it had enacted licencing regulations under its abo-

RESEARCH

Notwithstanding (past prohibitions) we have caught and sold our fish

ERNIE CREY

"

riginal fisheries strategy which would allow native Indians to sell fish under certain conditions.

And the Sto:Lo signed an agreement Friday — the same day the court ruling was handed down — with the department of fisheries and oceans setting an allocation for Indian fish sales.

The department of fisheries had no comment on the Appeal Court decisions or the Sto:Lo allocation agreement.

The Van der Peet ruling was one of eight landmark decisions handed down Friday. Five of the eight concerned fishing rights.

Besides the Van der Peet ruling,

It's the clarification we have been looking for for a long time

MIKE HUNTER

"

two others dealt with the sale of food fish. The court upheld the conviction of two Heiltsuk Indians for attempting to sell herring roe, and the conviction of a fish processor for unlawfully buying food fish.

Two other rulings upheld convictions which limit the right of Indians to exercise band bylaws over rivers and lakes.

The five fish-related decisions represent a setback for native aspirations to establish separate Indian regulated-fisheries.

"We got hammered," Gitksan and Wet'suwet'en leader Don Ryan said of the ruling against band bylaws.

"This has pushed us back to the

We got hammered. This has pushed us back to the high-water mark

DON RYAN

"

high-water mark."

Sto:Lo chief Ken Malloway, a relative of Van der Peet, said he is disappointed with the decision denying the right to sell fish. The issue will now go to the Supreme Court of Canada.

"It's not over," Malloway said.

Jack Nicol, former president of the United Fishermen and Allied Workers Union, said the federal government should scrap its aboriginal strategy, which he called "purely political."

"Now the courts have found there isn't a right, the government ought not to create a right that doesn't exist," he said.

Court Rulings 'Hammer' Natives, by Gordon Hamilton.

Under the Fisheries Regulations (Section 27(5)), "to sell or barter fish caught under such an Indian Food Fish license is an offense."

At trial, the Crown admitted that the fish sold by Vanderpeet were caught in keeping with *Stó:lō* people's Aboriginal right to fish. Vanderpeet claimed that this included the right to sell the fish. The right had not been extinguished and the Fisheries Act legislation that infringed on her right to sell was therefore invalid.

The trial judge heard a wealth of evidence about *Stó:lō* traditional practices of trading and bartering their fish. He concluded, however, that the trade which occurred prior to the colonization of B.C. was only incidental to food fishing and did not "take place in any regularized or market sense." Vanderpeet was convicted and fined $50.

Vanderpeet's appeal to the Supreme Court of British Columbia was successful. Justice Selbie ruled that the trial judge erred in considering contemporary tests for "marketing" to decide whether or not salmon was traded in Aboriginal B.C. He stated that the evidence presented led to the conclusion that the Aboriginal right to fish did indeed include the right to sell fish. He ruled that Aboriginal rights to trade are not "frozen" but instead have evolved to entitle Aboriginal people to sell for money.

It has been held that the Aboriginal right to hunt is not frozen in time so that only the bow and arrow can be used in exercising it - the right evolves with the times. So, in my view, with the right to fish and dispose of them, which I find on the evidence includes the right to trade and barter them. The Indian right to trade his fish is not frozen in time to doing so only by the medium of the potlatch and the like - he is entitled, subject to extinguishment or justifiable restrictions, to evolve with the times and dispose of them by modern means, if he so chooses, such as the sale of them for money. It is thus my view that the Aboriginal right of the *Stó:lō* peoples to fish includes the right to sell, trade or barter them after they have been caught.[27] 😊

Because the trial judge did not consider whether the right to sell had been extinguished, Justice Selbie returned the matter to the trial court. This issue had not been decided in **Sparrow** because the Supreme Court of Canada had ruled only on the food fishery, not on the right to trade or sell fish.

The government appealed the decision. The BC Court of Appeal's judgment in June 1993 was made at the same time as the ruling in the **Delgamuukw** case and six other cases concerning hunting and fishing rights. In a 3-2 decision, the Appeal Court ruled in favour of the government, stating that the right to fish does not include the right to sell fish.

Two of the concurring judges held that the sale of fish

to the Hudson's Bay Company in the period 1820-40 was not a logical progression of the traditional trading practices of the *Stó:lō*, because "selling" was not an Aboriginal tradition; so Vanderpeet could not argue that she was exercising an Aboriginal right when she sold the fish. The third concurring judge looked to the results of affirming an Aboriginal right to sell fish, and found that Aboriginal people would then be entitled to priority in the commercial fishery. He argued that such a result would incorrectly interpret the intention of Section 35, which was not meant to enlarge "existing aboriginal rights" beyond those recognized at the time the Crown asserted sovereignty over B.C.

The two dissenting judges upheld the lower court's verdict. One of these judges rejected the proposition that "aboriginal rights describe pre-contact life." He stated that at the time of the Crown's assertion of authority in B.C., the *Stó:lō* had been exercising their pre-existing right to fish for commercial purposes as well as subsistence purposes for several years. The other dissenting judge ruled that the right to trade or sell fish is an unextinguished evolving right which was exercised lawfully by Vanderpeet when she sold the salmon.

The Vanderpeet case went to the Supreme Court of Canada at the end of November, in 1995. As of August 1996, a decision has not yet come down.

Concluding Comments from the *Stó:lō* Nation Special Chief's Council Portfolio Holder for Aboriginal Rights and Title:

There never was an agreement between First Nations and the government of Canada that we shouldn't be able to barter our fish...and we've always practiced our right. I'm just speaking for Sumas here. We have many, many, many charges...my father and probably his father before him, and even my mother, were charged for selling fish. So we have many charges on this reserve and we've always practiced our rights even though it was... people call it Black Market or whatever. Some of my people here on the reserve, that's their only extra money gained throughout the year.
(Chief Lester Ned, 1995)

Recommended Further Readings:

"Law 12 Source File, Unit 1, Introduction to Law" Technology and Distance Education Branch, Ministry of Education, Victoria, B.C. November 1993.

Dianne Newell, *Tangled Webs of History,* Toronto: University of Toronto Press, 1994.

Tennant, Paul, *Aboriginal People and Politics: The Indian Land Question in British Columbia,* Vancouver: University of British Columbia Press 1990.

Peter Usher, "Some Implications of the Sparrow Judgement for Resource Conservation and Management," Alternatives 18, 2 (1991).

Reuben Ware, *Five Issues Five Battleground,* 1983.

Footnotes

1   Immemorial: extending back beyond record, memory or knowledge.

2   Excerpt from Ernie Crey, executive-director, Lower Fraser Aboriginal Fisheries Commission, November 7, 1993 to "Action Agenda for Self-Government" conference, 1.

3   Paul Tennant, *Aboriginal Peoples and Politics,* p.11.

4   View World Wide Web Virtual Library-Law for Constitution. Also Annotated Indian Act 1994.

5   Chief Joe Mathias, "Conspiracy of Legislation," from unpublished paper, January 21, 1986, p.1.

6   Robert T. Boyd, "Demographic History, 1774-1874," 136. Robert M. Galois, "The Native Population of the Fort Langley Region, 1780-1857: A Demographic Overview," contracted by Parks Canada, Canadian Heritage Department, 1995. See also Cole Harris, "Smallpox around of Georgia in 1782," *Ethnohistory* 41, 4 (Fall 1994)618, ftn. 112.

7   Dianne Newell, *Tangled Webs of History,* p.29.

8   In 1831, the Hudson's Bay Company cured 300 barrels of salmon traded from the Aboriginals (each containing 60-90 fish). In 1849, when major markets for cured salmon in the Sandwich Islands (Hawaii) had been established, the company was curing 2610 barrels. [*Evidence considered by Judge Scarlet: Appendix E Tab 5 of Exhibit 29 by Mary Cullen, for Vanderpeet in 5 WWR (1993), p.490]. (See Chapter 3 this volume.)

9   Crey, "Aboriginal rights," *Legal Perspectives,* (April/May 1992), p4.

10 Newell, *Tangled Webs,* p.29; see also Cole Harris, "Smallpox around the Strait of Georgia," p.607.

11 Cited in Newell, *Tangled Webs,* p.48.

12 In 1993, the New Democratic Party government of B.C. whose election promise was to negotiate claims with Natives and recognize Aboriginal rights, formed the B.C. Treaty Commission. Results indefinite at this point.

13 Mathias, "Conspiracy," p.5.

14 Crey, speech, p.3.

15 Newell, p.65.

16 Reuben Ware, Five Issues Five Battleground, p.21.

17 Crey, speech, p.3.

18 Newell, p.62.

19 Cited in Ware, p.23.

20 BCARS. Royal Commission on Indian Affairs for the Province of B.C. 1913-1915, Union of B.C.Indian Chiefs, pp157-58.

21 Newell, p.146.

22 Cited in Newell, p.147: from Vancouver Sun, 29 November 1967.

23 Cited in Newell, p.147: from Vancouver Province 16 April 1968.

24 Tennant, p.221.

25 Newell, p.218.

26 Newell, p.21.

27 Reasons for Judgement of the Honourable Mr. Justice W.S. Selbie in the Supreme Court of British Columbia between Her Majesty the Queen and Dorothy Marie Vanderpeet, August 14, 1991. pp.9-10.

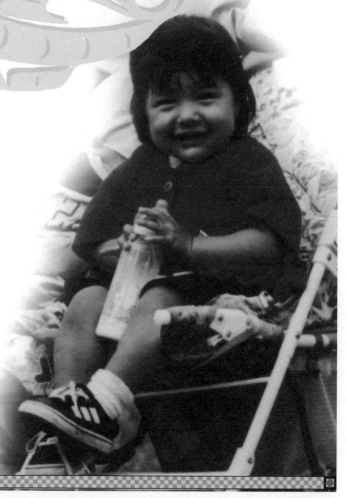

CHAPTER 9

Salmon *and* Aboriginal Fishing *on the* Lower Fraser River

Present Day

Management Issues, Concerns, *and* Impacts

Vince Harper

INTRODUCTION

The *Stó:lō* have a close kin relationship with salmon. Not only do the salmon provide nourishment, they also occupy an important role in *Stó:lō* culture and spirituality. *Stó:lō* management of their salmon fisheries was effective for thousands of years before the arrival of *Xwelítem* to the Fraser Valley. Although the *Stó:lō* have never surrendered their right to fish, their control over the fisheries has undergone profound shifts since the arrival and settlement of *Xwelítem* into the Fraser Valley. Today, salmon and salmon habitat resources are at tremendous risk, due to impacts related to urbanization and industrialization. This chapter illustrates why innovative management options that draw on traditional *Stó:lō* fisheries management must be identified and adopted in order to ensure the future of this valuable resource.

Fraser River.

1 THE RESOURCE AT RISK ■

Through extensive enhancement projects in the last few decades, species such as sockeye and pink salmon appear to be holding their own. Others such as the coho and chinook salmon are not doing as well. A frequently cited problem for declining fish stocks is decreased quantity and quality of fish habitat.

Salmon are well adapted to the variable natural habitats of the north temperate zones. They are, however, very environmentally sensitive fish, particularly in terms of habitat and water quality requirements during the incubating and rearing portions of their life cycle. Typical food items for those species that utilize streams for nursery purposes are terrestrial and aquatic invertebrate animals, whose own life cycles depend on similar habitat and water quality values as salmonids.

In general, the freshwater phase of the salmon life cycle requires fairly cool, well-oxygenated water, with clean gravel on the bottom, and abundant shade and cover to hide in. Special conditions are required for successful spawning, the development and hatching of eggs, and the growth and survival of their young. Small salmon travel around to different habitats as they get older, and therefore need to have access up and down the streams and into smaller tributaries including wetlands, side-channels, and swampy areas. When spawning, they need to be able to move up the streams and have suitable water levels and quality available in order to complete their life cycles.

The range of environments that salmon live in during their life cycles makes them very susceptible to environmental changes, especially those changes that affect water use and impacts of land use activities on the aquatic environment. Habitat use by salmonids varies widely not only with species, but also within runs of species, between discrete populations, or even between individuals of the same population. This makes any generalization about

Harrison River showing log booms.

their areas of preference and habitat requirements difficult. Damage to habitat was evident by the 1950's with many of the salmon streams only producing a fraction of their original run sizes. Although more regulations are currently in place than ever before, the fish habitat in British Columbia is still very much at risk.

2 IMPACTS ON FISH HABITAT ■

Historical Examples

When the Canadian Pacific Railway started work in the 1880s through the Fraser Canyon, a large amount of rock was dumped into the Fraser River from the adjacent hillsides, filling in important back-eddies which the salmon used as resting areas when they moved through this section of the river. There is no evidence that this had any significant effect on the salmon from the 1880's through to 1912. However, new railroad construction in 1911-12 started a chain of events which, when combined with a huge commercial catch in 1913 of 32 million sockeye (a record catch never since repeated), were to have a catastrophic impact on the salmon runs to the Fraser River system.

This new construction resulted in such an enormous quantity of rock being dumped into the river that flow patterns through Hell's Gate (Hell's Gate is an extremely narrow section of the Fraser River Canyon, located 200 km from the mouth of the river. Here, the drainage from 134,400 square kilometres of central British Columbia passes through a constricted area only 33 meters wide) were significantly altered. Only a few sockeye made it upriver to spawn, and most failed in their struggle. There was some removal of rock in September of that year, but it was too late for many of the fish. For example, the Salmon River had only a 1,000 sockeye return, all of which were speared by new Canadian set-

tlers. Only 600 sockeye entered Eagle River, and of these, only 100 were females. A single dead male sockeye was found on the beach of Adams Lake.[1]

The next winter, a large slide of rock at the same location made conditions at Hell's Gate even worse. A railroad tunnel under construction through a rock cliff over the eastern bank of the river collapsed, and 75,000 m³ of rock tumbled into the river. The width of the river was reduced to 25m with a 5m vertical drop over this distance. By 1915, it was estimated that 55,000 m³ of rock had been removed, 36,800 m³ dumped in the river and 18,000 m³ moved to high ground along the bank. However, the river bed never returned to normal. The rock deposited in 1913 produced a drop of 1.5m (5 ft); the rock slide of 1914 increased this to 4.5m (15 ft). The best that engineers could do at the time, was reduce the drop in water level through the gate from m to 2.75m (15 to 9 feet).

Finally, in 1946 and 1948, two fishways were built, one on each side of the river, and many of the upriver runs have experienced a partial restoration to their previous run sizes. Although the Hell's Gate slide of 1913 did impact sockeye stock, it should be noted that massive overfishing that year also played a significant role in diminishing subsequent salmon runs.

Contemporary photo of CPR at Hells Gate

Dam Construction

To date, the 1400 km stretch of the Fraser River mainstem in B.C. has managed to remain damless, but talks have been going on since the early 1900's. In 1912, a proposal to construct a dam across the Fraser about two and a half miles upstream of Yale was presented, but never carried through. If this project had gone ahead, the upriver salmon stocks would have surely been wiped out forever. However, some dams were built on several of the smaller tributaries flowing into the Fraser River, some of which once had salmon stocks in them, while others did not. For example, the effects of the Quesnel (removed in 1921) and Adams River (1908) dams on salmon populations in the Fraser River continue to the present day.

The devastating impacts that dams may have on migratory salmon stocks can be appreciated by looking at the Columbia River in the northern U.S. Over a dozen dams are built along the length of this river, and the sockeye salmon runs that once made it back into Canada through the Columbia River system are now basically extinct.

Forestry Impacts

One of the most common problems associated with decreasing salmon stocks has been the loss of salmon habitat due to poor forestry practices in the province. Most often, these impacts are due to logging too close to rivers and streams, or improper road construction built to gain access to forest resources.

Riparian area refers to land adjacent to the normal high water line in a stream, river or lake, extending to the portion of land that is influenced by the presence of the adjacent ponded or channelled water. Riparian areas typically exemplify rich and diverse vegetation which reflects the influence of available surface water. The importance of stream side vegetation to the health of the stream has

resulted in the development of Fisheries Sensitive Zones (FSZ) along aquatic habitats. FSZ are defined as instream aquatic habitats, as well as out-of-stream habitat features such as side channels, wetlands, and riparian areas.

A thriving riparian plant community is very important to the health of the water in the rivers and creeks for several reasons:
■ The density of vegetation in the riparian zone affects the amount of sunlight that reaches the stream, which in turn affects the temperature of the water. A dense cover of vegetation over a stream will trap most light before it reaches the water, and therefore prevents drastic increases in temperature which may be lethal to developing salmonids and other fish;
■ The root systems of the stream side plant communities are what hold together the stream bank soils preventing them from erosion. Surface erosion is controlled by the root mats of grasses and shrubs, while the roots of larger trees help maintain the structural integrity of the banks. Roots and organic debris also filter surface runoff which separates out suspended solids before they reach the stream channel;
■ The riparian zone is both a direct and indirect source of fish food. Insects fall into the water from overhanging vegetation which provides a direct source of food for fish. The organic material from the shrubs and trees such as leaves and needles are consumed by plant-eating invertebrates in the water, which in turn are eaten by salmonids and other fish species;
■ Vegetative cover also provides for protection from predation for developing juveniles and spawning adults.

Unfortunately, many of the same plant species targeted by the forest industry tend to grow best within the riparian zones of rivers and streams. As well, many forestry roads are also designed to parallel rivers and streams, because these are often the cheapest and easiest ways to gain access to lumber supplies. Although some of the destructive forest practices such as using rivers to transport logs downstream are no longer allowed, more work remains to be done to minimize the impacts of forestry on fish and fish habitat.

Agriculture

Agricultural practices have impacted salmon and salmon habitat in several ways. Some of these impacts include:
■ clearing of land next to streams or wetlands destroying the riparian zone;
■ use of herbicides and pesticides on agricultural crops or weeds which can enter the aquatic ecosystem through surface or groundwater runoff;
■ over-fertilizing land which causes excessive plant growth in streams leading to decreased oxygen levels for fish and

You Are Asked To Witness

other aquatic organisms when plants die and decompose;

■ use of ground and surface water for irrigation causing decreased levels of water in streams and wetlands for fish; and,

■ livestock using the water for drinking or grazing along the stream banks causing destruction of stream side vegetation, changes in the shape of the stream channel, changes to the water itself such as increases in temperature, suspended solids, and bacteria and destabilization of the stream banks through trampling and erosion.

Urbanization

Urbanization has the potential to seriously degrade and destroy fish habitat and impact fish populations. Two components of urbanization, are land developments and land use change. Some of the potential impacts that may be caused by urbanization are:

■ changes to the way in which water is cycled through a drainage basin by the removal of ground cover and forest canopy, which help to slowly release precipitation into streams through shallow subsurface flow or ground water. This leads to dramatic increases in the amount of water entering a stream following a storm event, which can lead to erosion of the stream channel and destruction of spawning and rearing habitat;

■ changes to the riparian vegetation by development or increased access by humans;

■ reduction in habitat complexity by decreasing the amount of pools in a stream and replacing them with more riffle areas;

■ loss of high and low water refuge areas; and,

■ degraded water quality through the introduction of sediments, nutrients, bacteria, oxygen-demanding substances, heavy metals, petroleum hydrocarbons, and synthetic organics.

There are also additional factors which compound the problem of managing and protecting the salmon stocks. Federal, provincial, regional, and municipal jurisdictions often overlap in habitat management. Also, it is uncertain how many fish are lost over time through habitat destruction as this is hard to measure. Another problem is the provincial Water Act which governs management of water does not take the needs of fish into account. Finally, the amount of productive habitat - in existence or lost - is largely unknown. Even though extensive efforts are being put forth to collect this data, the relationship between fish production and habitat is still uncertain.

3 GOVERNMENT INTERVENTION

Salmonid Enhancement Program (SEP)

Although enhancement techniques to augment salmon production, such as the building of hatcheries, were originally proposed over 100 years ago, it was not until the late 1960's and early 1970's that the federal government started to take a real interest in salmon enhancement in Canada. By the time the *Salmonid Enhancement Program (SEP)* was officially initiated in 1977, Canada already had 11 chinook and coho hatcheries in B.C. and over 20 years of experience with spawning channels and fishways.

The purpose of SEP was to attempt to rebuild salmon stocks to the levels that were present at the turn of the century. The intent was to double the catch of salmon over 30 years from an anticipated public sector investment of $30 million ($1976) per year.[2]

Various methods have been deployed which are forms of salmonid enhancement. These include: hatcheries, spawning channels, salmon fishway passages, incubation units, lake enrichment through fertilizer applications and other forms of habitat improvements.

There have been several biological concerns identified with respect to "enhanced" versus "wild" stocks. Some of the concerns cited include:
■ "enhanced" fish tend to be bigger than "wild" fish of the same age and may out- compete the wild stocks for food;
■ "enhanced" stocks may warrant larger harvests, while at the same time create a greater impact on the bi-catch of smaller, wild stocks; and
■ the dilution of wild gene pools by hatchery fish.

Peter Pearse of the Canadian Wildlife Federation has indicated that the SEP should be reoriented to put more emphasis on rehabilitating natural stocks through habitat improvement, rather than expanding hatcheries.[3] He has also suggested that SEP should focus on meeting specific management objectives for particular fisheries. Finally, he suggests re-evaluating the effectiveness and efficiency of the program from both a scientific and socio-economic standpoint.

According to Edgar Birch, a former federal SEP employee, "Salmon aren't like steers or chickens. With hatcheries, you get a lot of fish, but every year they come back weaker."[4]

Fisheries Mismanagement

According to Terry Glavin, salmon fishing technologies must be specific and selective in order to be sustainable. Instead of managing salmon stocks generally, the Department of Fisheries and Oceans should have been managing specific, distinct populations of salmon. "The large-scale management models that govern B.C. salmon fisheries, and the non-selective gears deployed in these fisheries, by their very nature tend to produce unsus-

tainable harvests whenever fisheries are conducted in "mixed stock" situations."[5] Glavin goes on to explain that each salmon run can sustain various degrees of fishing pressure. Runs with higher ocean survival rates and higher fry to smolt survival rates can sustain higher harvesting rates. So that by harvesting fish within an industrial large scale model it is impossible to consider variables in runs. Fishing equipment like trawl gear, or gillnets fisheries are what Glavin deems "the most dangerous non-selective fisheries on the B.C. coast." Unfortunately, much of the equipment used on the B.C. coast can be described as non-selective.

4 FUTURE MANAGEMENT OPTIONS ■

Applying Traditional Methods to Current Harvesting

The current management challenge of the fishery is to ensure enough fish of each species reach their spawning grounds in order to maintain the population. The number of excess fish, called the surplus, has to then be allocated among the various harvesters. In Canada, this is the responsibility of DFO. However, some of the salmon stocks that spawn in Canada pass through U.S. waters and are intercepted by U.S. fishermen and vice versa. To deal with this problem, Canada and the U.S. have formed the Pacific Salmon Commission, which has the responsibility to allocate the catches of these stocks between the two countries for those fisheries taking place in the treaty area (roughly the Strait of Juan de Fuca and the southern part of the Strait of Georgia). Outside of this area each country's fisheries department manages their respective fisheries.

While the tribes of Washington State are closely integrated with the Washington State Department of Fisheries, as a result of the Boldt Decision in 1974 which gave Aboriginal groups half of the salmon catch, the same cannot be said for the Aboriginal people living in Canada. Although the results of the Sparrow decision and other court cases have recognized that Aboriginal people have first rights of access to the fish after conservation, we still have a long way to go in order to catch up to the level of co-management currently seen in parts of the U.S. The Aboriginal Fisheries Strategy is intended to address this issue and more progress is expected in the future to reach this level of cooperation.

In-river Based Fisheries

Traditional in-river based methods like those practiced by the *Stó:lō* have been recognized as effective by biologists who see the need for a change in how the West Coast fisheries are currently administered and managed. They feel the use of devices such as weirs and/or traps at strategic locations along the mainstem and tributaries of major salmon producing rivers like the Fraser, would be

of considerable help in addressing some of the common recurrent problems seen in the fishery today such as dwindling numbers of wild stocks, accidentally catching threatened or endangered species, and more competition between the various stakeholders for their "fair share" of the fish. Supporters of a change to in-river fisheries say this would make the management of the fishery easier to control and predict. The use of in-river weirs and traps would enable fishery managers to obtain more accurate estimates of the size of the various fish runs on a stock by stock basis while at the same time, reduce or even eliminate the accidental deaths of those species or stocks considered threatened or endangered.

Another argument for change is that many of the current harvest methods are not selective in what they catch. This means that while targeting a certain type or stock of fish, other species or stocks that are considered threatened or in danger of extinction may inadvertently be caught at the same time. This is referred to as bycatch. Seine and gill net fisheries usually kill or at least badly injure fish, and therefore survival rates of released fish are often very low. A classic example of a fish that is faced with this problem every year are the Thompson River steelhead. These world-renowned sportsfish are extremely vulnerable to the commercial and aboriginal fisheries, because they tend to co-migrate with the fall chum runs up the Fraser River system. Due to the status of the stock (only 900 adult spawners were counted several years ago), the commer-

cial and aboriginal net fisheries are often limited or even shut down during the steelhead migrations to prevent accidental bycatch of these endangered species. These groups who are forced to cut back on their fishing time feel they are being treated unfairly, because a catch-and-release sports fishery continues to operate in the upper rivers for these same fish. Recent studies have found that 10% or more of the fish caught in a catch-and-release fishery will likely die due to the stress and energy loss caused by angling.

Some people argue that changing the major commercial catch from an ocean-based fishery to an in-river based fishery using traditional methods once employed by the *Stó:lō* and others, would alleviate much of the expense and uncertainties associated with the current commercial fishery. It seems ridiculous to invest millions of dollars in boats, gear, and manpower to chase around fish that are going to return to the rivers anyway. The in-river supporters including the *Stó:lō* argue "why not wait until the fish return and then harvest them?" In this way, there could be a more reliable count of how many salmon are returning on a stock by stock basis, which would make it easier to develop sustainable harvest levels on a stock by stock level. This would give added protection to the weaker endangered or threatened stocks by limiting the harvest levels while the protected fish are passing through. By using devices such as weirs or traps, those stocks identified as needing protection could be released more or face less harm, while the others could be harvested. Increasing reliable estimates of the numbers of fish returning on a stock by stock basis, would give fishery managers important information regarding where money needs to be invested in order to increase the populations of the various species and stocks. This in turn should result in more fish being produced, which would lead to increased harvest levels in the future. As mentioned, although the numbers of jobs related to the direct harvest of the fishery would most likely decrease, supporters for an in-river based fishery argue there would be more and more jobs created in processing the fish as the size of salmon runs increase over time.

Common Property

Despite the fact that Aboriginal people have never surrendered their fish to the Canadian government, the Pacific fisheries are managed as common property. This means that although the number of participants is limited by the Department of Fisheries and Oceans, the fish

do not belong to any one group or individual, they are regarded as the property of all Canadians. As a result, the share of the fish is decided by a catch-as catch-can fishery. Despite restrictions, the various B.C. fisheries have built bigger, faster, and more efficient fishing vessels. This means more money is being spent to catch the fish without there being a proportional increase in the number of fish to catch. To keep the level of harvest under control, fishery managers are faced with imposing more and more restrictions on the fisheries. This results in shorter, more hectic (and dangerous) seasons, greater fleet concentration, excesses of fish, and even more incentive to race for fish.

Individually Transferable Quotas

Recently, fisheries managers have looked at a new form of management based on the concept of individually transferable quotas (ITQ's). The idea is to divide the catch between harvesters based on a pre-season allocation of fish (or other species) to each harvester or vessel. ITQ's have been used in the past to deal with fisheries that have expe-

Fraser Valley logging has had a major impact on fish habitat.

Salmon weir.

rienced common property problems, such as overcapitalization (too many, too powerful boats); wasteful and dangerous fishing practices; chaotic, short seasons; overfishing pressures and conflict between users. New Zealand, for example, uses ITQ's for managing over 30 different species of marine resources. In the Pacific Region, geoducks (type of clam), sablefish, and halibut are now all managed by ITQ's with positive results. Each has demonstrated improved financial performance and as a result, the value of the licenses required to fish these species has increased dramatically. In turn, the resources are worth more on the market, and fishing costs have decreased as vessels use more economical mixtures of labour and capital.

However, ITQ programs have some drawbacks. If fees are not imposed at the beginning of the program, those people who already own licenses can often gain substantial profits. Also a transfer of quotas may lead to quota concentration in a few hands. ITQ programs may reduce employment although the length and stability of those employed may increase. Also, people may be inspired to dump lower grade fish (few survive) and keep the higher grade fish to fill their quotas. ITQ programs require extensive moni-

toring and enforcement to make them successful. Historian James McGoodwin notes, "in most cases, rights of access or rights over marine resources and marine properties should be conferred on fishing communities, not on individual fishers, particularly when communities are fairly homogenous."[6]

Fresh salmon from the Fraser Canyon.

Stó:lō fishers.

5 FUTURE OF THE RESOURCE ■

The future of the salmon fisheries in this province lies not only with ensuring that there is proper management and administration of the fisheries, but also ensuring the cooperation and support of Aboriginal fishers. Traditional *Stó:lō* fishing technology and management ideas must be drawn upon. As the *Stó:lō* have not surrendered their right to fish, their input into fisheries management is essential. We know that changes have to occur with management of this resource, and that the implementation of the changes will not be easy. Alternatives to current levels of harvest and harvest locations are only part of the answer. Public education is the rest. It is up to us to ensure there are salmon for future generations to come. The salmon depend on it; our children depend on it.

Recommended Further Readings:

Duff, W., **The Upper Stalo Indians,** (Victoria: Anthropology in British Columbia, Memoir No. 1, British Columbia Museum, 1952).

Glavin, Terry, **Dead Reckoning, Confronting the Crisis in Pacific Fisheries,** (Vancouver: Greystone Books, 1996).

Hewes, G.W., "Indian fisheries productivity in pre-contract times in the Pacific salmon area" **North West Anthropol: Res. Notes** pp.133-155.

Stewart, Hilary, **Indian Fishing: Early Methods on the Northwest Coast,** (Seattle and London: The University of Washington Press, 1977).

Roos, John F., **Restoring Fraser River Salmon: A History of the International Pacific Salmon Fisheries Commission,** (Vancouver: Pacific Salmon Commission, 1935-1985).

Footnotes

1   John F. Roos, **Restoring Fraser River Salmon: A History of the International Pacific Salmon Fisheries Commission, 1935-1985** (Vancouver: Pacific Salmon Fisheries Commission, 1985).

2   ARA Consulting Group, Inc. **Program Review: Salmonid Enhancement Program** (Ottawa: Prepared for Internal Audit and Evaluation Department of Fisheries and Oceans, 1993).

3   Peter H. Pearse, **Rising to the Challenge: A New Policy for Canada's Freshwater Fisheries** (Canadian Wildlife Federation, 1988).

4   Terry Glavin, **Dead Reckoning: Confronting the Crisis in Pacific Fisheries** (Vancouver: Greystone Books, 1996), p.84.

5   Ibid., p.86.

6   Ibid., p.141.

Changing Land Use *in* S'ólh Téméxw

(O u r L a n d) :
Population, Transportation,
Ecology and Heritage

Brian Thom & Laura Cameron

INTRODUCTION

The lower Fraser Valley has been occupied continuously for the past 10,000 years. Yet, it has only been within the last 150 years that a tremendous population boom has occurred with the movement of *Xwelítem* people into the region. Human transformations of the landscape from a bountiful ecosystem to one of developed roads, buildings, sewers, power lines, parks, and a dense population, have created new issues and concerns for *Stó:lō* people. This chapter examines urbanization within the lower Fraser River watershed (the region between Vancouver and Yale). It discusses the development, the population in the area, and provides a framework for understanding the many ecological and social impacts this has had on *Stó:lō* communities. The ramifications of the urbanization process extend beyond *Stó:lō* communities, and by using this as a focus for discussion, a broader understanding of the impacts on all communities emerges.

Imagine what the lower Fraser Valley was like before the development of cities. Imagine uninterrupted expanses of Douglas fir, cedar, and hemlock trees covering the uplands, while poplar trees and berry bushes grow in low lying areas closer to the river. The Fraser River was free of pollution, while its many streams and tributaries wound their way through the landscape.

Every year tens of millions of salmon spawned up the river. Elk and deer could always be found throughout the forests. Sturgeon, salmon and waterfowl occupied the shallow waters of Sumas Lake. Specially trained *Stó:lō* people burned some of these patches every few years to ensure rich berry picking and root harvesting soils in the seasons to come. *Stó:lō* villages dotted the landscape, particularly at the convergence of the many smaller waterways with the Fraser River. A few trails provide overland routes, but the streams, creeks, and rivers were the "highways" of the people. The Fraser River was the communication artery for the entire region. At least until the late 1700s, between 7,000 and 28,000 *Halq'eméylem* speaking people (the *Stó:lō*) were easily supported by the region's vast renewable resources.[1]

Now think of the current situation in the lower Fraser Valley, as seen from the window of a car on the Trans-Canada Highway. On a warm sunny day, the eastern valley skyline is a brown haze - the mountains sometimes completely obscured, the result of various gases produced by cars and industry. The highway roadside is dotted with signs, advertising the newest housing developments being constructed in the forested hillsides. The old Sumas Lake bed is home to livestock and heavily fertilized vegetables. A *Xwelítem* population of two million people have settled throughout the vast expanse of the now clear-cut forests, and are rapidly expanding onto the hills and mountains along the valley's fringe. Nineteen cities and twelve towns are linked by a complex series of roads that redefine the landscape. Urban underground infrastructure providing fresh water and sewage disposal have replaced streams and creeks. Forests and farmland are being encroached upon from all sides, as the region experiences urbanization.

1 POPULATION HISTORY & POPULATION PROJECTIONS ■

One of the most useful ways of understanding the changes in land use and the process of urbanization is by examining population trends. The *Stó:lō* have experienced this process of changing land use and urbanization. Prior to the first *Xwelítem* settlement, Fort Langley, established in 1827 by the Hudson's Bay Company, the *Stó:lō* occupied permanent villages during the winter throughout the Fraser Valley. In the summer, family groups moved from these villages to temporary summer camps for fishing, hunting and gathering of food and materials. The population of the Fraser Valley swelled every fall, when many groups of Aboriginal people from Vancouver Island, the Interior Plateau and Puget Sound travelled to locations along the Fraser River to trade goods and fish for salmon.[2]

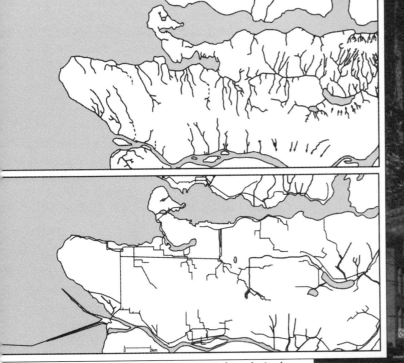

(Top) The system of natural streams and creeks in the Lower Mainland prior to 1880.

(Bottom) The current system of natural streams and creeks in the Lower Mainland. Notice how the drainage patterns have changed.

The *Stó:lō* population is estimated to have been between 7,000 and 28,000 prior to the first diseases in the late 1700s. Following the arrival of *Xwelítem* to this region and the introduction of numerous diseases, the population steadily declined. It reached its lowest level, slightly

(Top) Granville Street, looking north, 1885.

(Bottom) Granville Street, looking north, 1995.

Chapter 10: Changing Land Use in *Sólh Téméxw* (Our Land)

165

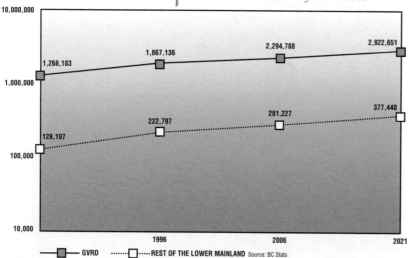

Population Growth, 1976-2011 by Regional District

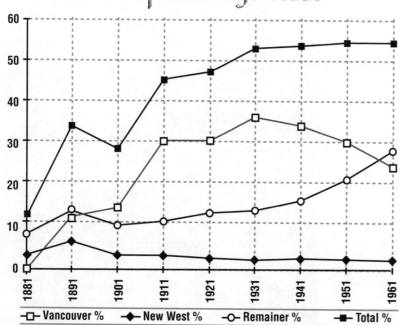

Growth of General Population by Decade as a percentage of the Province.
Note the rapid recent growth in the non-Vancouver/New Westminster area.

under 1,300 people, in 1928, and has since risen steadily to the 1993 level of about 5,700.[3]

The population history of *Xwelítem* people has been very different. Between 1827 and the Fraser River gold rush in 1858, the *Xwelítem* population hovered at less than 100 people settled centred around Fort Langley. Fort Hope and Fort Yale were the only permanent settlements for a few short years before 1858, and Victoria was the closest town. As a result of the gold rush, the *Xwelítem*

population boomed to over 30,000 people, the majority of whom were American men who had travelled to the Fraser Canyon between Hope and Hell's Gate. This drastic increase in population lasted only two years. By 1871, the permanent *Xwelítem* population was no more than 1,500, with almost one-third centred in New Westminster. The *Xwelítem* population grew steadily, particularly in the urban centres around New Westminster and later Vancouver, and to a lesser extent in the mostly rural Fraser Valley.[4]

The 1991 Canadian Census recorded a population of 2.7 million within *s'ólh téméxw* (the traditional territory of the *Stó:lō* people). The Aboriginal population comprised only 0.2% of this total figure. These shifts in population, during which urbanization has been continuous, explain some of the processes involved in establishing the urban landscape, and the subsequent marginalization of the *Stó:lō* from the land and resources.

Land use patterns have shifted in a relatively short period in British Columbia. This has set the stage for how communities will develop into the future. Currently, the lower Fraser Valley is experiencing unprecedented population growth, and over the years has been growing at a faster rate than the more dense urban centres around Vancouver. Projected population figures for these regions are stunning, particularly in areas of Abbotsford, Surrey, and Chilliwack. It is estimated that the District of Abbotsford will grow from its present population of 80,000 in 1995, to 250,000 in 2010. The City of Surrey is predicted to soon surpass Vancouver as the largest city in the province. Neighbouring Langley will also experience intense population growth. Chilliwack, situated on the edge of the commuter's circle to other major urban centres, is estimated to see a slightly less intense increase in population. Hope and Agassiz will surely feel the residual effects of the nearing urban sprawl, as more people move to these communities in an attempt to escape from the city.[5]

We need to consider how these tremendous population increases will affect people's lifestyles. The landscape is being profoundly transformed. How it is shaped is everyone's concern. Understanding the concerns and perspectives of *Stó:lō* people in this changing population, may help all of society better understand the process of urbanization, and provide some ideas on how to successfully manage this growth.

You Are Asked To Witness

Population Projections to the Year 2010

IN THOUSANDS

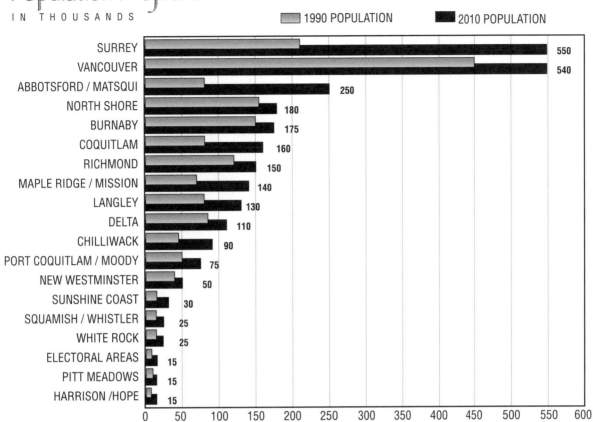

Population Projections to the Year 2010 in thousands.

2 STÓ:LŌ RELATIONSHIPS WITH THE LAND AND RESOURCES ■

Stó:lō people have a unique and long-standing relationship to the land and resources. First, the lower Fraser River region has been the home of the *Stó:lō* people and their ancestors for the past 10,000 years. The *Stó:lō* have a big stake in what happens here. Their stories and histories and ancestors connect them to this place. This long-term commitment the *Stó:lō* have to the land and resources provides them with a unique perspective - one where decisions about the future of what happens to the land and resources are made with the knowledge that their children and grandchildren will be there to live with those decisions.

With respect to this, the *Stó:lō* have developed a system of resource management through family connections. Many places where *Stó:lō* people get foods (fishing spots and productive root locations) are managed by families who have ancestral obligations to these places. People who can trace their ancestry to previous owners of these locations have access rights today. Often, these rights and privileges are acknowledged during naming ceremonies, where young people are given family-owned, ancestral names. During these naming ceremonies, a speaker will often describe the places and resources which the previous

owner of that name had access to. Decisions about the use and management of those important resource locations are made within the family.

In addition to inherited rights to these important places, *Stó:lō* people have a deeper, spiritual connection to the land and resources. Many stories passed down by Elders tell of how some of the ancestors of the people were transformed by *Xexá:ls* (the powerful "Transformers" who changed the world in ancient times) into the animals, plants and places which are found in the world today. People living today are descended from those people who are now the salmon, eulachon, sturgeon, cedar tree and so on. These ancestral relationships to the land and resources are another important consideration that *Stó:lō* leaders take into account when making land-use decisions.

Today, urbanization and development have effectively removed responsibility for much of this land and resources from the *Stó:lō*. *Stó:lō* people are out-numbered and have very rarely been part of the mainstream *Xwelítem* land-use planning process – a process which has transformed the very nature of the land, air, water and lives of living things in the lower Fraser River region. To shed light on some of these processes, several examples are presented below: urban transportation systems, impacts on *Stó:lō* heritage sites and, changes in ecosystem.

3 "THE FIBRE OF THE WEB" – TRADITIONAL AND URBAN TRANSPORTATION SYSTEMS ■

To better understand how the process or changing land-use effects the lives of *Stó:lō* people, we can examine one small example – transportation systems – which provides a looking-glass into many of the broader issues around this change. *Stó:lō* communities are located along the Fraser River and at the major tributaries which run into it. These communities were established according to traditional *Stó:lō* settlement patterns, which focus around the river and the utilization of its resources. The river, streams and sloughs connect *Stó:lō* people to the resources that are important to them. Their family and social networks have also traditionally been maintained by these "water-highways." This network was wide and vast, as people paddled up and down the Fraser River, to destinations as far away as Vancouver Island and Puget Sound. The river provided the means for people to maintain their economic, social and spiritual links with one another.

A *Stó:lō* canoe on the Fraser River in front of the new town of New Westminster, 1871.

Stó:lō people used and maintained trails, criss-crossing the land and providing connections to resources and people. Trails opened the heavily wooded prairies and hillsides for hunting and gathering expeditions. Trails through mountain passes and at portages between rivers connected more distant communities for trading, social and ceremonial life. These rivers, creeks sloughs and trails have made up the fibre of the web of the *Stó:lō* social, cultural and economic network.

Today, because of our heavy reliance on automobiles, roads have become the focal point of communities. They are the links by which we organize ourselves in relation to the people around us. In this way, analyzing roads provides a useful method of measuring urbanization. By looking at the development of road intensity (see next page), we can see where the urban setting has been most dense, and in which areas it has yet to expand. Urbanization has been heaviest near the mouth of the Fraser River, particularly in the primary urban centre of Vancouver. It becomes less dense as one moves away from this "core," but occurs at more intense, regular intervals, which can be called "secondary urban centres." These secondary centres provide all the essential services of the primary centre, in addition to many other market functions. Communities, such as Langley, Abbotsford, Chilliwack, Mission, Agassiz, and Hope, are often more important to the people living in rural areas around them, than the primary centre of Vancouver.

The impressive developments of roads and freeways in the Fraser Valley also shows how communities have shifted from a river-centred group of towns and villages, to a massive urban sprawl over almost the entire Fraser Valley. Early Hudson's Bay Company "brigade trails" and some early roads followed the trails established by the *Stó:lō*. By 1931, most areas of the region were accessible by road or trail. The wide-open landscape, once heavily forested, became transected by roads. By 1966, the vast web of road and freeway networks completely enmeshed communities from Hope to Vancouver and beyond.

Besides being a useful measure of urbanization, roads themselves have particular social implications to *Stó:lō* people. The location of *Stó:lō* villages along the river does not fit into the market-driven model which shaped the placement of the *Xwelítem* communities. As roads were built to access the different areas of urban population, old transportation routes were shifted away from the waterways and became more land-based. For the *Stó:lō* this shift occurred slowly. Canoes were still the main source of transportation for the *Stó:lō* well into the 20th century. As recently as the 1960s, many people who lived in Chehalis at the base of Harrison Lake, regularly travelled down the Harrison River and across the Fraser River to Chilliwack by canoe, for everyday occasions such as shopping and visiting family and friends.

Although *Stó:lō* communities are located along major rivers and sloughs, these are no longer the main means of travelling between communities. Some of these communities, now off the major arteries of transportation, receive few services and attention. Others have major highways, railroads and roads going right through the middle of their already small reserves. However, *Stó:lō* culture defiantly lives on in the late 20th century. During summer months, it is common to see Salish-style canoes tied to the top of trucks, vans, cars and trailers travelling

You Are Asked To Witness

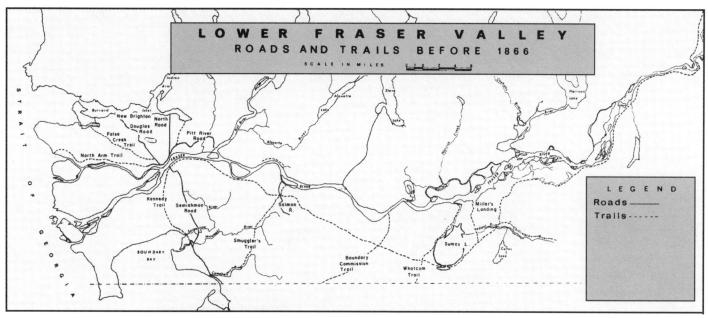

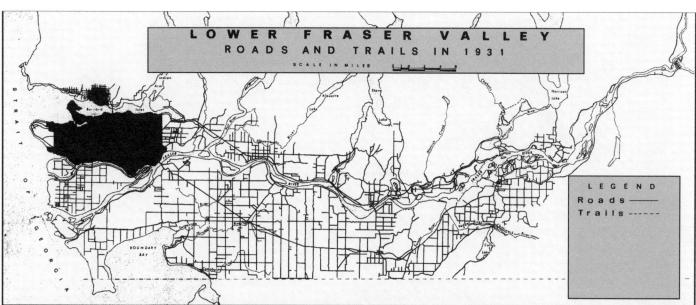

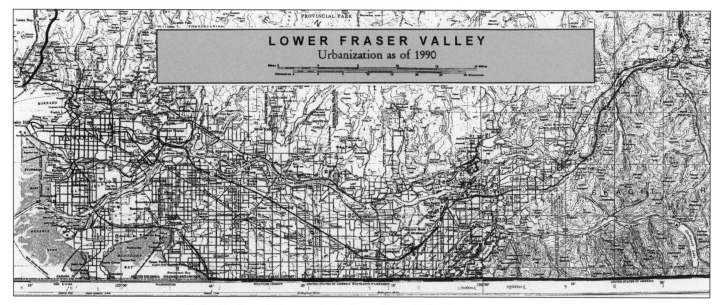

Trails, Roads, and Freeways in the lower Fraser Valley, from 1866 to 1990.

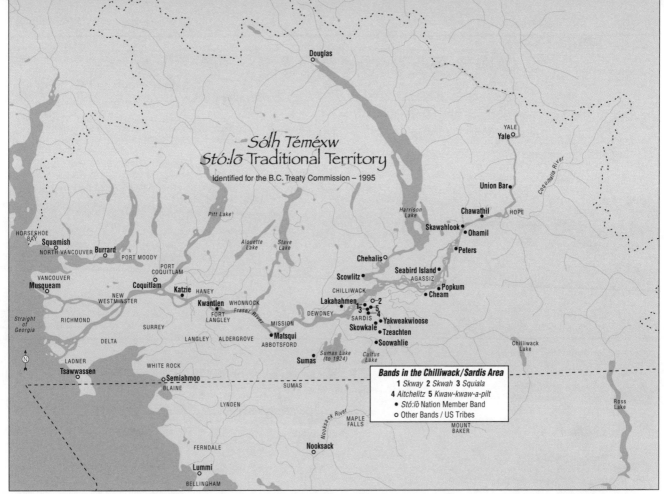

Map of contemporary *Stó:lō* Bands. Many of the reserves where bands are located were established at traditional village sites, reflecting the settlement pattern of the years when the reserves were made *(B. Thom, 1995)*.

down the freeway on their way to attend racing competitions. Many *Stó:lō* hunters go to the mountains by car to find their game along logging roads. Roads now are the main link between people in the far-flung communities which participate in the *smílha* or "winter ceremonies".

The development of these transportation systems have, in may cases, been detrimental to the landscape and the lives of the people who are dependent on it. Cars and trucks produce immense amounts of pollution that adversely affects the health of people living in *sólh téméxw*. Old stream channels are also affected by drainage culverts put in to allow roads to cross. These measures often make streams uninhabitable for returning salmon. Such problems are critical to the *Stó:lō* whose lives are so connected to the land and resources. Remember too, roads are but one example of the countless systems that provide support for major urban populations.

4 IMPACTS ON *STÓ:LŌ* HERITAGE SITES ■

Urban development also has a destructive impact on *Stó:lō* cultural heritage resources. "Archaeological sites" and "traditional use sites" are areas within the landscape that are irreplaceable, nonrenewable, heritage locations (they can never be replaced once they are destroyed). These sites are important and sacred to the *Stó:lō*. They represent direct connections to their ancestors and the spirit world. Urban development constantly threatens and impacts these types of cultural heritage resources.

Archaeological sites in the lower Fraser River area are the material remains of *Stó:lō* ancestors. They include the artifacts, homes, burial grounds, spiritual sites, and places where *Stó:lō* people obtained food. In many instances, archaeological evidence demonstrates that these places have been in use for thousands of years. The only way to

Figure 3   Land use in the Lower Fraser Valley 1986/87

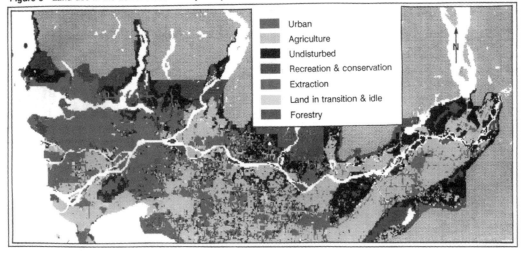

Urban
Agriculture
Undisturbed
Recreation & conservation
Extraction
Land in transition & idle
Forestry

This map was produced using SPANS, a micro-computer based Geographic Information System (GIS)

Scale 1:600 000

0   20 km

Land Use in the lower Fraser Valley 1986/1987. This map was produced using SPANS, a micro-computer based Geographic Information System (GIS).

preserve these heritage sites is to leave them undisturbed. If they must be disturbed, they can be best understood by careful and sensitive archaeological excavation, directed by *Stó:lō* cultural experts and spiritual leaders.

Traditional use sites are places the *Stó:lō* visit to practice aspects of their cultural heritage. They include sites with spiritual or ceremonial significance, as well as productive fishing sites, hunting locations, and plant gathering areas. Those sites associated with spiritual power often embody a special relationship between the *Stó:lō*, their ancestors and the natural environment.

Developments in urban areas often occur without consideration of the region's cultural heritage resources, even though places with heritage value are protected in the *British Columbia Heritage Conservation Act*. The Archaeology Branch and Heritage Branch of the Province of British Columbia have the power and authority to protect these resources and sites, but this task is extremely challenging. Developers with their own agendas also contribute to the destruction of these kinds of heritage sites, as they remain unaware of their value, and in many cases, their very existence. Preserving this type of heritage costs developers money, and is time consuming when archaeological investigations are required. These factors combine to make managing *Stó:lō* heritage sites very difficult.

5 CHANGING THE ECOSYSTEM, DIMINISHING LAND AND RESOURCE BASE ■

The lower Fraser Valley is one of the most important and complex ecosystems in the country. It boasts of one Canada's richest agricultural lands, as well as diverse wildlife and forests. The conversion of these natural ecosystems to urban areas through the growth of cities has irreversible, long-term impacts on the landscape and people. Many *Stó:lō* feel the most critical concern about the process of urbanization is its impact on ecosystems and their diminishing land and resources. These resources have been the foundation of *Stó:lō* culture for thousands of years. As urbanization continues, *Stó:lō* culture and livelihood is threatened.

The Canadian Wildlife Service estimates that the Fraser River and its tributaries are home to approximately 80 species of fish and shellfish. The Fraser River is the single largest salmon producing waterway in the world. This area supports the highest density of waterfowl and shorebirds in Canada, while acting as an important "stop-over" for migratory birds. The diverse forested mountains which border the Fraser River provide habitat for a variety of species of plants, birds, mammals, reptiles, amphibians and insects. Figure 9 illustrates land use in the lower Fraser Valley in 1986/87, as compiled by a Geographic Information System. As seen in this computer-generated map, few areas of the Fraser Valley are left undisturbed, and urban expansion through the forests and agricultural land is extensive.

Innumerable impacts on the ecosystem have occurred due to the growth of cities within the lower Fraser Valley. Only a very few examples are listed here: Five B.C. Hydro power plants which have flooded lands and blocked salmon habitat; the ever-increasing use of forest lands for logging have disrupted animal, plant and fish habitat; the dyking of wetland and bog areas has endangered many kinds of life and choked out many plants which convert greenhouse gasses to oxygen; urban sewage and agricultural waste contaminate clean drinking water (like the Abbotsford Aquifer) and have closed all shell-fish beds permanently in the Fraser River watershed; massive expansion of sub-urban communities onto surrounding, forested hill-sides into agricultural land reserves brings in more people to put more stress and drain on the resources already being rapidly used up. These things affect all communities. The Stó:lō have been at a disadvantage historically because they have had little say in how these processes develop.

A healthy ecosystem is full of many diverse plants and creatures. In order to maintain it, we must develop a long-term perspective on the resources of the Fraser Valley, and seek to understand the linkages that exist between the human and the non-human. Similarly, a healthy understanding about the place where we live involves opening ourselves to diverse ways of comprehending history and geography. We must strive to find these connections. An examination of stories about Sumas Lake provides us with a useful example.

6 SUMAS LAKE: A CASE STUDY IN CHANGING LAND USE ■

Sumas Lake was drained in the 1920s with the aid of political will, nearly four million dollars and some of the largest pumps then draining (or what used to be called "reclaiming") lands in the British Commonwealth. In the winter of 1828, a Hudson's Bay Company expedition noted an encampment of 300-400 Aboriginal people situated near the lake, a body of water they estimated to be over 16 kilometres long and almost ten kilometres wide.[6] In 1919, Canada's Commission of Conservation discovered that the lake was nearly 3 metres deep at low water and over 10 metres deep at high water. At its low water depth, the lake was 10 kilometres long and over 6 kilometres wide.[7] The size and shape of Sumas Lake was changeable. Engineers report that before the lake was drained, it would spread to well over 25 km in length.

All lakes are continually being filled in by sand, gravel, and sediments. Set in a large time-frame and assured the absence of human or divine intervention, Sumas Lake would have eventually become land, filling up over the centuries to the height of the Fraser River floodplain.[8] But this lake had some special features. It was a tidal lake, open to the Fraser River through the Sumas River, therefore subject to the tidal action of the Pacific Ocean eighty kilometres away. Sumas Lake was also a flood lake meaning its size changed seasonally, expanding during spring freshets and winter rains as its tributaries swelled with water, then returning to its former size. The Fraser River, which drains 1/3 of B.C., could feed tremendous amounts of water into the lake during freshets.

7 WAS THE LAKE WORTH PRESERVING? ■

Incoming European settlers to Canada commonly believed what we now call "wetlands" including bogs, swamps, and marshy edges of lakes, were wastelands. Impossible to farm and full of mosquitos - surely the wise course of action was to drain, plough, and "manage" them. With these sentiments, thousands of hectares of wetlands were destroyed through dyking and drainage activities throughout the lower Fraser Valley in the last century.

In 1935, Stó:lō historian Xáxts'elten, Peter Pierre of Katzie, likened the Fraser River of earlier times to "an enormous dish that stored up food for mankind."[9] Today we are learning just how fragile the "food dish" in the Fraser system has become. Ecologists tell us that wetlands, such as those that were drained in the Fraser floodplain, sustain more life than most good farmland.

Wetlands cover only six percent of the earth's surface, but they are integral to maintaining the stability of the world's environment. Like the forests on the West Coast, they replenish the air's oxygen as they take in carbon dioxide.

Retaining and slowly releasing vast quantities of water, wetlands also slow the progress of river water to the sea, trapping sediments and pollutants.[10] Wetlands help to sustain the earth's biological diversity as they provide rearing habitat for fish and other creatures. Marsh grasses, rushes, sedges, and flowering surface vegetation all specially adapted to flood cycles, support and shelter a complex web of animal and insect life. The big open grasslands around the lake provided territory for wildlife to fly and run. Prior to drainage, members of the

Sumas Lake, 1901.
A picnic party and sail boat at Sumas Lake Ridge.

You Are Asked To Witness

Sumas Lake ecosystem included dabbling ducks, whistling swans, and the now endangered Pacific Salamander. The lake was transcontinentally important as a stop-over for migratory birds and as part of the spawning route of salmon. It very likely provided rearing habitat for salmonoid offspring. Sumas Lake also contained many other varieties of fish, such as sturgeon, dolly varden trout, as well as catfish.

The destruction of Sumas Lake, a community of creatures in both its deep and shallow waters, was a great ecological tragedy. But we must understand that Sumas Lake was hardly a pristine environment, "untouched" by humans. People have been living in the Sumas Lake area since time immemorial. After hearing/reading some lake memories, we will discuss territorial and resource management conflicts which were occurring at Sumas Lake decades before the drainage ever occurred.

8 A SUNDAY OUTING ■

The family of *Stó:lō* Elder, Edward Kelly at Kilgard (the Sumas Indian Reserve #6), lived by Sumas Lake. Although sent to the Coqualeetza Indian Residential School, he was able to spend his summer vacation with his family prior to the lake's disappearance. In 1987, he was asked by Janelle Vienneau of the Matsqui Sumas Abbotsford Museum Society "what do you remember about Sumas Lake?"[11]

Kelly: Sumas Lake... I mentioned about the sturgeon and all varieties of salmon and trouts and the ducks were out there by the millions - way out, ducks and the geese. And the people had the small canoes in those days, and they - like for a Sunday outing- they would they would go out, like from the small slough into the big slough, then into the Sumas Lake and they would have a picnic, just family affair. I'm referring to my family. Mother used to make up the lunches and my dad would bring his rifle along and if we needed deer, he'd kill a deer. But the deer had to be down right near the water. If the deer was up a little, up on the side of the mountain he just won't... He just overlooks that deer because there's always deer all

around. But the deer must be near the water before he would shoot it. Then he would bleed a deer and put his rifle away. And dad always brought his fishing line and dad would be trolling around up and down, mother would be knitting and us kids would be swimming in the lake. That's a Sunday outing.

Vienneau: Before we go any further you had mentioned something to me about sweet potatoes.

Kelly: Oh, yes. This Sunday outing. Just across the big slough, there's a small slough, and just across the big slough from the Kilgard brick plant is where the sweet potatoes grew every year. And the people would dig the potatoes – they're small with a sort of sweet flavour. And when the lake was drained, there was no longer any high water time and the wild potatoes disappeared.

9 DIFFERENT SEASONS, DIFFERENT ACTIVITIES ■

Edward Kelly's childhood memories provide a unique window on Sumas Lake, illustrating the activities people did there when he was a child. Kelly recalled that in the winter he and his friends would skate across the frozen lake. When Gus Commodore, the older man who accompanied them, yelled "it's time to go home" the "north wind blows so hard it is very easy getting home because we'd just put out our coats for sails, sail back home again on the ice."

Before the lake was drained, Kelly's mother would can the many varieties of fish that inhabited the lake, along with duck and deer meat. The preservation of these foods ensured that the family would have plenty to eat during the rest of the year.

In the low-water months, both Aboriginal and *Xwelítem* families with cattle were particularly thankful for the lake's existence, because its surrounding grasslands were common grazing areas and a place to harvest natural fodder. Cattle farmers from as far away as Chilliwack would bring their cows and sheep here to graze. Many of these people opposed any proposal to drain of Sumas Lake because they anticipated that once the lake was gone and the lands sold, their cattle would be denied access to the lands that were presently open to them during the low water season. Kelly recalls the following memories of his father's use of the Sumas grasslands.

Edward Kelly at Sumas, B.C., 1912.

"Why buy the land? When we could use the land for free?" Said, "there are no fences." The cattle, all the stock, ran out on Sumas Prairie. Say when my dad, now when it's milking time in the evening, would go out looking for the cows. The milk cows -if we see one cow we know our cows are there. And same with the horses, the needing any of the horses for any type of work, we would have to go out on the Sumas Prairie. If we see one horse we know our horses are there.

Then for milking cows - my dad, when through milking, he would let the cows out of the barn. Then the cows would go out with the rest of the cattle and in the morning we had to look for them again.

10 LAKE PLEASURES/ MOSQUITO CHALLENGES ■

Picnic At Sumas Lake, "Abbotsford Post" June 4, 1920

On May 24th a party of Ridgedale people were the guests of Messrs J. Saunders and C. Farr on a motor boat picnic to Sumas Lake. Two boats carrying about 45 persons left the landing at 9 am with Capt. Kelleher at the wheel of the leading craft. The weather man favoured the day with his best goods and the sail up the river and lake were most delightful. All were ready for the picnic dinner which was spread on Spoon Island, after which the party moved to the head of the lake where there was a delightful picnic ground. Games were engaged in by some of the younger people, while many of the gentlemen were busy with hook and

line. A slight shower slightly shortened the day of sport. Laden with wild flowers and the spoil of the day, the return trip was made in less than two hours, a choppy sea on the lake adding to the excitement. All agreed that a most enjoyable day had been spent and that Claude and Johnny were 'jolly good fellows'

Boat trips to the lake, such as the one described in the above newspaper article "Picnic At Sumas Lake" were pleasurable outings, remembered as a way to escape from the mosquitoes. Mr. and Mrs. Kelleher, both of *Stó:lō* heritage, were interviewed in Matsqui in 1966 by Fraser Valley historian Oliver Wells.

Wells: The draining of the lake made a difference in the country, didn't it?

Mrs. Kelleher: Oh, my, yeah. My, we used to have a good time up on that lake, when we had the gas boat, and we'd get a crowd and go way up there to get out of the mosquitoes.[12]

Mrs. Kelleher's comments are interesting because Sumas Lake was not viewed by the new "scientific" insect experts in the early twentieth century as a refuge from mosquitoes. In fact, politicians who hoped to drain the lake for profitable farmland were supported by leading entomologists (insect experts) who strongly advocated the drainage of Sumas Lake, in part because it was said this flood lake encouraged the production of these biting flies. For at least one month in the summer, mosquitos could be extremely numerous throughout the Fraser Valley, especially in Mission. Although they are potentially painful nuisances for humans and other mammals, mosquitoes are also part of the food chain, eaten by fish, birds, and other insects like dragonflies.

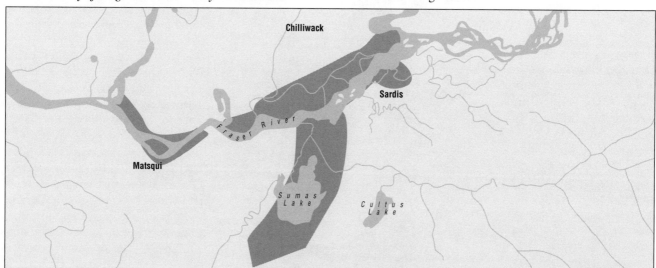

In 1919, the National Research Council of Canada in cooperation with the Dominion Department of Agriculture, sponsored an investigation of the lower Fraser Valley mosquito populations. The study continued until 1921, when the Canadian Air Board and the Department of Agriculture sent aircraft to conduct one of the first entomological surveys in Canada's history. Eric Hearle, Assistant Entomologist in charge of mosquito investigations for the Dominion Department of Agriculture, asserted that "the abundance of mosquitoes in the Lower Fraser Valley, British Columbia, has forced itself upon the notice of all those who have settled there since the first white man to penetrate into the district from the East left his record of the severity of the pest... The dyking and draining of the huge flood-water breeding areas are most important."

174

E.W. Carlson on deck of the dredge Col. Tobin.

Aboriginal people in the Sumas area certainly "noticed" the mosquitoes. The name *Qwá:l* meaning mosquito, is the name of a warrior from the Sumas Band who was famous for his "in and out" style of attack.[13]

During "mosquito-time" *Stó:lō* people developed innovative, non-destructive solutions to cope with the biting flies. They burned "smudges" to keep the mosquitoes at bay. They also simply and effectively left the mosquito-infested areas.

Stó:lō Elder Dan Milo spoke of *Snaníth*, a village built on stilts on the lake where the *Stó:lō* went to escape the mosquitos.[14] They rarely fly far across large bodies of water, as the Kellehers demonstrated when they took their boat to the lake in order flee from the mosquitos at their home in Matsqui. Decades before, Aboriginal people actually lived on the lake during "mosquito-time." John Keast Lord, an English naturalist on the International Boundary Survey which mapped the boundary's northwest region from 1858-1860, describes a village located out on the waters of the lake built by people he calls "savages.":[15]

Endowed with an instinct of self-preservation, mosquitoes seldom venture far over the water after once quitting their raft - a fact the wily savage turns to his advantage. Rarely can an Indian be tempted ashore from his stage during mosquito time; and when he is, he takes good care to whip out every intruder from his canoe before reaching the platform. These quaint-looking scaffolding, scattered over the lake, each with its little colony of Indians, have a most picturesque appearance. Fleets of canoes are moored to the poles, and the platform reached by a ladder made of twisted bark. To avoid being devoured, and to procure the sleep requisite for health, I used very frequently to seek the hospitality of the savages, and pass the night with them on their novel place of residence.

11 SUMAS DYKING ACT ■

In April 1878, the first legislation relating to the drainage of Sumas Lake was written and adopted, allowing Ellis Luther Derby "to drain Sumas Lake and other lands" in the Chilliwack, Sumas and Matsqui districts.[16] Authorized by the Act, Derby began his dyke in Matsqui and planned to run it across the Sumas Indian Reserve. All the Crown lands near the "Chillukweyk, Sumass and Masquee Reserves" were to be granted to Derby for his efforts. Yet, by granting lands surrounding the reserves to Derby, the Sumas Dyking Act would make it impossible to extend those small reserves any further. For that reason, Gilbert Sproat, a government official charged with the job of judging the sufficiency of reserve allotments, recommended disallowance of the Act.

Sproat also challenged Ottawa on behalf of the Matsqui people who "had been told by white men that if they or their cattle injured the dyke they would be put in prison..." The people felt not only that the dyke was useless, but that the reserve was unsuitable.

The effect of draining lakes and diverting the course of streams touching or near the Indian reserves has also to be considered: in short, the whole question preeminently requires the well considered sanction of the Dominion Government and requires it now.[17]

The point was made but the debate was cut short. The provincial government reassured Prime Minister John A. Macdonald that drainage of the lake was a good idea, and promised to amend the Act stating that

The draining of Sumas Lake. This photo is the dredge 'Col. Tobin' about half way up the Vedder Canal, Marsh Construction Co. was the constructor, Sumas Prairie.

Aboriginal people would not have to pay for the drainage or dyking. The "sufficiency" of the reserves was then judged not on the basis of the current land base but on what the size the reserves would be if they were drained. The *Stó:lō* were given no choice or voice in the matter. Many Indian agents and Indian Affairs officials would thereafter assume that the *Stó:lō*, on their increasingly tiny pieces of dry land, not only favoured, but required drainage.

Hop-picking, one of the early successful crops on the lake bottom was hops. After the lake was drained, Aboriginal families responded and adapted to the changed environment, continuing to play an important role in the resource economy of the province.

Sumas Lake, as seen from the B.C. Electric substation on Vedder Mountain, ca. 1916.

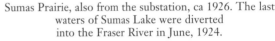

Sumas Prairie, also from the substation, ca 1926. The last waters of Sumas Lake were diverted into the Fraser River in June, 1924.

12 CONFLICTS WITH *STÓ:LŌ* RESOURCE USE ∎

Along with their new *Xwelítem* neighbours, the *Stó:lō* continued to enjoy the benefits of Sumas Lake. They used the lake's wildlife resources for food, ceremony, and trade, but these activities became increasingly threatened. Regulation of fishing practices began in 1878 when Ottawa banned the use of salmon nets in freshwater. In 1888, federal authorities created the "Indian food fishery" when they passed legislation stating that the aboriginal fishery was only to provide food for personal consumption. Other legislation, such as the banning of weirs, undermined *Stó:lō* fisheries management in Sumas Lake.

A federal concern with wildlife conservation in Canada originated very late in the nineteenth century. Hunting regulations were basically provincial matters until "The Treaty for International Protection of Migratory Birds" was signed with the United States in 1916. The federal government was thus empowered to make rules enhancing the protection of migratory birds, establishing closed seasons, issuing hunting permits and designating endangered species. But conservation for whom? Although they ignored aboriginal rights to hunt, British Columbia representatives asserted their frontier rights to hunt wherever, whenever, and whatever they wanted.[19] After the drainage in the 1920s, weekend hunters from Vancouver continued to stop at the Sumas Lake "shooting range" until the lake bottom was divided into private fields after the drainage.

13 McKENNA-McBRIDE COMMISSION: SUMAS PEOPLE SPEAK OUT ◼

In September 1912, Victoria and Ottawa agreed to participate in the McKenna-McBride Royal Commission. The joint Provincial-Federal venture was created to "finally adjust all matters relating to Indian Affairs in the Province of British Columbia." They excepted from these matters the overriding concern of Aboriginal people - title to their homelands and waters.[20] The Commissioners travelled for three years, from 1913-1916, visiting most places where Aboriginal people lived, including the area of Sumas Lake.

When the commission visited Sumas Indian Reserve 6 on January 12, 1915, Chief Ned of the Sumas Band was called as the primary witness.[21] A confident oral speaker, he attempted to establish his own agenda and standards of trust at the outset of the public hearing.

> I am glad to see you people come into this house, and I am going to tell you the truth of what I am going to say. ...That is the land and that is what the old people know, that is what they used to say. The Indians have always been poor, that is the reason I have always been worrying because I know the old people used to say that the White people will be shoving you around all over this open prairie to get our food. We used to get our meat, ducks and fish out in this lake (Sumas) and on the prairie. We go out on the Fraser and catch our fish, and we go out on the mountains on each side of this lake and get all the meat we want; but today it is not that way anymore. We can't get what we want. If I go out and take my gun there is always someone to round me up and have me arrested. If I go out and catch a fish the policeman comes out after me with a gun. Every year that we use a net they come out and take it way from us, and that is what worried me all the time - that is all on that part...

Chief Ned stated that he and his people make "half our living" from the "fish and ducks and things like that."[22] He judged that most of their land was subject to overflow at high water. Yet he did not want to have their land dyked.

Q: *Do you get plenty of hay?*

A: We don't get hardly any timothy hay – we depend upon the wild hay.

Q: *Could there be any land reclaimed here by dyking?*

A: I could not say. I am against the dyking because that will mean more starvation for us.

Q: *Why do you think that you would be starved out if this land were dyked?*

A: Because the lake is one of the greatest spawning grounds there is and this dyking would cut it off and in that way would cut off our fish supply.[23]

14 THE DRAINING OF SUMAS LAKE ◼

Much territory was reduced from the Sumas people in the midst of the lake drainage project (1920-1924). Eleven hectares of the twenty hectares Aylechootlook (Sumas Reserve #5) were "wiped out" by the dyke, constructed by the authority of the Land Settlement Board (L.S.B.) to divert and contain the Vedder River. The L.S.B. chairman felt that he owed nothing to the Aboriginal people whose remaining nine hectares obviously was "improved" owing to the construction of the dyke.[24]

A deeper Sumas Lake story does not begin and end with the story of the drainage. It started thousands of years ago and continues today. You can think about it every time you are driving down the Transcanada Highway between Chilliwack and Abbotsford, because a long stretch of your journey involves travelling over and alongside the bottom of Sumas Lake. It is a tragic story, because it involves the destruction of enormous tracts of wetlands and the dispossession of land and water resources from the original occupants of the Fraser Valley. But, it is also a story of *Stó:lō* people's resilience, as they continue to strengthen their communities and meet tremendous challenges posed by the past and the future on the dynamic floodplain.

15 CONCLUSIONS ◼

The long-term process of urbanization has clearly revealed that Aboriginal people have had little voice in determining the future of *s'ólh téméxw* - the world which has sustained their communities for thousands of years. The population history shows that the *Stó:lō* make up only a small fraction of the overall expanding population in the lower Fraser Valley. Transportation networks have redefined the valley's cultural landscape, creating an orientation away from the river. What were once community centres are now often marginal reserves. Reserves that are surrounded by cities have in some cases become "urban ghettos." Resources once used and managed by extended family networks are now often alienated by private ownership, or even completely lost, as with Sumas Lake. Ecosystems are being disrupted and changed at an increasingly rapid level in all areas of this region. If they are lucky, cultural heritage sites like *Xá:ytem* near Mission are being made into small, bounded parks. More often than not, however, places like this which are important to the *Stó:lō* are being completely destroyed. Until recently, the *Stó:lō* have rarely been given the power to make decisions about development or even the voice to influence the decision makers.

Because treaties have never been signed with Aboriginal people in most of British Columbia, the alienation of their land has been illegal and unconstitutional. Recently, Aboriginal people throughout the province have been asserting their Aboriginal rights and title to the land and its resources. Land claims negotiations are on-going, and aimed at shifting how decisions regarding land management take place. However, unless further measures are taken to ensure that development occurs cautiously in *s'ólh téméxw*, children (both *Stó:lō* and *Xwelítem*) of future generations, will face a profound loss of opportunities.

There is a place for traditional *Stó:lō* culture within this development and urbanization. Ethnographer Michael Kew and ecologist M. Griggs have suggested that understanding how Aboriginal people have successfully managed the environment, lands and resources for thousands of years, can provide a model from which society at large can also manage this system. They are not advocating that we live in ways Aboriginal societies did over 200 years ago. Instead, they acknowledge that a great deal of knowledge can be gained from understanding *Stó:lō* models of resource management.[25]

The key features of traditional *Stó:lō* systems of land and resource management involve:

(1) relatively **few people,** with similar broad perspectives on the land and resources make decisions that impact the ecosystem;

(2) **local control** of the resources in the environment and;

(3) a real **commitment** to the local place (having respect for and a long-term connection to the land).

As discussed earlier, *Stó:lō* people have developed an adaptable and flexible economy and society which fulfils these three key points.

In traditional *Stó:lō* society, non-local interests had little influence on how local resources were used. Other than through barter, exchange, and occasional raids, neighbouring groups did not have regular permanent, large-scale population moves into this region. Influence and interest remained at the level of local control, and communities were largely self-sufficient. Family leaders maintained their position of status and social order in communities, largely through their own strong values of respect and ethical behaviour. Their family-centred society connected people to place through birth, marriage and inherited names. These connections remained intact through life and even after death. Loyalty and obligations to communities were strong and locally centred.

This contrasts with present-day urban society.

Tiffany Silver, Spindle Whorl Dancer

Multi-national corporations and foreign investors control a great deal of the region's economy and resources. Decisions about what happens in and around local communities are often made in provincial and federal capitals, located hundreds of kilometres away. Individual people and families who live in cities and towns are connected by property ownership, not kinship, and are generally far more migratory than *Stó:lō* communities have ever been.

In the future, people in the lower Fraser Valley can learn a great deal about successful land and resource management within and around urban centres by understanding what impacts local communities. Focusing on *Stó:lō* communities provides a unique vantage from which to understand these impacts on a variety of levels, and suggests a number of cultural alternatives to the current development path. Knowledge of these complex issues will allow for more careful and sensitive decision making in the future.

Recommended Further Readings

Wilson Duff, *The Upper Stalo Indians of the Fraser Valley, BC,* 1952.

Alfred Siemens, *Lower Fraser Valley: Evolution of a Cultural Landscape,* 1968.

Kathleen Moore, *Urbanization in the Lower Fraser Valley,* 1980-1987, Canadian Wildlife Service Report 120, 1990

Oliver Wells, *The Chilliwack and Their Neighbours,* 1993.

Footnotes

1   Gordon Mohs, "The Upper *Stó:lō* Indians of British Columbia: An Ethno-Archaeological Review", unpublished ms. *Stó:lō* Nation, 1990.

2   Wilson Duff, *The Upper Stalo Indians of the Fraser Valley, B.C.,* Memoir No. 1 (Victoria: British Columbia Provincial Museum, 1952).

3   As discussed elsewhere in this book, the early population of the *Stó:lō* people is very difficult to determine. Census taking did not become a regular practice in British Columbia until the late 1800s. The mortality of many of the diseases which inflicted *Stó:lō* communities brought on a steady, if not somewhat varied population decrease until the 1920s. Estimates of the pre-European population have been made by extrapolating back from the mortality rates of the epidemics that came through the area and by estimating the number of *Stó:lō* villages and their average population. Even at the lowest estimates, however, there were many, many *Stó:lō* people living in the lower Fraser River region prior to the first smallpox epidemics.

4   Cole Harris, "The Lower Mainland 1820-81", in *Vancouver and its Region.* edited by Graeme Wynn and Timothy Oke (U.B.C. Press, Vancouver), 1992.

5   M. Seeling and A. Artibise, *From Desolation to Hope.* U.B.C. School of Community and Regional Planning, Vancouver, 1991.

6   Cited in Bruce Ramsey, *Five Corners: The story of Chilliwack* (Vancouver: Agency Press, 1975), p.15. See UBCSPE, *Journal of Fort Langley Commencing With Voyage from Fort Vancouver June 27, 1827, to July 30, 1830, 97-94.*

7   Arthur V. White, Water Powers of B.C. (Dominion Commission of Conservation, 1919), pp.45, 233.

8   Valerie Cameron, "The Late Quaternary Geomorphic History of the Sumas Valley," (M.A.) Department of Geography, SFU, 1989, p.111.

9   J.E. Michael Kew and Julian R. Griggs, "Native Indians of the Fraser Basin: Towards a Model of Sustainable Resource Use" in Anthony Dorcey, ed. *Perspectives on Sustainable Development in Water Management: Towards Agreement in the Fraser River Basin, 1991.*

10 William A. Niering, *Wetlands of North America,* (Charlottesville, Virginia: Thomasson-Grant, 1991), p.15.

11 M.S.A. Museum Archives, Edward Kelly. AH# 97, 1987.

12 Wells, *Chilliwack,* 189.

13 Wilson Duff, *The Upper Stalo Indians of the Fraser Valley, B.C.,* Memoir No. 1 (Victoria: British Columbia Provincial Museum, 1952) pp.82, 96.

14 Oliver Wells, "Vocabulary of Native Words in the Halkomelem Language," (Vedder B.C.: Wells, 1965), p.27.

15 John Keast Lord, *At Home in the Wilderness:* What to Do There and How to Do It: A Handbook for Travellers and Emigrants (London: Hardwicke & Bogue, 1876), pp.279-280.

16 British Columbia, *Sumas Dyking Act* Statutes of B.C. 1878, c.6.

17 NAC, RG 10, Vol. 7538, file 27, Sproat to Supt. General, 25 January 1879.

18 NAC, RG 15, Vol. 778, file 540515, *Extract from a report of the Committee of the Honourable, the Privy Council, approved by His Excellency on the 21st October, 1896.* The Dominion actually had title to the lake bottom as the province administered water rights in the railway belt: however, this issue is controversial. For further reading see Claudia Notzke, *Aboriginal Peoples and Natural Resources in Canada* (York: Captus University publications, 1994), p.15.

19 Wildfowl could be shot by sportsmen with permits after March 31 "if injurious to agriculture" which Hewitt admitted was an unlikely occurrence; the 5-year closed season on wood duck was rescinded and B.C. was specially exempted from a 10-year closed season on cranes, swans and curlews.

20 McFarland, "Cut-offs," p.45.

21 BCARS, Add MSS 1056, *Royal Commission on Indian Affairs for the Province of B.C.* 1913- 1915 (Union of B.C. Indian Chiefs), p.152.

22 Ibid., p.157.

23 Ibid., p.155

24 NAC, RG 10, Vol 7886, file 36153-13, Ditchburn, Chief Inspector of Indian Agencies to Secretary, Dept of Indian Affairs, 31 Oct. 1923.

25 See the chapter 9 this volume.

CHAPTER 11

Spoken Literature
Stó:lō Oral
Narratives

M. Teresa Carlson ■ Keith Thor Carlson ■ Brian Thom ■ Albert "Sonny" McHalsie

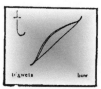

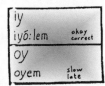

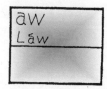

Halq'eméylem alphabet.

INTRODUCTION

Stó:lō culture and traditions are expressed primarily through elaborate oral narratives, the contextual meanings and usages of which are not always evident to people outside of that culture. This chapter is designed to assist people with little or no background in *Stó:lō* culture navigate their way through *Stó:lō* oral literature available in print and other formats. Every effort has been made to consult and collaborate with *Stó:lō* storytellers during the composition of this chapter. However, the primary authors of are not *Stó:lō* and therefore, the perspective remains that of outsiders looking in.

Throughout this chapter the expression "oral traditions," is used to refer to all aspects of "spoken" *Stó:lō* society. "Oral narratives" comprise one important facet of the broader oral traditions, and may be thought of as spoken "stories" which embody the history, philosophy, and moral teachings of *Stó:lō* culture. The expression "oral literature," by contrast, refers to those oral narratives which have been "captured" and recorded, especially in written format. In the *Halq'eméylem* language of the *Stó:lō* there are two categories of oral narratives:

1) *sxwōxwiyám*– myth-like stories set in the distant past which usually explain, among other things, how *Xexá:ls* (the Transformers) came to *Stó:lō* territory to "make things right" for the present generation; and

2) *sqwélqwel* – "true stories or news," which typically describe experiences in people's lives.

This chapter seeks to expose the depths of meanings imbedded in *Stó:lō* oral narratives (those explicit in the stories themselves and those attached by their narrators and audiences). To do this the authors suggest a framework to permit an understanding of *Stó:lō* narratives within an indigenous context. Readers are introduced to the *Stó:lō* categories of *sxwōxwiyám* and *sqwélqwel* and encouraged to familarize themselves with what these distinct literary genres mean to *Stó:lō* people. The lessons implicit in the oral narrative surrounding the transformer rock at *Xá:ytem* serve as vehicles to appreciate the general features found in all *sxwōxwiyám*. The "warm and witty" writings of Hank Pennier serve as the focus for the discusion of *sqwélqwel*. The authors bring four diverse backgrounds to their collective study (literary, historical, anthropological and traditional *Stó:lō*). As such, they have sought to bridge the methodological gap which often separates students of different disciplines. Readers will be presented with techniques which can be used to better understand the interactive and dynamic "performance art" aspects of oral narratives. The authors also explore the issue of contextual cultural knowledge and discuss the association between knowledge of oral narratives, local history and social status. In doing so they make apparent the multiple levels at which oral narratives can be appreciated. The authors go to great lengths to caution readers against judging true *Stó:lō* oral narratives (as they continue to be shared by living Elders in real life situations) by what is presented in the "captured" medium of written oral literature. This caution should not discourage people from reading and enjoying the many wonderful examples of *Stó:lō* oral literature available in print.

Finally, readers may find the shifting spellings of *Halq'eméylem* words presented throughout this chapter somewhat confusing. This is a reflection of the non-literary nature of the *Halq'eméylem* language, and the ineffective manner in which people not fluent in the *Stó:lō* language have struggled over the years to capture the oral essence of *Halq'eméylem* and translate it into written English. A standardized *Halq'eméylem* "Upper *Stó:lō* alphabet" and writing format was developed in the late 1970s, and subsequently adopted by the *Stó:lō*.[1] This standardized orthography has been applied throughout, and added in squared parenthesis [ ] within quotes.

1 THE RELEVANCE OF ORAL TRADITIONS TO CONTEMPORARY *STÓ:LŌ* SOCIETY ■

The continuing relevance of oral traditions to contemporary *Stó:lō* becomes immediately apparent to anyone who has had the privilege of attending a traditional *Stó:lō* gathering, such as a spirit dance, potlatch, naming ceremony, wedding, or funeral. On such occasions, recordings (written, audio, and/or visual) are prohibited. Before anything can begin, members of the host family "cover" the shoulders of a prominent speaker (who is almost always male) with a blanket, identifying him as the master of ceremonies who will conduct "the work." The

Stó:lō Speaker *Tixwelatsa* (Herb Joe) wearing a blanket.

speaker talks to the audience on behalf of the host family, and at the same time he is guided by his *shxwelí* – life force or spirit. Good speakers speak sincerely and with emotion, evoking similar responses from those gathered. They project their voice, punctuating the end of each phrase with a pause and a raise in pitch; statements are made with authority, ensuring that those gathered absorb the meaning of the words. A speaker's voice must be powerful enough to reach everyone within the large *Stó:lō* longhouses where many of these events continue to be held. The longhouse itself is an important component in the ceremonies, as are the gathered Elders and the burning fires. *Stó:lō* traditions maintain that the spirits of the ancestors can communicate with the physical world through fires. So, while wearing the blanket, and in the presence of the Elders and the spirits of the ancestors, speakers know that they must speak truthfully.

The first task of every speaker is to call witnesses. Beginning in one corner of the longhouse and moving

counter clockwise, certain respected guests are identified by a member of the host family and called as witnesses by the speaker. When the speaker calls out the witness' *Halq'eméylem* name he is careful to use the prescribed invitation: "*Xó:lhmet te syóysthet tset, há:kweles chap i tló slát,*" which translates as "please witness, respectfully watch, and carefully remember the events you are going to see and hear this evening." If the witness does not speak *Halq'eméylem* the standardized English phrase "you are asked to witness the work that is being done here," is substituted. As they are called, each witness stands and acknowledges the speaker. It is a great honour to be called as a witness, and so each *Halq'eméylem* speaking witness responds by rising and extending their arms in front of them, elbows bent, palms turned inward, at head level (in the typical *Stó:lō* manner of showing deferrential respect) and says, "*Ō Sí:yá:m, yalh yuxw kw'a's hóy tl'o kw's su me ó:thòx*" (a solemn expression of thanks and respect). If the witness only speaks English, they typically just stand up, raise their hands, and respectfully bow their head. Before calling the next witness the speaker pauses as members of the host family (typically women) approach the witness who has just been called and thank them by clasping their right hand and leaving a few coins in their palm. Witnesses fully understand that if in the future any question arises as to what occurred during the ceremony, (for instance, confusion over the right to a name that has been bestowed), they can be called upon to recall what they had seen and heard in an accurate and truthful manner.

After all the witnesses have been called the "work" (ie. a naming ceremony) begins. After each person involved in the work finishes speaking they are given money by members of the host family. After all the "work" has been completed the floor is opened to the witnesses, each of whom has the right to speak. Elders and the most respected witnesses always speak first. Each witness comments on the work which has been done, and usually reminds those gathered to keep *Stó:lō* oral traditions strong.

While not an example of an oral narrative, the preceding description does provide a context for understanding the continuing relevance of oral traditions to the *Stó:lō*.

2 STÓ:LŌ ORAL NARRATIVES AS LITERATURE ■

Stó:lō people characterize oral narratives as either "*sxwōxwiyám*" or "*sqwélqwel*." At the risk of oversimplifying what is in reality a complex and sometimes subtle distinction, *sxwōxwiyám* can be thought of as stories set at or just before the arrival of the Transformers (*Xexá:ls*), in the distant "mythological" past. *Xexá:ls* is the collective name for the powerful transformer siblings – the three sons and one daughter of black bear and red-headed woodpecker. Sometimes Elders will use the singular term *Xá:ls* when referring to just one of the brothers. Some contemporary Elders substitute the name *Xá:ls* with the term "Transformer," "Magician," "Changer," "Great Spirit," or "Little Christ." *Sqwélqwel*, by contrast, typically deal with more contemporary stories relating personal or community experiences. Usually, *sxwōxwiyám* are "more formal in style" than *sqwélqwel*; both are meant to educate as well as entertain.

Respected *Stó:lō Sí:yá:m* speaking to the people gathered to witness First Salmon Ceremony.

When studying *Stó:lō* oral narratives we recommend using the *Stó:lō* categories of *sqwélqwel* and *sxwōxwiyám* rather than trying to fit this oral literature into European categories such as "biography," "myth, "legend," or "folktale." For example, despite the appearance of seemingly similar plots, a *sxwōxwiyám* about the "world of the dead" should not be casually categorized with "Orpheus myths" prevalent in western literature. Instead, a cross-cultural comparison which recognizes and emphasises the distinct origins of these genres might be a more useful exercise. Such a comparison provides readers with a better understanding of the cultures and traditions of the people who generated them, and brings the stories "more authentically alive in translation than by adding storytelling techniques from English which are not present in the Halkomelem."[2]

The point of studying *Stó:lō* oral literature is to gain an appreciation of these stories, not in the commonly thought of tradition as written works of prose, but as a unique style of literature which gives a sense of shared experience between the readers and the *Stó:lō*. These traditional narratives can bring to life for readers the landscape and culture around them. Indeed, once appreciated within their cultural context *Stó:lō* oral literature can become a form of expression which reaches audiences of different generations, and transcends ethnic and cultural barriers.

Features of *Sxwōxwiyám*

Sxwōxwiyám provide a means through which *Stó:lō* existence in, and relationships with, the world are explained within a historical context. They also have shared meanings with all "Coast Salish" people. As the anthropologist Wayne Suttles explains, *sxwōxwiyám* are set in:

An age when the world was different, its people were like both humans and animals of the present age, and it was full of dangerous monsters. ...[This] age ended when xé'ls [Xá:ls] the Transformer came through the world, transforming monsters and other myth-age beings into rocks and animals, and setting things in order for people of the present age... [In these stories we are] usually told how [a community's] founder [came to find his] winter village or summer camp, where the Transformer gave him technical or ritual knowledge, and where he established special relationships with local resources. ...as in the Katzie... [sxwōxwiyám] of the ancestor who married a sockeye salmon woman and was taught how to perform the rite that ensures the return of her people, the summer run of sockeye salmon....[3]

In other words, *sxwōxwiyám* express in a creative way:
1) the fundamental values and accepted behaviour of the *Stó:lō*; how to live (for example, why gluttony and laziness are unacceptable).
2) the chaotic and shifting nature of the world during the period which existed before the arrival of the *Xexá:ls*, and their necessary appearance to "make the world right."

3) the emergence/origin/growth of a community of people (for instance, the "original" ancestors of the Katzie people).

4) explanations for the intimate kinship between certain resources and various *Stó:lō* communities, (ie. sturgeon, mountain goats and sockeye salmon) and also explanations for the origins of specific geographical features (ie. a large stone in the landscape or whirlpool in a certain part of a river).

5) the origin and character of animals and plant resources (for instance, dog salmon are striped because as people they wore striped blankets and lived in houses painted with stripes; today the cedar tree provides people with many things because originally he was a man who was generous to all).

The First Salmon Ceremony.

The First Salmon Ceremony.

6) the inherent characteristics of certain resource procurement areas (the salmon baby story illustrates where good salmon can be caught and why salmon in other areas taste bad or cure poorly).

It is also important to note that while many *sxwōxwiyám* describe the origin of various things (salmon, deer, wolves, fire, the sun, moon, death, etc.), unlike the Judeo-Christian "Genesis" story, *sxwōxwiyám* did not traditionally include "creation" narratives outlining the beginning of the world.[4] The myth-age world in which *sxwōxwiyám* are typically set was already in existence prior to the times described in the narratives.[5] For instance, while *sxwōxwiyám* contain "origin stories" about each *Stó:lō* community's "first people," such stories are prefaced by an account describing some tragedy wherein nearly all people in the Fraser Valley die leaving only one man and one woman alive. These two survivors, who reside in separate villages, eventually find one another and repopulate the land – thereby becoming the "first people." Thus, in *Stó:lō sxwōxwiyám* the expression "origin" or "first people" has a culturally specific meaning not immediately apparent to outsiders. *Sxwōxwiyám* acknowledge the existence of people who lived before the "first people."[6] This suggests a world view in which people are aware that their lifetime experiences are only a few of the many which have come before, those which will come after, and those which are continually occurring around them.

Another feature of *sxwōxwiyám* which *Xwelítem* audiences sometimes find disconcerting is that, unlike stories told in the Aristotelian tradition, *sxwōxwiyám* do not always have a clearly defined beginning, middle and end.

Gathering cedar bark.

The Lessons of
<u>X̱á:ytem</u> – Strategies
for Understanding
and Studying
Sx̱wōx̱wiyám

Of the countless
Stó:lō sx̱wōx̱wiyám which
have been passed down
from generation to gen-
eration, probably the
best known among
mainstream society is
the story surrounding
the large <u>X̱á:ytem</u> boul-
der near Mission. The
following story is the
sx̱wōx̱wiyám relating to
the site as shared by *Stó:lō* Elder Bertha Peters:

A person from Chilliwack Landing told me
this story: The Great Spirit [X̱á:ls]
travelled the land, sort of like Jesus, and he
taught these three *sí:yá:m,* (these three
chiefs) how to write their language. And they
were supposed to teach everyone how to
write their language, but they didn't. So they
were heaped into a pile and turned to stone.
Because they were supposed to teach the
language to everyone, and because they
didn't, people from all different lands will
come and take all the knowledge from the
people. Because they wouldn't learn to write
they lost that knowledge.[9]

Stó:lō spiritual leaders explain that the *shxwelí*, or life
force, of the three *sí:yá:m* continues to exist within the
<u>X̱á:ytem</u> boulder.

Like all *sx̱wōx̱wiyám*, the story of the three *sí:yá:m* who
were transformed into the <u>X̱á:ytem</u> stone conveys multiple and textured meanings to those who hear it. Each lis-

Available sources suggest that prior to contact the *Stó:lō*
thought of *sx̱wōx̱wiyám* not as a series of short independent stories, but rather as one incredibly long and complex story. What sometimes appears to outsiders as
confused narrative is actually a reflection of the non-lin-
ear (non-European) manner in which the *Stó:lō* view time
and history. Over the past 150 years Europeans have
extracted pieces of the larger story and recorded them separately, artificially breaking up and truncating the greater
narrative.[7] Recently, some *Xwelítem* people have taken
these individualized stories and attempted to "correct"
what they saw as flaws, gaps, or "lost knowledge and information" by inventing episodes to fill in the supposedly
missing pieces.[8] While mainstream secular beliefs stress
the beginning and end of all biological life, *Stó:lō* beliefs,
by contrast, emphasize the continuity of existence
beyond the life span of the biological creature. As such,
sx̱wōx̱wiyám give expression to the intimate "living" connection between the *Stó:lō* past, present, and future. *Stó:lō*
existence, therefore, is a never ending story in which the
ancestors of the past interact with people of the present
in shaping the future.

X̱á:ytem, transformer rock.

tener brings their own knowledge and life experience to the story. Likewise, speakers or storytellers "know" their audiences and subtly adapt their *sxwōxwiyám* to suit their circumstances and situation. As *Halq'eméylem* linguist Dr. Brent Galloway explains, *sxwōxwiyám* are highly individualistic. They "depend greatly on the style of the speaker, what the speaker and hearer know together about the topic (or know each other knows), how informative the speaker wishes to be, and how open the speaker is to questions from the hearer."[10] The greater the shared life experiences and understanding between the storyteller and audience, the more effectively the speaker will communicate meaning through a *sxwōxwiyám*. Yet, the objective of a *sxwōxwiyám* is not necessarily to convey prescribed sets of uniform messages or lessons. While that may sometimes be the case, *sxwōxwiyám* are meant to fulfill the much larger task of assisting their audience acquire the necessary cultural knowledge needed to make healthy decisions in a variety of situations. Some of the meanings conveyed by the *sxwōxwiyám* of the three *sí:yá:m* who were turned into the stone at *Xá:ytem* form the basis of our model for studying *Stó:lō* oral narratives.

The Interactive Performance Aspect of *Sxwōxwiyám*

The most explicit message derived from the *Xá:ytem* story is that the *Stó:lō* need to be innovative in their approaches to preserving their cultural knowledge. However, as is apparent from the carefully prescribed manner in which *sxwōxwiyám* have traditionally been shared, the most effective innovations in preserving the stories retain the ability to convey meaning in a dynamic and interactive fashion. Ideally, *Stó:lō* oral narratives are shared between a speaker and audience who speak *Halq'eméylem*

and have similar cultural knowledge derived from common life experiences. The sharing of stories in this context becomes an interactive performance, wherein the audience is an active participant, rather than just a passive listener. In one of the most standardized features of this interaction the audience is expected to encourage the storyteller to continue speaking by periodically saying, "*I'ó:y,*"[11] which means, "keep going a little" / "I'm awake."[12]

In this context, certain audiences are excluded from particular variations of a story based upon their age, understanding of the culture and history, their position in society, and so on. For example, simpler versions of a *sxwōxwiyám* are told to children at bed time, while more sophisticated forms are related to adult audiences with the teller being very conscious of using precise words and details in the story, according to tradition.[13] Likewise, a sensitive *Stó:lō* storyteller visiting an elementary school Language Arts class tells a slightly different version of a *sxwōxwiyám* than they would ordinarily share among adult family and friends around the kitchen table over a game of cards.[14] This can also be observed when the main theme, plot, or story line of a *sxwōxwiyám* remains constant while the supporting material around the main subject(s) changes depending upon the context in which the narrative is being told. In other words, the scene of the telling, including who the teller and audience are and the time and setting of the telling, will all affect the version, length, and performance of the story. In light of this dynamic interaction, readers must bear in mind that when a story is written down it becomes less fluid.

Stó:lō Spindle Whorl dancers.

Whereas both a written narrative and a spoken story may be interpreted in different ways by various audiences, only in the context of the sharing of an oral narrative does the speaker retain effective control of the medium. When a storyteller shares a *sxwōxwiyám* with a live audience all of the speaker's expressions and gestures, the audience's responses, and the implied references combine to provide "meaning" and context. This "atmosphere" adds to the total expression of the oral narrative, embodying performance with story. Witnessing or participating in the performance of an oral narrative allows for vocal subtleties to be perceived such as intonations, pronunciations, and variations in voices (used primarily to distinguish between characters), as well as hand gestures, facial expressions, dances, drumming, and so on. These performances are used not only to entertain an audience (although certainly this element is present in the events), but also, among other things, to instil and reinforce appropriate and socially acceptable behaviour in community members. As a result, these narratives convey aspects of *Stó:lō* culture which are often lost when frozen on audio tape or in written text (media which usually record a story in isolation). The experience of witnessing an oral narrative performed versus simply reading one, is akin to seeing live theatre versus silently reading the script.

Take for example, the following excerpt from "The Mink and *Qals [Xá:ls]*" story as recorded at Scowlitz by turn-of-the-century ethnographer Charles Hill-Tout:

When he had gone, the *Qals [Xexá:ls]* came out from their hiding place and questioned the boy, asking what he does when his grandfather brings in the fish. He replies: "I dance down to the shore like this with the roasting spit and stick it through the flounders." When he had so said, one of the *Qals [Xexá:ls]* took him and shook him so that his bones fell out of his skin, which *Qals [Xexá:ls]* now put on, so that he may appear to be the old man, whom he desires to trick, as his grandson.

When *S'kwam* returns *Qals [Xexá:ls]* takes the roasting-spit and dances down to the landing and attempts to thrust the spit through the flounders as the boy was accustomed to do, but he was clumsy over the operation and the old man called out and told him that he was tricking him and was not his grandson...[15]

In Hill-Tout's recounting of this story we are not privileged to view and hear the movements and music of the dance as they would have been shared by the original *Stó:lō* speaker. Likewise, we cannot see the special thrusting motions of the roasting-spit, or listen to the changing intonations of voice as the grandfather becomes aware of the trick that has been played upon him. The intended

meanings or lessons of the original teller are removed. In Hill-Tout's account the thick layers of meaning conveyed through expression and intonation are shaved away, leaving a less satisfying non-interactive text.

The analogy of *sxwōxwiyám* being like a theatre play is appropriate in another sense as well. Take, for example, a study of William Shakespeare's **Hamlet**. The play was designed to be performed and to evoke emotional responses from a live audience. Actors playing various parts bring certain perspectives to their roles. To an even greater extent, the director creates certain messages in his specific rendition of the play, some of which may not have been explicitly intended by Shakespeare, but which do not involve an abandonment of the the original script. For example, in some performances of Hamlet the hero is portrayed as insane, while in others, he is calculating and in full control of his faculties. In some versions, the appearance of Hamlet's father is real and necessary for Hamlet to learn the truth (that the King was poisoned by Hamlet's uncle). Other directors portray the ghost as a figment of Hamlet's imagination which he himself conjours to justify his own suspicions about a natural death he refuses to accept? All of these variations, and more, exist within Shakespeare's original text. What was Shakespeares original intent? While historically interesting, determining the meaning is not as important as understanding the meaning delivered in each new performance. Likewise, *Stó:lō* Elders take pains to retain the "original" content of *sxwōxwiyám*. They use oral footnoting to carefully explain who they learned the story from, and in that way establish the validity of the story's content. Like the director who bends meaning within the unaltered text of Shakespeare, gifted *Stó:lō* story tellers use the same narrative to stress different points, depending upon their intent, their audience and circumstance.

Authorship and Upperclass Status

The story of *Xá:ytem* reminds us that, unlike Hamlet, *Stó:lō* oral narratives do not have a single author; the only "authority" that emerges is that given to the teller of a story by his or her community.[16] This does not, however, imply that *sxwōxwiyám* are in the public domain and open to carefree revision. As mentioned, *Stó:lō* storytellers recognize that the *sxwōxwiyám* they share are part of their extended family's heritage, and treasured windows into their history and culture. Storytellers, therefore, carefully explain to their audience from whom they originally learned the story, and in other ways indicate how the story was passed on to them in a legitimate fashion from a respected family member who knew the importance of "keeping the stories right."

Drawing this connection to respected Elders or ancestors is an important feature of *Stó:lō* society; it is regarded as a sign of being high class, or *smelá:lh*. Those people who do not know *sxwōxwiyám* or who have in other ways forgotten their history and the lessons of their Elders are considered to be *s'téxem* – of lower status – as are all peo-

Gwen Point, respected *Stó:lō* speaker.

ple who come from families who have "lost their history."[17] For example, notice how carefully Hank Pennier, in the following extract from his book *Chiefly Indian*, explains how he learned a particular *sxwōxwiyám* and the context of its telling. By explaining that his step-father was a *Stó:lō* Elder who continued to practise such traditional customs as plucking out his facial hair, Pennier adds legitimacy to his version of the story:

My step father... was an old guy, but he never had a whisker on his face. If a whisker popped out, out it came roots and all, with his little knife. He was a nice old man and my brothers and sisters and I saw quite a lot of him.

At night he use to tell us long stories of the past. Especially in the long winter evenings with us sitting around the wood stove to stay warm we listened... and I guess that was when I started to be proud I was a Indian or at least part of one. If I was smarter I would have listened a lot harder and learned a lot more, but of course I was still quite young.

The story I liked best was about... [Hank Pennier's story then goes on to relate a *sxwōxwiyám*.][18]

Cultural Knowledge and Context

Another lesson stemming from the *Xá:ytem* stone story is that people must be careful when preserving a *sxwōxwiyám* to ensure that cultural knowledge and context can continue to be communicated effectively. The various permanently recorded and published examples of *Stó:lō* literature vary in the degree to which they effectively communicate the original and indigenous meaning of each *sxwōxwiyám*. Some written versions have had so many layers of meaning shaved away that they become all but culturally unintelligible. Take, for example, the following cryptic summary of "The Transformer Story" recorded and published nearly eighty years ago by the ethnographer James Teit:

The Transformer came to Yale, and there he saw a man smoking. He asked him what he was doing, and he answered that he was smoking. The Transformer said to him, "you must die;" and the man answered, "Very well, but do not put me into the water. I want to remain here, so that the people may see me and talk to me, and that I may see them." When he finished speaking, he was transformed into a stone, which may be seen there. It is shaped like a man.

Near Yale, the Transformer met a man who was hunting deer. He transformed both hunter and deer into rocks in the water.

A little below Yale he met some women who were making salmon-oil. He transformed them and their kettle into stones, which may be seen at that place.[19]

You Are Asked To Witness

In such a summary, not only are readers deprived of the original performance aspects of the narrative, but the cultural context and intended meanings are minimized. All written accounts are interpreted with some degree of context by readers. However, the greater the shared experiences of the teller and the audience, the richer the shared meaning. An informed audience will have the special knowledge to appreciate even the most cryptic of summaries. In this case, for example, informed readers would bring background information to the summary about the "Transformer" and the personalities and lives of those with whom he came into contact. They would metaphorically transform the "tale" from a foggy window, barely permitting a glimpse of *Stó:lō* society, to an open doorway whereby shared memories of similar stories are recalled and used to reinforce a common world view. When reading oral literature it is important to keep in mind that the more stories that are read, the easier it will become to understand this common world view. In a sense, readers will begin to recognize and appreciate cultural messages within the stories.

To clarify this point, and at the same time provide readers with a broader exposure to *Stó:lō* oral literature, we will now turn our attention to a recording made by Franz Boas. Boas was the father of modern North American anthropology and the first academic who seriously attempted to familiarize himself with the people and cultures of the Northwest Coast. In 1890 he visited the *Stó:lō* community of Chehalis and recorded the following story about how *Qoa'l'otlk'otl* (one of the *Xexá:ls* Transformer siblings) became engaged in a competition with a "very powerful man" (Indian doctor) named *SHa'i* who lived on the shores of Harrison Lake.[20] The compe-

titions took a number of forms, each of which *Qoa'l'otlk'otl* lost. Exasperated at his continual defeats, *Qoa'l'otlk'otl* ultimately determined not just to better *SHa'i* in another contest, but to kill him. To accomplish this he required special powers normally not available to him:

. . . Now *Qals [Xá:ls]* wanted to kill *SHa'i*. He asked his sister, "Could you give me some of your menstrual blood?" She said yes, and gave it to him. So he put it in the bottom of his pipe and heaped tobacco on it. The youngest of the brothers warned *Qoa'l'otlk'otl* [the oldest of the *Xexá:ls* siblings] and begged him to leave *SHa'i* alone, since he was so powerful. But *Qoa'l'otlk'otl* paid no attention to him. He went to *SHa'i* and said, "Yesterday when the canoe capsized and when it snowed afterwards, we were extremely cold. But the tobacco has warmed us very nicely. Won't you smoke some too?" And he offered him the pipe. But *SHa'i* refused, saying that he could not smoke. But *Qoa'l'otlk'otl* encouraged him to try, and finally persuaded him. He took a puff, and *Qoa'l'otlk'otl* told him, "You have to inhale deeply and swallow the smoke." He took three puffs and then fell dead. *Qals [Xá:ls]* ripped out his tongue and threw it away; it became a rock. He ripped out his stomach, tore off his arms, legs and head, and threw them away and transformed them into stone.[21]

Transformer rock *Tewít*, the hunter.

Read in isolation by someone unfamiliar with *Stó:lō* culture, Boas' recordings might leave readers with a negative impression about some of the activities described and their significance. For example, a contemporary mainstream Canadian reader might wonder why menstrual blood was used to ultimately defeat *SHa'i*. Does this imply that in traditional *Stó:lō* society women were considered particularly dirty or even toxic? A reader culturally fluent in *Halq'eméylem* would understand *Stó:lō* notions of "spirit power." For example, the *Stó:lō* explain that if a man wants to become an expert fisherman he goes on a spirit quest and receives special spirit powers to assist him. While fishing, he calls upon this spirit to assist him. A fisherman also inadvertently leave residual spirit power in his fishing equipment, canoe, and even his clothing – indeed, any of his personal possessions. Different people have varying strengths of spirit power depending on the acquisition and nurturing of their spirit. Men typically acquire spirit power through intense training. Women also acquire spirit power in this manner; however, they have additional inherent spirit power which is of a different nature. This special female spirit power is particularly potent during a woman's menstrual cycle and pregnancy. A woman is so spiritually powerful during these times that she will not touch her husband's fishing equipment for fear of over-riding and rendering impotent his special fishing spirit power. Although the greater message is more complex, the point here is that even though *Qoa'l'otlk'otl* was one of the powerful *Xexá:ls* siblings, his spirit power was insufficient to overcome those of the shaman *SHa'i*. Only with the assistance of menstrual blood from his spiritually potent sister could he defeat the powerful Indian doctor.

The preceding example clearly illustrates the role of cultural knowledge and context and the major drawbacks of freezing an oral narrative into oral literature. By assessing an audience and responding to the subtle messages given as they listened to the story, a contemporary *Stó:lō* storyteller would be able to relate the story of *SHa'i* and *Qoa'l'otlk'otl* so that even a *Stó:lō* cultural neophyte would be able to appreciate the concept of residual spirit power, so central to the narrative. This does however, also illustrate that once a reader becomes more familiar with *Stó:lō* culture, stories such as this can provide greater understanding, and therefore more sophisticated appreciations and readings of oral narratives.

Humour in *Stó:lō* Oral Narratives

Humour plays a vital role in the telling of many *sxwōxwiyám* (as well as many *sqwélqwel*, as will be demonstrated in the next section). This is not to say that *Stó:lō* oral narratives are all funny stories, or that they necessarily centre upon clown-like "tricksters," as is sometimes assumed with Aboriginal narratives. Rather, *sxwōxwiyám* are generally concerned with such subjects as the serious work of the Transformer siblings, *Xexá:ls*. However, humour plays an important role in the delivery of these stories.

Among other things, humour in *sxwōxwiyám* serves to bring stories to life by engaging the teller and listeners in an interactive emotional exchange.[22] Often, *sxwōxwiyám* express humour through discussions of sex, bodily functions, and death. Frequently, such humour occurs at the expense of one particularly unfortunate character. Such is the case in the numerous tragic misadventures of *Sqayéxiya*, Mink, the travelling companion of *Xexá:ls*, who repeatedly gets into trouble because of his lascivious nature. Such comic relief no doubt assists listeners in learning to distinguish between community standards of acceptable and unacceptable behaviour. Humor also makes the stories not only more memorable, but also more entertaining.

The humour in the following *sxwōxwiyám* is fairly typical of *Stó:lō* oral narratives. It was shared by Chehalis Elder Jimmy Charlie in the autumn of 1993 while he was visiting with a large group of family and friends around the family kitchen table. As they heard of Mink's misfortune Mr. Charlie's audience began to laugh, some so hard they had tears running down their face:

> ... Mink was travelling with *Xexá:ls* down the river when they came to a village where they planned to spend the night. As they got closer to the shore Mink saw a beautiful woman. She was the most beautiful woman Mink ever saw. Mink wanted to spend some time with her, and approached her... pretty soon they were "toolying," you know? – "toolying" After a while Mink was finished and wanted to stop, but when he tried to pull out he couldn't. The woman wasn't a beautiful lady after all. She was a *stl'áleqem* [a supernatural monster]. She just clamped on down there and Mink couldn't get away. He cried for help, and jumped and wiggled around, but he couldn't get away. Then he saw his friend, and he said, "get me some cut-grass, get me some cut-grass!" His friend ran down by the edge of the river and got some cut-grass and came back and gave it to Mink. Mink, he just grabbed it and "swoosh," dragged it between himself and the woman (the *stl'áleqem*). That was it, Mink lost it. He lost it you know. He had to just cut it off.[23] 😊

The narrative about Mink is both humorous and unfortunate. Yet, beyond being engaging, Mink's experiences also set up a model of "proper behaviour." As with other aspects of oral narratives discussed earlier, we see that there are multiple education techniques applied within the genre of the *sxwōxwiyám*. Humor is one of these.

Sqwélqwel

The second category of *Stó:lō* oral narratives, *sqwélqwel*, differ from *sxwōxwiyám* in that they usually deal

You Are Asked To Witness

Stó:lō Elder Rosaleen George.

mance (ie. adaptation to situation and circumstance, and special cultural knowledge), can occur. However, like the *sxwōxwiyám* captured as literature, written *sqwélqwel* can also prove extremely enjoyable as an educational and entertainment tool. The following excerpt, one of the few published *Stó:lō sqwélqwel*, was written by Scowlitz Elder Hank Pennier in his 1974 book *Chiefly Indian*.

. . . That reminds me I have not told you about how the Indians kept warm in the old days. They didn't put on a Cowichan sweater like my wife knits for us all now. They would make a thin cord from cedar bark which is fine and stringy and can be used for all sorts of useful things. They then would use this to hang up a large rock about the size of a man's head about three feet off the ground. They would then lie down underneath this rock at night time and just thinking about what would happen if the fine cord would break would make them sweat and stay warm all night.[25]

In this short *sqwélqwel*, Pennier illustrates his knowledge about traditional uses of cedar rope and the importance of retaining cultural knowledge. Within the story also is humour which becomes a medium for communicating subtle messages of "how to". The richness of this humour however, reaches beyond its function as a tool, and provides a glimpse into humour as an important aspect of *Stó:lō* society.

The Reality of *Sxwōxwiyám* and *Sqwélqwel* to the *Stó:lō*

Although *sqwélqwel* usually relate what non-*Stó:lō* readers might interpret as more recent, "real" events and *sxwōxwiyám* discuss the distant mythical past during the time of the Transformers, it is important to note that cross-overs between the elements of the two types of narratives are not uncommon. Thus, it is not always easy to classify a story as either *sxwōxwiyám* or *sqwélqwel*. This stems primarily from the fact that both types of narratives illustrate various realities that often exist simultaneously. The narratives shared by the *Stó:lō* often do not make a distinction between a distant history that was and a contemporary history that is, or a distant history that is unreal and a contemporary history that is real. There is no line drawn between the mythical/supernatural/spiritual and the natural/ordinary that cannot be bent. Even the inferred difference between the past and the present, or a supernatural versus a natural experience, can be blurred (yet the distinction between a *sxwōxwiyám* and a *sqwélqwel* are clear to *Stó:lō* Elders).

with more contemporary or recent history. Often they are referred to as "true stories" or "news."[24] Moreover, *sqwélqwel* also differ in that they are neither delivered in a prescribed manner, nor are audiences formally expected to subtly persuade the teller to continue. *Sqwélqwel* offer accounts and understandings of everyday or life events in terms of a *Stó:lō* epistemology or knowledge base. Both *sxwōxwiyám* and *sqwélqwel* are used to illustrate lessons, to teach and entertain, and to explain to the listener how the world works. *Sxwōxwiyám* do this within the framework of the myth age, and *sqwélqwel* within the realm of "history" or life experience.

Most of the guidelines for appreciating oral narratives discussed above in relation to *sxwōxwiyám*, apply equally to *sqwélqwel*. Ideally, a *sqwélqwel* is also shared between a live speaker and audience so all the elements of perfor-

While the events which unfold in a *sxwōxwiyám* are actually dependent upon a touching of the "earth world" and the supernatural, in contemporary *sqwélqwel* people who are already in fixed or grounded forms sometimes still experience an ephemeral connection with the supernatural world. One way of trying to grasp this concept is to think of a house with several rooms, in which different realities are occurring. The hallways and stairs in the house are "grey areas," in which beings from different rooms can meet, unexpectedly or in a predetermined fashion, and experience situations that would not normally occur had they remained in their own rooms. Periodically, entire walls or floors disappear, and whole worlds of realities intermingle to create various effects. Of course, these walls and floors reappear (although sometimes not in their original locations), and so the worlds which were opened are closed off, or are not accessible in the same way. In other words, access may still be available, but sometimes not all of the necessary elements are still present to allow the same results. In all of these instances, the house is real, each room is real, and each "grey area" is real, although only one or two of these realities may be evident to people at one time.

For instance, a contemporary person might tell a "real" story in which they acquired the spirit power of a bird during a spirit quest, but cannot physically and permanently transform into the bird as happens in a *sxwōxwiyám*. The following excerpt is taken from Diamond Jenness' *The Faith of a Coast Salish Indian*, as told by Peter Pierre:

My daughter Margaret once became ill, and I diagnosed her malady as spirit sickness... a cousin from Hammond chanted the white-owl song. Then she showed signs of life, and after he had danced and chanted a second time, she began to sing the *skokok* [a mountain-bird] song. A day or two afterwards, when she performed her dance, the people had to tie a rope around her waist to keep her from flying away. Even with the rope holding her down, her feet rose a foot or two from the floor.[26]

Likewise, a contemporary storyteller may tell of an encounter with a supernatural *stl'áleqem*, or monster like a sasquatch [*sásq'ets*], but such a story would be no less "real" to the teller or audience than one describing a contemporary hunter's encounter with a moose. Take as an example, the following *sqwélqwel* shared by Chawathil Elder Bill Pat-Charlie in the summer of 1992:

Two of my cousins went up Harrison Lake in a canoe to hunt deer. That was about 1935. They landed on a log booming ground and climbed up a hill. When they had almost reached the top of the hill they saw a large hairy man. The "thing" stood at the top of the hill and looked down on them. My cousins became afraid and shot at his head with their 30:30 rifles, but it didn't effect him at all. He just wiped his head where the bullets had hit, then he started to come after them. My cousins kept shooting, but the "thing" did not slow down. It just kept coming. My cousins ran back to their canoe as fast as they could. They paddled away very quickly, while the thing ran back and forth on the booming grounds. Soon after, one of my cousins drowned (the other is still alive). If someone sees a sasquatch you know they will die, or someone close to them.[27]

Inner cedar bark being prepared for use as clothing.

You Are Asked To Witness

3 CONCLUSIONS - SPOKEN LITERATURE ■

The oral traditions of the *Stó:lō* are clearly a central facet of their culture. Sharing these stories allows the speaker and the audience to share in the communally held experiences, histories, beliefs, and philosophies of the *Stó:lō* people. "Spoken literature" takes place in both formal and everyday settings, recalling a variety of cultural experiences from the supernatural world of the *X̱exá:ls* (*sx̱wōx̱wiyám*) to the happenings of one's life (*sqwélqwel*). Both tellings embody the important cultural knowledge of "how to live" – information which is extremely important to pass on "properly" in an oral society.

As we have outlined, the context in which the story is told – including the prior cultural knowledge of the teller and the listener – is important, as is the way the story is represented, particularly when it is written down. A great deal of loss of cultural knowledge can occur when transcription and translation are not carefully approached. And yet, one of the best ways of acquiring this cultural appreciation is through oral narratives and oral literature.

In order to become more informed and familiar with *Stó:lō* traditional culture, it is advisable that the first chapter of this book be read in conjunction with the oral literature in this chapter. Although it may seem daunting, we encourage people to read as much *Stó:lō* oral literature as possible; with each reading comes greater appreciation and understanding not only of particular stories in the greater literature, but also of *Stó:lō* society in general.

Recommended Further Readings

Franz Boas, *Indian Myths and Legends from the North Pacific Coast of America,* Berlin: A. Asher & Co., 1895.

Julie Cruikshank, Dän Dhá Ts'edenintth'é: *Reading Voices,* Vancouver: Douglas and McIntyre, 1991.

Brent Galloway, A *Grammar of Upriver Halq'eméylem,* Berkley: U of California Press, 1993.

Charles Hill-Tout, *The Salish People,* Volume III: The Mainland Halkomelem, Vancouver; Talonbooks, 1978.

Dell Hymes, "Mythology" in *Handbook of North American Indians,* Vol. 7, North West Coast, Washington, DC: Smithsonian Institute, 1990.

Diamond Jenness, *The Corn Goddess and Other Tales from Indian Canada,* Canada: National Parks Board, 1956.

Diamond Jenness, *The Faith of a Coast Salish Indian,* Victoria: Province of B.C., 1955.

Norman Hart Lerman, *Lower Fraser Indian Folktales,* Seattle: University of Washington, 1950-1951.

Ralph Maud, *A Guide to British Columbia Indian Myths and Legends,* Vancouver: Talonbooks, 1982.

Henry Pennier, *Chiefly Indian,* Vancouver: Greydonald Graphics Ltd., 1972.

Eloise Street, *Sepass Tales, Songs of Y-ail-mihth,* Chilliwack: Sepass Trust, 1974.

Wayne Suttles, *Coast Salish Essays,* Vancouver: Talonbooks, 1987.

James A. Teit, *Folk-Tales of Salishan and Sahaptin Tribes.* Chapter VII. "Tales from the Lower Fraser River," New York: The American Folklore Society, 1917.

Oliver Wells, *Myths and Legends of South Western British Columbia: STAW-loh Indians,* Sardis, 1970.

Oliver Wells, *The Chilliwacks and Their Neighbours,* Vancouver: Talonbooks, 1987.

Gwen Point and Helen Joe working cedar bark.

Footnotes:

1 Brent Galloway. Wisdom of the Elders, The Structures of Upriver *Halq'eméylem* , a Grammatical Sketch, (Coqualeetza Education Training Centre: Sardis, BC, 1980).

2 Galloway, Brent. "An Upriver Halkomelem Mink Story: Ethnopoetics and Discourse Analysis." Unpublished manuscript, *Stó:lō* Nation, Archives, p.159.

3 Wayne Suttles, "Central Coast Salish" Handbook of North American Indians, Vol. 7, p.466.

4 Eloise Street's book *Sepass Tales*, includes a *sxwōxwiyám* which outlines the creation or genesis of the world. Other versions of genesis stories are told by contemporary *Stó:lō*, possibly reflecting the changing cultural environment in which people found themselves in the past century – an environment heavily influenced by Christian missionaries, in which the *Stó:lō* developed innovative and adaptive ways of viewing their changing world.

5 In this way *Stó:lō sxwōxwiyám* are similar to Greek mythology, set in the times of the gods Zeus and Apollo. We know that the Titans existed before Zeus, but we are told nothing about how the Titans came to be.

6 There are several "original stories" in *Stó:lō* oral tradition. For two version see, Oliver Wells *The Chilliwacks and their Neighbours*, (Talonbooks: Vancouver, B.C., 1987), pp.48,50.

7 This is the impression Sonny McHalsie, Cultural Researcher at *Stó:lō* Nation, has been left with after having numerous conversations with different *Stó:lō* Elders.

8 This observation is made after a thorough examination of all published and most unpublished *Stó:lō sxwōxwiyám*, and after numerous discussions with various elementary school teachers and high school literature teachers who wanted to provide their classes with "exposure to another culture." See also the comments of Elli Maranda in "B.C. Indian Myth and Education: A Review Article" in BC Studies,Spring, 1975. p.130.

9 Conversation between Bertha Peters and Albert "Sonny" McHalsie, September 1995.

10 Brent D. Galloway. *A Grammer of Upriver Halkomelem*, (U. of Calif. Press: Berkley, LA, London, 1993), p.613.

11 Pronounced similar to the sounds made by the letters "E-I."

12 Brent D. Galloway. *A Grammer of Upriver Halkomelem*, (U. of Calif. Press: Berkley, LA, London, 1993), p.613.

13 Ibid.

14 We refer here to our experience with two Elders from the Chehalis community on Harrison Lake. To the obvious delight of all present, the Elders began sharing somewhat explicit and earthy *sxwōxwiyám* about Mink and *Xeχa:ls* during the course of a crib game. On having a subsequent opportunity to listen to one of the same Elders share one of the same *sxwōxwiyám* with a group of high school student during a "cross   cultural awareness workshop" the story was significantly modified to suit the young audience.

15 Charles Hill-Tout, "The Salish People," Vol. III, p.156.

16 See D.H. Hymes. *In Vain I Tried to Tell You: Essays in Native American Ethnopoetics.* (U of Pennsylvania Press: Philadelphia, 1981)

17 See Wayne Suttles, "Coast Salish Private Knowledge,", In *Coast Salish Essays*. p.4.

18 Henry Pennier. *Chiefly Indian*, pp. 17-18.

19 James Teit, "Tales From the lower Fraser River," *Memoirs of the American Folk-Lore Society*, Vol.XI, 1917. p129.

20 Franz Boas' term "a very powerful man" refers to "Indian doctors." In *Halq'eméylem* there are two types of Indian doctors: *shxwlá:m*, meaning healers; and *shxwí:n*, or people who had the power to inflict harm. It is unclear in the oral narrative related here as to what kind of doctor *SHa'i* was.

21 Franz Boas. *Indian Legends from the North Pacific Coast of America.* (A. Asher & Co.: Berlin, 1895), pp.31-32.

22 This is the impression Sonny McHalsie has been left with after numerous conversations with *Stó:lō* Elders.

23 Conversation between Jimmie Charlie and Keith Carlson, Chehalis October, 1995.

24 Galloway, 1993, p.614.

25 Henry Pennier, **Chiefly Indian,** chpt. 1.

26 Diamond Jenness, *The Faith of a Coast Salish Indian*, p.55.

27 Conversation between Bill Pat-Charlie and Keith Carlson, in Mr. Pat-Charlie's living room at Chawathil, July 29, 1992.

Halq'eméylem Names for present-day Indian Reserves in *Stó:lō* Traditional Territory[1]

Reserve Name and Number	*Halq'eméylem* name	"literal meaning of name"
Aitchelitz 9	*Áthelets*	"edge at bottom" or "place where two rivers meet"
Albert Flat 5	*Ó:ywoses*	"on both sides"
Aylechootlook 5	*Texqéyl*	"always going dry"
Aywawwis 15	*Iwówes*	"something that does not want to show itself"
Barnston Island 3	*Qelesílhp*	"water goes right by"
Burrard Inlet 3	*S'èthnets*	"bay"
Capilano River 5	*Xwmélets'then*	"horseflies at the mouth"
Chawuthen 4	*Chowéthel*	"land sticking way out"
Cheam 1	*Chiyó:m*	"always wild strawberries"
Chehalis 4/5/5a	*Sts'a'í:les*	"laying on the chest"
Coquitlam 2	*Setlámqemen*	"when the tide's high, we can go"
Coquitlam 1	"*Slakǝyánc*"	"young sockeye"
Greenwood Island 3	*Welqámex*	having to do with an eddy
Holachten 8	*Thewelhem*	meaning not recorded
Hope 1	*Ts'qó:ls*	"bare" or "bald"
Katzie 2	*Xwthéxth'exem*	"always nettle place"
Katzie 1	*Q'éyts'i*	"moss"
Kawkawa 16	*Q'éwq'ewe*	meaning of name associated with two loons
Kaykaip 7	*Halq'eméylem* name not recorded	
Klaklacum 12	*Lexwtl'atl'ekw'em*	meaning not recorded
Kuthlalth 3	*Xelhálh*	"injured person"
Kwawkwawapilt 6	*Qweqwe'ópelhp*	"lots of wild crab apples"
Lakahahmen 11	*Leq'á:mel*	"level place" or "place that is visited"
Lakaway 2	*Láxewey*	"lots of people drowned"
Lelachen 6	*Lexwlaxel*	"always fishing platforms"
Lukseetsissum 9	*Spópetes*	"blowing" or "always windy"
Matsqui 4	*Mómeqwem*	"a mossy place where lots of berries and *meqwem* tea grown"
Matsqui Main 2	*Máthkwi*	"easy travelling"
McMillan Island 6	*Sqwàlets*	"the river went through"
Mission 1	*Slhe'án'*	*Snichim* (Squamish) name for "head of bay"
Musqueam 4	*Xw'ichum*	meaning not recorded
Musqueam 2	*Xwmèthkwiyem*	"place of the plant *méthkwey*'"
Peters 1/1a/2	*Skw'átets*	"water trickling through"
Pitt Lake 4	*Tl'eltl'elsále*	meaning not recorded
Popkum 1/1a	*Pópkw'em*	"puffballs"
Puckathoetchin 11	*Peqwchō:lthel*	"river bank caving in"
Qualark 4	*Qw'elóqw'*	"cooked heads"

Ruby Creek 2	*Halq'eméylem* name not recorded	
Schelowat 1	*Sxelá:wtwx*	"painted house"
Schkam 2	*Sqám*	"calm water"
Scowlitz 1	*Sq'éwlets*	"turn at bottom"
Sea Island 3	*Sqwsatsun'*	meaning not recorded
Seabird Island 1	*Sq'éwqel*	"turn in the river"
Semiahmoo 1	*Tá'telew'*	"little creek"
Seymour Creek 2	*S'á:mámet*	"lazy people"
Shxw'owhamel 1	*Shxw'ōwhámél*	"where the river levels and widens"
Skawahlook 1	*Sq'ewá:lxw*	"on both sides" or "a bend/turn"
Skawahlum 10	*Sq'ewílem*	"go arouund a bend in the river"
Skowkale 10/11	*Sq'ewqéyl*	"going around a turn"
Skumalasph 16	*Qemlólhp*	"maple tree"
Skwah 4	*Sqwá*	"to go through"
Skwahla 2	*Sqwá:la*	"where you come up the slough out into the open"
Skwali 3	*Sqwáli*	meaning not recorded
Skway 5	*Shxwhá:y*	"a lot of people died"
Skweahm 10	*Skwiyám*	word comes from the name of a man
sold (New Westminister Band) . . .	*Qiqá:yt*	"resting place"
Soowahlie 14	*Th'ewá:lí*	"melting or dissolving away"
Spuzzum 1	*Spíyem*	meaning not recorded
Squakum Creek 3	*Sqwéxem*	"silver Harrison/Chehalis River spring salmon"
Squeah 6	*St'élxweth'*	"to move in a semi-circle with the current"
Squiala 7/8	*Sxwoyehá:lá*	"container of a lot of dead people"
Stullawheets 8	*Lexwtl'ikw'elem*	"place where there are lots of red knickanick berries"
Sumas Cemetary 12	*Halq'eméylem* name not recorded	
Swahliseah 14	*Lexwyó:qwem*	"always smells like rotten fish"
Three Islands 3	*"Pook-chen-nus"*	meaning not recorded
Trafalgar 13	*Qíqemqèmèl*	"tide" and "a little bay"
Tsawwassen 1	*Stsewòthen*	"seaward edge"
Tseatah 2	*Siyét'e*	meaning not recorded
Tunnel 6	*Xelíqel*	"steep"
Tzeachten 13	*Ch'iyáqtel*	"fish weir"
Upper Sumas 6	*Kw'ekw'e'í:qw*	"sticking up"
Wahleach Island 2	*Xwelích*	word comes from the name of a man
Whonnock 1	*Xwéwenaqw*	meaning not recorded
Williams 2	*Xwítxiyl*	having some reference to "feet"
Yakweakwiooose 12	*Yeqwyeqwí:ws*	"burned out many times"
Yale 20	*Q'alelíktel*	meaning not recorded
Yale 1	*Xwoxwelá:lhp*	"willow tree place"
Yale 23/24	*Lexwts'okw'á:m*	"always skunk-cabbages"
Yale 22	*Íyem*	"strong"
Yale 21	*Aseláw*	meaning not recorded

4-1/2 Mile . . . . *Halq'eméylem* name not recorded
Chehalis Graveyard 6 . . . . *Halq'eméylem* name not recorded
Douglas 8 . . . . *Halq'eméylem* name not recorded
Grass 15 . . . . *Halq'eméylem* name not recorded
Inlailawatash 4a . . . . *Halq'eméylem* name not recorded
Katzie Graveyard 2 . . . . *Halq'eméylem* name not recorded
Kwantlen 3 . . . . *Halq'eméylem* name not recorded
Kwantlen 5 . . . . *Halq'eméylem* name not recorded
Kwantlen 2 . . . . *Halq'eméylem* name not recorded
Kwantlen 4 . . . . *Halq'eméylem* name not recorded
Lakway Cemetery 3 . . . . *Halq'eméylem* name not recorded
Papekwatchin 4 . . . . *Halq'eméylem* name not recorded
Peters 2 . . . . *Halq'eméylem* name not recorded
Saddle Rock 9 . . . . *Halq'eméylem* name not recorded
Sahhacum 1 . . . . *Halq'eméylem* name not recorded
Spuzzum 7 . . . . *Halq'eméylem* name not recorded
Spuzzum 1a . . . . *Halq'eméylem* name not recorded
Stout 8 . . . . *Halq'eméylem* name not recorded
Tipella 7 . . . . *Halq'eméylem* name not recorded
Yaalstrick 1 . . . . *Halq'eméylem* name not recorded
Yale 18 . . . . *Halq'eméylem* name not recorded
Yale 25 . . . . *Halq'eméylem* name not recorded
Yale 23 . . . . *Halq'eméylem* name not recorded
Yale 19 . . . . *Halq'eméylem* name not recorded
Zaitscullachan 9 . . . . *Halq'eméylem* name not recorded

1   Information obtained from Sonny McHalsie's, Rosaleen George's, Matilda Gutierrez's and Amelia Douglas' personal knowledge, compiled with assistance from Brian Thom and Kevin Washbrook. The following written sources were also consulted: Wilson Duff, The Upper Stalo Indians of the Fraser Valley, British Columbia, (Victoria: *Anthropology in British Columbia*, *Memoir 1*, British Columbia Provincial Museum, 1952); Brent Galloway, Albert Phillips and Coqualeetza Elders Group (1976-1979) *Stó:lō* Place Names File, Ms. (*Stó:lō* Nation Archives, [SNA] Chilliwack); George Gibbs (1858) United States Boundary Survey Map, unpublished map, (Copy on file at SNA); Charles Hill-Tout "Ethnological Report for the StsEe'lis and Sk'au'lits Tribes of the Halkomelem Division of the Salish," *Journal of the Royal Anthropological Institute*, 1904; Walter Kenyon *An Archaeological Survey of the Lower Fraser from Chilliwack to the Strait of Georgia*, Graduating Essay, University of British Columbia, 1953; Wayne Suttles Katzie Ethnographic Notes *Anthropology in British Columbia, Memoir 2*. (Victoria: British Columbia Provincial Museum, 1955); Wayne Suttles "The Central Coast Salish," in *Handbook of North American Indians, Volume 7, Northwest Coast*. Edited by W. Suttles, (Washington: Smithsonian Institution Press, 1990); Wayne Suttles *"Linguistic Evidence for Burrard Inlet as Former Halkomelem Territory"* (Papers for the 31st International Conference on Salish and Neighbouring Languages, U.B.C., August 1996); Oliver Wells *A Vocabulary of Native Words in the Halkomelem Language* (Sardis: 1965).

— Photo Credits —

CHAPTER SIX

p. 110 Chilliwack Museum and Archives, #p.coll.120 file 243; **p. 111** Courtesy of British Columbia Archives and Records Service, #HP-70053; Courtesy of British Columbia Archives and Records Service, #E-5553; **p. 112** Courtesy of Royal British Columbia Museum, #PN6371; Gary Feigehen, #P-18A; Courtesy of Royal British Columbia Museum, #PN6259; **p. 113** Keith Carlson and Kim Stevenson; Courtesy of British Columbia Archives and Records Service, #A-04313; **p. 114** E.W. Carlson; Courtesy of British Columbia Archives and Records Service, #A-03579; **p. 115** Courtesy of British Columbia Archives and Records Service, #D-06815; Courtesy of British Columbia Archives and Records Service, #G-00802; **p. 116** Courtesy of British Columbia Archives and Records Service, #A-03868; Courtesy of British Columbia Archives and Records Service, #A-03928; Chilliwack Museum and Archives, #p-1365; **p. 117** Courtesy of British Columbia Archives and Records Service, #B-02522; Courtesy of British Columbia Archives and Records Service, #D-08907; **p. 118** Courtesy of British Columbia Archives and Records Service, #A-06839; Chilliwack Museum and Archives, #p-1363; **p. 119** Courtesy of Royal British Columbia Museum, #PN7585; Chilliwack Museum and Archives, #add mss 362 file 287(a); Chilliwack Museum and Archives, #p-5324; **p.120** Courtesy of British Columbia Archives and Records Service, #D-07548; **p. 121** Courtesy of Royal British Columbia Museum, #PN6258; **p. 122** Courtesy of British Columbia Archives and Records Service, #A-03874; **p. 123** Courtesy of Royal British Columbia Museum, #PN7587; Chilliwack Museum and Archives, #p-1479; Laura Cameron.

CHAPTER SEVEN

p. 126 E. Labinsky with Wesley Sam; **p. 127** Field Museum of Natural History; Ann Mohs; **p. 128** E. Labinsky with Robert Bobb; **p. 129** Ann Mohs; Courtesy of British Columbia Archives and Records Service, #D-08911; **p. 130** Ann Mohs; **p. 131** E. Labinsky with Harold Wells; **p. 133** Department of Indian and Northern Affairs; **p.134** Ann Mohs; **p. 135** Tracey Joe, #T1-20; **p.136** Paul Kane, *War Party*, Juan de Fuca, Watercolor on paper, 5.25" X 8.78", 1846, Stark Museum of Art, Orange, Texas; **p.137** Ann Mohs; **p. 138** Gary Feigehen, #AA-9A.

CHAPTER EIGHT

p. 141 Gary Feigehen, #U-27; **p.142** Courtesy of Royal British Columbia Museum, #PN1380; **p. 144** Chilliwack Museum and Archives, #p.coll.199 file 283; **pp. 146-147** Courtesy of British Columbia Archives and Records Service, #E-05964; **p. 150** Article reprinted courtesy of the Vancouver Sun, Gordon Hamilton; **p. 151** Gary Feigehen, #C-25A; **p.152** Gary Feigehen, #F-23A.

CHAPTER NINE

p. 154 Gary Feigehen, #B-15A; **p. 155** Gary Feigehen, #AA-31A; Gary Feigehen, #U-4; **p. 156** Gary Feigehen, #V-8A; **p. 157** Courtesy of British Columbia Archives and Records Service, #A-03874; Gary Feigehen, #V-5A; **p.159** Gary Feigehen, #Q-16; **p. 160** Courtesy of British Columbia Archives and Records Service, #F-08715; **p. 161** Courtesy of Royal British Columbia Museum, #PN878; Gary Feigehen, #U-15; **p. 162** Gary Fiegehen, #B-7A.

CHAPTER TEN

p. 164 Chilliwack Museum and Archives, #p-1007; **p. 165** Courtesy of UBC Press and Dr. Graeme Wyn. Originally printed in Wynn, Graeme and Oke, Timothy. Vancouver and Its Region. Vancouver: UBC Press, 1992; **p. 166** Greater Vancouver Regional District; Ryan Ross; **p. 167** Population projections reprinted from Artibise, Allan. From Desolation to Hope. Vancouver: UBC School of Community and Regional Planning, 1991, p.8; **p. 168** Courtesy of British Columbia Archives and Records Service, #A-03330; **p. 169** Maps reprinted from Meyer, Ronald H. "The Evolution of Roads in the Lower Fraser Valley" in Seimens, A. Lower Fraser Valley Evolution of a Cultural Landscape. Vancouver: Tantalus Research Ltd, 1968; This map is based on information taken from the National Topographic System map sheet numbers 92G and 92H, Copyright 1990. Her Majesty the Queen in Right of Canada with permission of Natural Resources Canada. **p. 170** Ryan Ross and Brian Thom; **p. 171** Map reprinted from Moore, Kathleen E. *Urbanization in the Lower Fraser Valley.* Enviroment Canada, Canadian Wildlife Service, December 1990; **p. 172** Courtesy of Royal British Columbia Museum, #PN9522; Chilliwack Museum and Archives, #p-7077; **p. 173** Matsqui Sumas Abbotsford Museum, #p-1554; **p. 174** Reproduction by Jan Perrier; **p. 175** E.W. Carlson; E.W. Carlson; **pp. 176-177** Chilliwack Museum and Archives, #p-3564; Matsqui-Sumas-Abbotsford Museum, #p-4998; Matsqui-Sumas-Abbotsford Museum, #p-5005; **p. 179** Gary Feigehen, #F-8A.

CHAPTER ELEVEN

p. 182 *Stó:lō* Nation *Halq'eméylem* Language Program; **p. 183** *Stó:lō* Nation *Halq'eméylem* Language Program; **p. 184** Gary Feigehen, #D-23A; **p.185** Tracey Joe, #T1-15; **p. 186** Tracey Joe, #T1-27; Tracey Joe, #T1-28; **p. 187** Gary Feigehen, #E-28A; Gary Feigehen, #H-5; Gordon Mohs; **p. 188** Gary Feigehen, #P-34A; **p. 190** Gary Feigehen, #N-4A; **p. 191** Gary Feigehen, #X-19A; **p. 192** Gary Feigehen, #C-29A; **p. 194** Gary Feigehen, #P-4A; **p. 195** Gary Feigehen, #P-2A; **p. 196** Gary Feigehen, #I-17A

— Index —

Trutch reductions 74
twin tracking, Canadian National Railway 82, 83
unemployment, *Stó:lō* 110, 123, 124
Union of British Columbia Indian Chiefs 104 (illus)
upper-class
  see smela:lh
urbanization
  see also Fraser Valley; pollution; transportation
  general effects of 62, 64, 82, 164, 165 (illus), 178-179
  traditional *Stó:lō* culture as a model for development 179
  as reflected by urban transportation systems 168-170, 169 (maps)
Uslick, Harry 23
Uslick, William 99
Vancouver, George 28, 35
Vanderpeet, Dorothy M. 149, 151
veterans, *Stó:lō* 18
  see also stómex
  exemption from the draft 128-130
  leadership roles in *Stó:lō* communities 136-137
  "life without racism" 132
  lost benefits 132
  marginalization of by other *Stó:lō* 133-136
  prior to 1900 127
  racism toward and *stómex* stereotypes of 126, 131, 132-135
  Remembrance Day ceremony 137
  World War I 128
  World War II 127 (illus), 128-132, 130 (illus)
Vienneau, Janelle 173
villages 16
wage labour economy
  see capitalist economy
wage labour, *Stó:lō*
  see also farming, *Stó:lō*; hop picking; salmon canning
  the 1881 census and 120
  income levels 124
  mining 115 (illus)
  the 1991 census and 124
  road and railway construction 115
  steamship/paddle wheel labour 118
  and unemployment 123
War of 1812 127
warriors
  see stómex
Wells, Harold 62, 131-132, 131 (illus)

Wells, Oliver 15, 16, 174
"White Paper" (1969) 103-104
Wili:léq, Fred 23
Wili:léq, Saul 23
Williams, Allan 6
winter dance
  see smílha (gathering of the winter dance) or *syúwél* (winter dance)
women, *Stó:lō* 47 (illus)
  and the economy 113, 116, 118
  gold miner's mistreatment of 62-63
  menstrual cycle and spritual power of 191-192
  and spiritual leadership 92
  as traders 44
World War I 127
World War II 127 (illus), 128-132, 130 (illus)
writing
  see Halq'eméylem
Xá:ls
  see Xexá:ls
Xá:ytem 56, 71, 183
  lessons of 97 (illus), 187-188, 187 (illus), 189, 190
Xá:ytem Longhouse Interpretive Centre (Mission, B.C.) 5, 15, 123
Xexá:ls (Transformers) 56, 167, 185
  see also Transformer rocks; *Xá:ytem*
  cedar tree 55, 56-57, 56 (illus), 186
  "The Mink and *[Xá:ls]*" 189
  Mink's tragic misadventure 192
  Mt. Cheam and Mt. Baker story 56
  Qoa'l'otlk'otl vs. SHai 191-192
  gift of salmon 140, 185
  "The Transformer Story" (James Teit) 190-191
  lessons of *Xá:ytem* 187-190
Xeyteleq, the story of 9-10
Xwelítem (people of European ancestry)
  see also cross-cultural relations, *Stó:lō-Xwelítem*
  immigration of 65, 72 (illus), 121, 166
  origins of the expression 51, 54
Yale 62 (illus), 115 (illus)

— Notes —